Count Down Your Age

Count Down Your Age

Look, Feel, and Live Better than You Ever Have Before

FREDERIC J. VAGNINI, M.D.

DAVE BUNNELL

New York   Chicago   San Francisco   Lisbon   London   Madrid   Mexico City
Milan   New Delhi   San Juan   Seoul   Singapore   Sydney   Toronto

Library of Congress Cataloging-in-Publication Data

Vagnini, Frederic J.
    Count down your age : look, feel, and live better than you ever have before / Frederic J.
Vagnini and Dave Bunnell.
       p.   cm.
    Includes bibliographical references.
    ISBN-13: 978-0-07-147807-6 (alk. paper)
    ISBN-10:   0-07-147807-8
    1. Health.   I. Bunnell, Dave.   II. Title.

RA776.V12   2007
613—dc22   2007001149

1 2 3 4 5 6 7 8 9 10 11 12 13 14 15 16 17 18 19   FGR/FGR   0 9 8 7

ISBN-13: 978-0-07-147807-6
ISBN-10:   0-07-147807-8

Interior design by Monica Baziuk

The information contained in this book is intended to provide helpful and informative material on the subject addressed. It is not intended to serve as a replacement for professional medical advice. Any use of the information in this book is at the reader's discretion. The authors and publisher specifically disclaim any and all liability arising directly or indirectly from the use or application of any information contained in this book. A health-care professional should be consulted regarding your specific situation.

This book is printed on acid-free paper.

Contents

Preface

Paul McCartney turned 64 on June 18, 2006. He was only 16 when he wrote the lyrics for "When I'm 64"—recorded nine years later on the Beatles' greatest album, *Sgt. Pepper's Lonely Hearts Club Band*. Sir Paul still has a fine head of hair, and though we doubt he rolls in at "a quarter to three," he has the energy and good looks of a much younger man. We suspect McCartney's perception of older people has changed. According to an article in the *New York Times*, half of those over 64 consider themselves middle-aged or young. To be old, you have to be 104.

Some of our favorite people are actually 100 years old or older (centenarians). The ones Dave has interviewed for his LongLife-Club website (longlifeclub.com) are vigorous, alert, and mostly independent. Some still drive, and at least one is still mountain climbing. By the middle of this century, there will be approximately 800,000 centenarians in the United States. Even so, if you live the perfect lifestyle, your odds of reaching 100 are still only about 1 in 10,000. Genetic factors and the age of your mother when you were born are probably more important than how much broccoli you eat.

We have a different, more achievable concept: instead of worrying about being 100, why not be younger now? Combing the most recent scientific and observational knowledge of nutrition, fitness, lifestyle, and medicine with Dr. Fred Vagnini's real-world experience as a cardiologist and holistic wellness doctor, we have developed a customizable health program that will slow and even reverse the aging process. Here's how. Let's assume you are an average 64-year-old person. Take the extensive self-test in Chapter 1 of this book, read Chapters 2 through 5, and then in Chapter 6, create your personal health plan. If you follow the plan, when you are 65 years old, you will have actually reduced your *functional* age to that of someone *younger* than 64. You will be counting *down* your age.

We believe you can count down your age by as much as 20 years. Research proves there are at least 10 biomarkers of aging that you can control and even reverse. No matter what your age, you can increase your muscle mass, speed up your metabolic rate, reduce your body fat percentage, improve your aerobic capacity, and lower your cholesterol. Do these, and guess what: everyone will start remarking on how great you look.

Most people imagine they will live to be at least 80 years old, but they worry that degenerative diseases, including Alzheimer's disease, will make their last years miserable. They don't want to be dependent on other people or live in an "old folks" facility. We imagine that if you're reading this book, you may want to live beyond 80 years, but more important than longevity, you are concerned about the *quality* of your remaining days. You want to stay young, have a sharp mind, be energetic and disease free, and live a meaningful, enjoyable, fun-filled life! If so, you share our passion; these are the exact things we want for ourselves.

Dave is an overachieving boomer with a background in the computer world. Thanks to some inspiration supplied by his grandmother and the help of his friend "Dr. V" Dave reinvented himself as an advocate of healthy living. Starting in the late 1950s, Dave's grandmother practiced yoga, grew her own organic vegetables, took supplements, and passed out free copies of Adelle Davis's book *Let's Eat Right to Keep Fit* to anyone who would listen to her mildly scolding message about how to live and what foods to eat. People poked fun at her as a "health nut," but Dave looked up to her, and at the age of 56, he decided to take up her mission. Along the way, he interviewed Dr. V for an article on wellness centers, and they later met at an antiaging conference. The two of them have been collaborating ever since.

Dr. V is a unique physician and health educator. After practicing for 25 years as a heart, lung, and blood vessel surgeon and operating on thousands of patients, he became interested in health education, preventive medicine, and clinical nutrition. Because of his vast experience in the area of heart disease and nutrition, he became a frequent guest speaker and has appeared regularly on local and national radio and television. The author of several books and host of his own radio show, Dr. V still sees 30 to 40 patients a day.

Writing this book, we mostly used plural pronouns to refer to ourselves, but in some instances we felt compelled to convey information about one of us individually, such as, "Dave eats fruit for breakfast" and "Dr. V prefers to eat his fruit at night for dessert." This has helped us accomplish our goals of telling our personal stories while also conveying a great deal of useful information, and we hope it works well for you.

We want *you* to reap the rewards of our evangelism. Our book is designed to provoke you into action. Some of our suggestions incorporate ideas you've known about for years, such as exercising and eating more vegetables, but perhaps have never implemented. Others, such as keeping a personal health journal and laughing your head off, may be quite novel. To get started, take the Count Down Your Age tests to give yourself an accurate picture of what you need to do to slow down or reverse aging. Who knows: maybe you have already counted down your age several years—in which case, you're off to a fantastic start.

You'll discover that the program we've created out of our personal experiences and extensive research is challenging and comprehensive. We have found that the ability to deal with stressful situations, for example, is every bit as important as taking your vitamins. And we believe it is our duty to not just tell you things but also show you how and give you all the reasons why. Based on what you learn from the test and the book, you should be ready for the fun part. We guide you through the process of building your very own personalized health plan covering the areas of nutrition, exercise, lifestyle, and medical care. With this plan, you will be able to increase the number of years you can count down your age. You will feel better than you *ever* thought possible.

Acknowledgments

Our sincere thanks to our very effective agent, Coleen O'Shea, and our editor, Johanna Bowman, for their help and advocacy, without which this project would not have been completed so successfully.

SPECIAL THANKS to my coauthor, David Bunnell. He introduced an amazing concept and has followed through with his genius from the computer world and an impressive writing ability to complete this important piece of work. As founder of the LongLifeClub, he has made a major contribution to the new field of antiaging medicine.

My staff at the Heart, Diabetes and Weight Loss Centers of New York, for helping me in caring for thousands of patients yearly as an antiaging physician and in the management of cardiovascular disease, diabetes, and weight reduction.

My nephew Daniel Cajigas, director of the Nutrition and Wellness Vitamin Division, for his exceptional work and support.

—Dr. Frederic Vagnini

SPECIAL THANKS to my friend Dr. V, who has proved to the world that doctors can not only fix hearts but have big hearts as well.

—Dave Bunnell

Count Down Your Age

8 4 3
5 2
6
3 6 7
1
6 3
5
2
8

1

The Antiaging Test

Take the Test, Find Out Where You Are, and Start Counting Down Your Age

To get started, it is extremely valuable to establish a baseline: where do you stand in terms of your current health? Perhaps you can already count down your age, but by how many years? Our test is designed to find out. People who take the test tell us it is informative and fun; it gives them added incentive to complete the rest of our program. Plus, you'll want to take it again as a way of measuring your progress. We recommend that you take this test now and then take it again every three to six months. The online version at countdownyourage.com will even store a scorecard each time for you so that you can refer back to it. (You can also find the online version at longlifeclub.com.)

The results of your test combined with the new knowledge you'll accumulate from reading this book will serve as the basis for your very own, personalized "Count Down Your Age Plan." You'll know where your strengths and weakness are, and you'll be able to set your own goals. If you want the energy, mental sharpness, and good looks of a healthy 45-year-old when you're 64, your Count Down Plan will allow you to achieve this—and we're not kidding. So, do it now!

■ **1. What do you think is the best diet for counting down your age?**
(Circle *best* answer.)

    Ⓐ Low carbohydrate (Atkins, South Beach, and so forth)
    Ⓑ Low fat (Ornish, SlimFast, Jenny Craig)
    Ⓒ Mediterranean
    Ⓓ Calorie reduction
    Ⓔ Vegetarian
    Ⓕ Vegan
    Ⓖ Subway sandwich
    Ⓗ No diet; just eat the right amount of the healthiest foods

Score: Ⓐ 40 Ⓑ 60 Ⓒ 80 Ⓓ 85 Ⓔ 90 Ⓕ 80 Ⓖ 10 Ⓗ 100

YOUR SCORE _____

■ **2. How often do you eat breakfast?**

    Ⓐ Every morning
    Ⓑ Five mornings a week
    Ⓒ Fewer than three mornings a week
    Ⓓ Hardly ever

Score: Ⓐ 100 Ⓑ 70 Ⓒ 30 Ⓓ 0

YOUR SCORE _____

■ **3. Which of the following foods do you eat on an average day?**
(Circle *all* that apply.)

    Ⓐ Whole grains (bread, cereal, or pasta)
    Ⓑ Raw fruit
    Ⓒ Beans
    Ⓓ Wheat germ
    Ⓔ Oatmeal or oats in another form
    Ⓕ Raw veggies
    Ⓖ Cooked veggies
    Ⓗ Broccoli, cauliflower, or cabbage

I Nuts, seeds, or both
J Tofu
K Pizza
L Cheeseburger
M Smoothie

Score: A 20 **B** 20 **C** 10 **D** 10 **E** 10 **F** 20 **G** 20 **H** 10 **I** 10
J 10 **K** 0 **L** 0 **M** 0

YOUR SCORE _____

■ **4. On an average day, which fruits do you eat? (Circle *all* that apply.)**

A Apple
B Banana
C Orange
D Blueberries (or other berries)
E Grapefruit
F Orange juice
G Grapefruit juice
H Melon
I Fruit smoothie
J Other fruit
K I don't eat fruit

Score: A 10 **B** 10 **C** 20 **D** 20 **E** 20 **F** 5 **G** 10 **H** 10 **I** 5
J 10 **K** 0

YOUR SCORE _____

■ **5. Which of the following best represents the breakfast you eat each day? (Coffee, tea optional.)**

A Eggs, toast, potatoes, perhaps bacon
B High-fiber ("healthy") cereal, fruit, nonfat or low-fat milk, and/or yogurt

⊙ Regular cereal (cornflakes, Rice Krispies, and so forth) and orange juice

⊙ Whole-grain toast, orange juice

⊙ White toast, orange juice

⊙ Bagel, cream cheese

⊙ Sweet roll, orange juice

⊙ Fast food, such as McDonald's McMuffin

⊙ Breakfast shake or bar

⊙ Cigarette, shot of tequila

Score: ⊙ 30 ⊙ 100 ⊙ 50 ⊙ 60 ⊙ 10 ⊙ 30 ⊙ 0 ⊙ 0 ⊙ 30 ⊙ 0

YOUR SCORE _____

■ **6. Approximately how many eggs do you eat?**

⊙ Two or more eggs every day

⊙ I eat eggs five times a week.

⊙ I eat only egg whites.

⊙ I eat eggs one to three times a week.

⊙ Seldom

Score: ⊙ 20 ⊙ 30 ⊙ 60 ⊙ 50 ⊙ 30

YOUR SCORE _____

■ **7. How often, in a week, do you eat bacon, sausage, or other cured meats (including lunch meats such as salami)?**

⊙ Once or twice

⊙ Two to four times

⊙ More than four times

⊙ Very rarely

⊙ Never

Score: ⊙ 30 ⊙ 10 ⊙ 0 ⊙ 90 ⊙ 100

YOUR SCORE _____

■ **8. How much coffee, including espresso drinks, do you consume?**

Ⓐ Equivalent of one or two cups of regular coffee (not decaf) in the morning

Ⓑ Equivalent of three to four cups of regular coffee (not decaf) a day

Ⓒ Five or more cups of regular coffee (not decaf) a day

Ⓓ Decaffeinated coffee

Ⓔ Never touch the stuff

Score: Ⓐ 80 Ⓑ 40 Ⓒ 10 Ⓓ 90 Ⓔ 100

YOUR SCORE _____

■ **9. If you drink tea daily, what kind and how much?**

Ⓐ Black or dark tea (two or more cups)

Ⓑ Green tea (two or more cups)

Ⓒ I love my herbal tea and drink at least two cups.

Ⓓ About one cup

Ⓔ Occasionally I drink tea.

Ⓕ I never, ever drink this foul, nasty liquid.

Score: Ⓐ 60 Ⓑ 100 Ⓒ 40 Ⓓ 20 Ⓔ 10 Ⓕ 0

YOUR SCORE _____

■ **10. Which of the following dairy products do you consume on a regular basis? (Circle *all* that apply.)**

Ⓐ One to three glasses of nonfat or low-fat milk daily

Ⓑ One to three glasses of regular milk daily

Ⓒ Regular milk occasionally (about three times a week)

Ⓓ Cream or half-and-half in my coffee or tea

Ⓔ Milk in my coffee

Ⓕ Cheese, including cottage cheese

Ⓖ I love yogurt and eat it most days.

Ⓗ Yogurt, occasionally

❶ Butter
❿ I love blood sausages.
❸ I don't eat dairy products because I'm lactose intolerant.
❹ I never eat dairy products.

Score: Ⓐ 50 Ⓑ 0 Ⓒ 20 Ⓓ 0 Ⓔ 40 Ⓕ 10 Ⓖ 90 Ⓗ 60 Ⓘ 10 Ⓙ 0
Ⓚ 0 Ⓛ 50

> YOUR SCORE _____

■ **11. How many servings of vegetables do you eat on an average day? (A serving is less than you might think: one serving of most fruits and vegetables is the equivalent of ½ cup in volume.)**

Ⓐ Most days, just one serving
Ⓑ Two servings a day
Ⓒ Three to four servings a day
Ⓓ Five to six servings a day
Ⓔ More than six servings a day
Ⓕ Does ketchup count?
Ⓖ None; veggies are for wimps

Score: Ⓐ 10 Ⓑ 30 Ⓒ 50 Ⓓ 90 Ⓔ 100 Ⓕ 0 Ⓖ 0

> YOUR SCORE _____

■ **12. Which of the following best represents your lunch on a normal day? (Circle *best* answer.)**

Ⓐ Hamburger, fries, and a Coke
Ⓑ Chicken nuggets, fries, milk shake
Ⓒ Sandwich on white bread
Ⓓ Sandwich on whole-grain bread with tomatoes, lettuce, or other vegetable, plus some meat, fish, or chicken
Ⓔ Veggie sandwich
Ⓕ Salad, some crackers or bread, iced tea or water
Ⓖ Raw veggies, nuts, and a drink

🅗 Fish (including sushi) or chicken, salad or some veggies, and a drink
🅘 Pizza
🅙 Two martinis and a cigarette

Score: 🅐 0 🅑 0 🅒 15 🅓 50 🅔 70 🅕 100 🅖 90 🅗 90 🅘 20 🅙 0

YOUR SCORE _____

■ **13. How much water do you drink daily? (Include water you might drink when you wake up, during meals, between meals, after exercising, in the evening, etc. A glass of water is eight ounces.)**

🅐 I drink eight or more glasses of water.
🅑 Six to eight glasses of water
🅒 Four to six glasses of water
🅓 Two to four glasses of water
🅔 I drink less than two glasses.
🅕 No water; soda instead

Score: 🅐 100 🅑 80 🅒 50 🅓 20 🅔 10 🅕 0

YOUR SCORE _____

■ **14. What are your sugar habits? (Circle *all* that apply.)**

🅐 I use jam or honey on my toast, or I add sugar to cereal or pour syrup on pancakes.
🅑 I drink one or two sodas a day.
🅒 I drink more than two sodas a day.
🅓 I add sugar to my coffee or tea.
🅔 I don't look at nutrition labels on packaged food.
🅕 I study the food labels and try not to buy anything that has added sugar or fructose or one of the many substitutes.
🅖 I eat sweets every day.
🅗 I eat dessert (not fresh fruit) most days of the week.
🅘 I eat dessert one or two days a week.

J I never eat dessert.

K I avoid sugar like the plague.

L I eat candy bars for snacks.

M A little sugar can't hurt you.

Score: A 0 **B** 0 **C** 0 **D** 0 **E** 0 **F** 90 **G** 0 **H** 0 **I** 40 **J** 100
K 100 **L** 0 **M** 0

YOUR SCORE _____

■ **15. How much wine, beer, or hard liquor do you drink on a daily basis? (Review the last three or four days before answering this question; then circle the *most correct* answer.)**

A One or two glasses of red wine

B One or two glasses of white wine

C One or two glasses of beer or cocktails

D Three to four drinks (wine, beer, or cocktails)

E Five or more drinks (wine, beer, or cocktails)

F Only on special occasions

G No alcohol—no way

Score: A 90 **B** 50 **C** 20 **D** 10 **E** 0 **F** 90 **G** 100

YOUR SCORE _____

■ **16. Which one of the following best represents dinner you eat on a normal evening?**

A Meat, potato, something green, plus dessert

B Meat, potato, something green, no dessert

C Meat, fish, or chicken; no potato, lots of vegetables, no bread, no dessert

D Three martinis, a couple glasses of vino, and a Subway sandwich

E Lots of wonderful vegetables, perhaps a little pasta or rice, and fruit for dessert

F Salad, fish or chicken, rice or potato, veggie, dessert

G Salad, fish or chicken, veggie, dessert
H Meal in **F** or **G** above, with a little raw fruit for dessert
I Rice topped with a curry dish
J Fried chicken or fried fish, chips, salad
K Cheeseburger, Coke, fries, and a large chocolate brownie
  with lots of chocolate sauce

Score: A 20 **B** 30 **C** 80 **D** 0 **E** 90 **F** 80 **G** 80 **H** 100 **I** 50
J 10 **K** much less than 0

YOUR SCORE _____

■ **17. Love dessert? (Circle *all* that apply.)**

A Dessert most days
B Dessert, but usually whole fruit
C I eat dessert three times or more per week.
D Less than three times a week
E Occasionally eat dessert
F Never eat dessert

Score: A 0 **B** 80 **C** 20 **D** 80 **E** 90 **F** 100

YOUR SCORE _____

■ **18. How frequently do you eat meat (including beef, lamb, pork, lunch meat, hot dogs, sausage, buffalo, and game meats)?**

A At least twice a day
B Most every day
C Three to five times a week
D Less than three times a week
E About once or twice a week
F Rarely eat the stuff
G Never eat meat

Score: A 0 **B** 10 **C** 40 **D** 80 **E** 100 **F** 100 **G** 100

YOUR SCORE _____

■ **19. How frequently do you eat fish? (Circle *best* answer.)**

Ⓐ Are you kidding? Fish stinks—never touch it.

Ⓑ I don't eat fish; I'm a vegetarian.

Ⓒ About once a week

Ⓓ Two to three times a week

Ⓔ Three to five times a week

Ⓕ Every day

Score: Ⓐ 0 Ⓑ 20 Ⓒ 40 Ⓓ 80 Ⓔ 100 Ⓕ 90

YOUR SCORE _____

■ **20. How much "starchy food" (potatoes, white bread, pastas, and rice) do you eat? (Circle *all* that apply.)**

Ⓐ Potatoes most every day

Ⓑ White rice all the time

Ⓒ Only white bread

Ⓓ Whole-grain bread, pasta, and rice

Ⓔ Pasta (and not that yucky whole-grain fake stuff)

Ⓕ Starchy foods three to five times a week

Ⓖ Starchy foods less than three times a week

Score: Ⓐ 0 Ⓑ 0 Ⓒ 0 Ⓓ 100 Ⓔ 20 Ⓕ 10 Ⓖ 60

YOUR SCORE _____

■ **21. What kind of cooking oil do you primarily use?**

Ⓐ Olive oil

Ⓑ Canola oil

Ⓒ Sunflower or safflower oil

Ⓓ Enova oil (Japanese salad and cooking oil combining soy and canola oils; its purported advantage over other polyunsaturated oils is a difference in chemical structure said to help reduce body fat.)

Ⓔ Grape seed oil (increasingly used by chefs as an alternative to olive oil because of its high flash point, approximately 320 degrees F; it is high in antioxidants and contains vitamin E and a group of bioflavonoids known as procyanadins)

Ⓕ Corn oil or cottonseed oil

Ⓖ Vegetable shortening

Ⓗ Butter

Ⓘ Margarine

Score: Ⓐ 100 Ⓑ 90 Ⓒ 60 Ⓓ 85 Ⓔ 90 Ⓕ 10 Ⓖ 0 Ⓗ 10 Ⓘ 0

YOUR SCORE _____

■ **22. Which of the following foods do you eat at least once every two weeks? (Circle *all* that apply.)**

Ⓐ Blueberries

Ⓑ Grapefruit

Ⓒ Almonds

Ⓓ Apples

Ⓔ Avocados

Ⓕ Beets

Ⓖ Broccoli

Ⓗ Cocoa

Ⓘ Cranberries or cranberry juice

Ⓙ Flaxseed

Ⓚ Garlic

Ⓛ Ginger

Ⓜ Olive oil

Ⓝ Onions

Ⓞ Oranges

Ⓟ Oats or oatmeal

Ⓠ Salmon

Ⓡ Soy

Ⓢ Tea
Ⓣ Tomatoes
Ⓤ Whole grains
Ⓥ Red wine
Ⓦ Beans
Ⓧ Sea vegetables (a.k.a. "seaweed")
Ⓨ Cabbage
Ⓩ Kale

Score: 10 points for each

YOUR SCORE _____

■ **23. Do you take a multivitamin? (Circle one.)**

Ⓐ You bet your sweet bippy.
Ⓑ No. Why—what's it to you?

Score: Ⓐ 100 Ⓑ 0

YOUR SCORE _____

■ **24. Which of the following supplements do you take on a daily basis? (Circle *all* that apply.)**

Ⓐ Omega-3 (fish oil)
Ⓑ Vitamin B complex
Ⓒ Alpha lipoic acid
Ⓓ Acetyl-L-carnitine
Ⓔ Curcumin
Ⓕ Vitamin D
Ⓖ Vitamin E
Ⓗ CoQ10
Ⓘ Magnesium
Ⓙ Selenium
Ⓚ SAMe

Ⓛ Phosphatidyl serine (PS)
Ⓜ Nattokinase

Score: 10 points for each

YOUR SCORE _____

■ **25. Do you exercise on a regular basis? (Circle one.)**

Ⓐ Yes
Ⓑ Not on your life

Score: Ⓐ 100 Ⓑ 0

YOUR SCORE _____

■ **26. How often, during an average week, do you exercise?**

Ⓐ Every day
Ⓑ Five to six days
Ⓒ Three to five days
Ⓓ One to two days
Ⓔ Never

Score: Ⓐ 100 Ⓑ 90 Ⓒ 70 Ⓓ 40 Ⓔ 0

YOUR SCORE _____

■ **27. On the following 6-to-20 scale, how would you rate the intensity of your exercise effort?**

6 None
7 Very, very light
9 Very light
11 Fairly light
13 Somewhat hard
15 Hard

17 Very hard

18 Very, very hard

Score: 6. 0 7. 0 9. 10 11. 30 13. 60 15. 80 17. 100 18. 80

YOUR SCORE _____

The Borg Scale Test

"How hard do you exercise?" Gunnar Borg, the famous Swedish exercise physiologist, demonstrated that a person's response to that question can be accurately rated on a scale of 6 to 20, where 6 represents no exercise and 20 represents pushing yourself to the limit. A score of 19 or 20, in our view, is not as good as a score of 15 to 18, because you can wear your body down, damage your joints, and create an excess amount of free radicals if you consistently push yourself to the limit. Hard but not "crazy" is best.

■ **28. How long is your average exercise session?**

Ⓐ Two hours or more

Ⓑ 90 minutes

Ⓒ 60 minutes

Ⓓ 45 minutes

Ⓔ 30 minutes

Ⓕ 15 minutes

Ⓖ 5 minutes

Score: Ⓐ 100 Ⓑ 100 Ⓒ 90 Ⓓ 70 Ⓔ 40 Ⓕ 20 Ⓖ 10

YOUR SCORE _____

■ **29. Stand on one foot and balance yourself for as long as you can, up to 2 minutes. How long can you do this? (Circle closest answer.)**

Ⓐ Less than 30 seconds
Ⓑ 45 seconds
Ⓒ 1 minute
Ⓓ 1 minute, 30 seconds
Ⓔ 1 minute, 45 seconds
Ⓕ 2 minutes

Score: Ⓐ 0 Ⓑ 20 Ⓒ 50 Ⓓ 70 Ⓔ 90 Ⓕ 100

YOUR SCORE _____

■ **30. Repeat the preceding exercise with your eyes shut. How long can you do this?**

Ⓐ I can't.
Ⓑ 10 seconds
Ⓒ 20 seconds
Ⓓ 30 seconds
Ⓔ 45 seconds
Ⓕ 1 minute or more

Score: Ⓐ 0 Ⓑ 10 Ⓒ 30 Ⓓ 60 Ⓔ 80 Ⓕ 100

YOUR SCORE _____

■ **31. How long can you hold your breath? (If you don't know, test yourself: First take several deep breaths through tightly pursed lips to expand your lungs and oxygenate your body. Take one final deep breath, again through tightly pursed lips, and hold it for as long as possible, timing yourself with a clock or any timing device.)**

Ⓐ 2 minutes or more
Ⓑ 90 seconds, up to 2 minutes

Ⓒ 60 seconds, up to 90 seconds

Ⓓ 30 seconds, up to 60 seconds

Ⓔ 15 seconds, up to 30 seconds

Ⓕ Less than 15 seconds

Score—If you are 75 years old or older: Ⓐ 100 Ⓑ 100 Ⓒ 100
   Ⓓ 90 Ⓔ 50 Ⓕ 10

Score—Age 65–75: Ⓐ 100 Ⓑ 100 Ⓒ 100 Ⓓ 50 Ⓔ 30 Ⓕ 0

Score—Age 55–65: Ⓐ 100 Ⓑ 100 Ⓒ 80 Ⓓ 40 Ⓔ 10 Ⓕ 0

Score—Age 30–55: Ⓐ 100 Ⓑ 90 Ⓒ 70 Ⓓ 20 Ⓔ 0 Ⓕ 0

Score—Under 30: Ⓐ 100 Ⓑ 80 Ⓒ 50 Ⓓ 20 Ⓔ 0 Ⓕ 0

YOUR SCORE ＿＿＿＿＿

Experts on Breath Holding?

Experts say that even if you are a nonswimmer but are in good physical condition, you can learn to hold your breath for the three minutes and 38 seconds that it took Tanya Streeter to break the world free-diving record. (Although, they concede that using that time to descend to 400 feet below sea level before swimming back to the surface, as she did, may be more of a challenge.) We think these "experts" must be referring to teenagers. Dave, who is an ardent swimmer, can hold his breath for 2 minutes, 15 seconds—3 minutes, 38 seconds seems impossible.

■ **32. How often do you engage in a true aerobic exercise (an activity in which you *continuously* exert some, if not all, of your large muscles, such as leg or arm muscles, for at least 20 minutes, during which your heart rate is elevated to 60 to 80 percent of its maximum capacity)? (Circle *best* answer.)**

Ⓐ Five to seven times a week

Ⓑ Three or four times a week

C Twice a week

D Once a week

E Once every two weeks

F Once in a while

G You're not my momma!

Score: A 100 **B** 90 **C** 70 **D** 40 **E** 10 **F** 0 **G** 0

YOUR SCORE _____

■ **33. How strong are you? (Circle *all* that apply.)**

A I can get up from a chair without effort.

B I seldom have difficulty opening the lid on a jar of food.

C I can easily carry two full bags of groceries.

D I have no difficulty lifting up a toddler.

E If my car stalled on the highway and I had to put it into neutral and push it, I could do this—no sweat.

F I can bench-press 200 pounds.

Score: A 5 **B** 30 **C** 20 **D** 20 **E** 60 **F** 100

YOUR SCORE _____

■ **34. How often do you do resistance training (exercise involving using your large muscles to move a weight, such as weight lifting, stretch bands, and certain body exercises)?**

A Every day

B Five times a week

C Three to four times a week

D Twice a week

E Once a week

F Once or twice a month

G Once in a blue moon

H Never

Score: Ⓐ 70 Ⓑ 90 Ⓒ 100 Ⓓ 90 Ⓔ 70 Ⓕ 30 Ⓖ 0 Ⓗ 0

YOUR SCORE _____

■ **35. Touch-your-toes test: Standing still with your knees locked, bend forward—how far can you stretch?**

Ⓐ I can put my head on my knees and my elbows on the floor.
Ⓑ I can put my hands flat on the floor.
Ⓒ I can touch the floor with my fingers.
Ⓓ I can reach my ankles with my fingers.
Ⓔ I can touch my shins.
Ⓕ You're killing me.

Score: Ⓐ ha-ha Ⓑ 100 Ⓒ 80 Ⓓ 50 Ⓔ 20 Ⓕ 0

YOUR SCORE _____

■ **36. How often do you really, really sweat (sauna, intense exercise, Bikram yoga—doesn't matter how)?**

Ⓐ About once a week
Ⓑ Daily
Ⓒ Two to three times a week
Ⓓ Four to six times a week
Ⓔ All the time, because my boss is a real hard-ass
Ⓕ Not often (less than once a week)

Score: Ⓐ 40 Ⓑ 100 Ⓒ 60 Ⓓ 90 Ⓔ 0 Ⓕ 0

YOUR SCORE _____

■ **37. Are you keeping your spine flexible? (Circle *all* that apply.)**

Ⓐ When I use my remote control, I always bend forward.
Ⓑ I practice yoga one time or more a week.
Ⓒ I do stretching exercises.

D I get regular adjustments from my chiropractor.
E I hang upside down.
F I sit up straight.
G I walk a lot.

Score: A 0 **B** 90 **C** 80 **D** 50 **E** 90 **F** 30 **G** 30

YOUR SCORE _____

■ **38. Do you dance? (Circle *best* answer.)**

A Hell no. Just what planet do this Dave dude and
Dr. Viola or whatever come from, anyway?
B I confess: occasionally.
C About once a month.
D Yes; it is great—I go dancing once every other week or so.
E I love dancing and try to dance once a week, sometimes
more.

Score: A 0 **B** 20 **C** 40 **D** 60 **E** 100

YOUR SCORE _____

■ **39. Do you have an exercise "routine" that works for you?**

A Yes
B No

Score: A 100 **B** 0

YOUR SCORE _____

■ **40. Do you exercise your eyes? (Circle *best* answer.)**

A Huh, well, no.
B Sometimes, yes, I exercise my eyes.

Ⓒ By staring at the television without blinking for hours and hours almost every day.

Ⓓ Yes, I exercise my eyes.

Score: Ⓐ 0 Ⓑ 50 Ⓒ 0 Ⓓ 100

YOUR SCORE _____

▪ **41. When did you last take up a new and demanding sport or exercise activity—one that requires careful attention and focus (for example archery, hang gliding, water polo, golf if you never played before, or any sport that is new to you)?**

Ⓐ Within the past three to five years
Ⓑ Within the past year or two years
Ⓒ In the past year
Ⓓ None of your bizwax
Ⓔ A long time ago (more than five years)
Ⓕ Never

Score: Ⓐ 30 Ⓑ 80 Ⓒ 100 Ⓓ 0 Ⓔ 0 Ⓕ 0

YOUR SCORE _____

▪ **42. Do you consciously exercise your brain?**

Ⓐ Yes
Ⓑ No

Score: Ⓐ 100 Ⓑ 0

YOUR SCORE _____

▪ **43. When did you last take up a new activity that requires you to use your mind in new and demanding ways (for example chess,**

Sudoko, bridge, taking an academic class, tutoring children, learning to identify plants or birds.)

Ⓐ Within the past three to five years
Ⓑ Within the past year or two years
Ⓒ In the past year
Ⓓ None of your bizwax
Ⓔ It's been a long time (more than five years).
Ⓕ Never

Score: Ⓐ 30 Ⓑ 80 Ⓒ 100 Ⓓ 0 Ⓔ 0 Ⓕ 0

YOUR SCORE _____

■ **44. Quickly read the following sentence once:** The purple rabbit played a guitar and ate a can of peaches with a spoon. **Without looking at or reading the sentence again, do the following:**

1. Close your eyes and sing "Happy Birthday" to yourself *twice.*
2. Count on your fingers to 17.
3. Take a long, deep breath.
4. Answer the following questions:
What animal was in the sentence you read?
What color was the animal?
What musical instrument was it playing?
What was it eating?
What utensil was it using to eat?
Now check your answers by rereading the sentence.

Score: All five answers correct—give yourself 100 points and thank the lord your short-term memory is still working great. If you missed only one question, give yourself 80 points. If you missed more than one question, you get no points.

YOUR SCORE _____

■ **45. On an average night, how much sleep do you get? (Circle *best* answer.)**

Ⓐ Four hours or less
Ⓑ Five to six hours
Ⓒ Seven hours
Ⓓ Eight hours
Ⓔ Nine hours
Ⓕ Ten or more hours
Ⓖ None—I don't sleep.

Score: Ⓐ 10 Ⓑ 20 Ⓒ 60 Ⓓ 90 Ⓔ 100 Ⓕ 100 Ⓖ 0

YOUR SCORE _____

■ **46. Have you *ever* fallen asleep while driving? (Be honest and circle the *best* answer.)**

Ⓐ Never
Ⓑ Once, more than a year ago
Ⓒ Within the past year
Ⓓ I almost fell asleep while driving, but I was able to "catch" myself before it was too late.

Score: Ⓐ 100 Ⓑ 20 Ⓒ 0 Ⓓ 10

YOUR SCORE _____

■ **47. Which of the following things do you smoke, if any? (Circle *all* that apply.)**

Ⓐ Cigarettes
Ⓑ Cigars
Ⓒ Pipe
Ⓓ Pot
Ⓔ Crack is my substance of choice.
Ⓕ Nothing

Score: Ⓐ 0 Ⓑ 0 Ⓒ 0 Ⓓ 0 Ⓔ 0 Ⓕ 100

YOUR SCORE _____

■ **48. Do you talk on the cell phone (portable or hands-free— doesn't matter) while you are driving? (Circle *most honest* answer.)**

Ⓐ Occasionally

Ⓑ I pull over to the side of the road.

Ⓒ Talking on the cell phone is an efficient way to use my time while driving, so what's it to you, Bud!

Ⓓ I don't have an obnoxious cell phone.

Ⓔ I don't drive.

Score: Ⓐ 50 Ⓑ 100 Ⓒ 0 Ⓓ 100 Ⓔ 100

YOUR SCORE _____

■ **49. Do you have trouble keeping your mind on what you are doing? (Circle *best* answer.)**

Ⓐ Rarely, or not at all

Ⓑ Some, or a little, of the time

Ⓒ Occasionally, or a moderate amount of time

Ⓓ Most of the time

Score: Ⓐ 100 Ⓑ 90 Ⓒ 40 Ⓓ 0

YOUR SCORE _____

■ **50. How often do you feel that your life is a "failure"? (Circle *best* answer.)**

Ⓐ Rarely, or not at all

Ⓑ Some, or a little, of the time

   Ⓒ Occasionally, or a moderate amount of time

   Ⓓ Most of the time

Score: Ⓐ 100 Ⓑ 90 Ⓒ 40 Ⓓ 0

YOUR SCORE _____

▪ **51.   How often do you feel you are enjoying life? (Circle *best* answer.)**

   Ⓐ Rarely, or not at all

   Ⓑ Some, or a little, of the time

   Ⓒ Occasionally, or a moderate amount of time

   Ⓓ Most of the time

Score: Ⓐ 0 Ⓑ 10 Ⓒ 50 Ⓓ 100

YOUR SCORE _____

▪ **52.   How would you assess the "quality" of your sleep? (Circle *all* the answers that apply—and come on, now: be brutally honest about it.)**

   Ⓐ I sleep like a baby and wake up totally refreshed.

   Ⓑ I have trouble falling asleep.

   Ⓒ My sleep is disturbed during the night.

   Ⓓ I snore like a choo-choo train.

   Ⓔ Sometimes I sleep well; sometimes I don't.

   Ⓕ I need sleeping pills to sleep.

   Ⓖ A bottle of brandy usually does the trick.

Score: Ⓐ 100 Ⓑ 0 Ⓒ 0 Ⓓ 0 Ⓔ 60 Ⓕ 20 Ⓖ 0

YOUR SCORE _____

▪ **53.   *Men only*: On average, how many orgasms do you currently have per week?**

🅐 50 or more

🅑 About 7; sometimes I get lucky and have more

🅒 More than 3, fewer than 7

🅓 At least 1 or 2

🅔 Fewer than 1 per week

Score: 🅐 0 for lying 🅑 100 🅒 80 🅓 40 🅔 0

YOUR SCORE _____

■ **54. *Women only*: How would you rate the quality of your sex life? (Circle *most correct* answer.)**

🅐 I see fireworks frequently.

🅑 My sex life is very satisfying.

🅒 Not the greatest, but somewhat satisfying.

🅓 Boring and not so great.

🅔 Not good at all.

Score: 🅐 100 🅑 100 🅒 60 🅓 20 🅔 0

YOUR SCORE _____

■ **55. How much of a role does humor play in your life? (Circle *all* that apply.)**

🅐 I don't see anything funny at all in this royally screwed-up world.

🅑 I love to laugh; it makes me feel great.

🅒 I watch at least one really funny TV show every week.

🅓 Really funny movies are the greatest.

🅔 I like really good jokes.

🅕 Seeing the humor in everyday situations is one of my most important gifts.

🅖 I have at least one favorite comedian.

Score: ⓐ 0 ⓑ 100 ⓒ 10 ⓓ 10 ⓔ 10 ⓕ 10 ⓖ 10

YOUR SCORE _____

■ **56. Do you practice meditation? (Circle *best* answer.)**

ⓐ I meditate for 15 minutes or more each and every single day.

ⓑ I meditate three to five times a week.

ⓒ I meditate once or twice a week.

ⓓ You can't be serious—meditation is a big, fat waste of time.

ⓔ No.

Score: ⓐ 100 ⓑ 80 ⓒ 40 ⓓ 0 ⓔ 0

YOUR SCORE _____

■ **57. How would you describe your relationship with your spouse or your "significant other"? (Circle *best* answer.)**

ⓐ Happy most of the time

ⓑ Stormy weather

ⓒ Good days, bad days

ⓓ I'm divorced or separated.

ⓔ My spouse or significant other died.

ⓕ I don't have one.

ⓖ I'm happy to live by myself.

Score: ⓐ 100 ⓑ 20 ⓒ 50 ⓓ 40 ⓔ 30 ⓕ 10 ⓖ 20

YOUR SCORE _____

■ **58. How big is your social network? (Circle *all* that apply.)**

ⓐ I have many good friends.

ⓑ I belong to a social club.

Ⓒ I have a large extended family.

Ⓓ I'm actively involved in one or more community organizations.

Ⓔ I regularly attend religious services.

Ⓕ I connect to a lot of people through the Internet.

Ⓖ My bridge club rocks (applies to any other type of social game, including poker).

Ⓗ Bingo is my game.

Ⓘ My buddies and I drink together and watch sports.

Score: 10 points for each

YOUR SCORE _____

■ **59. Does your life have meaning? (Circle *best* answer.)**

Ⓐ Yes; I am highly motivated to stay healthy and vital because the things I'm doing in life are very important to me.

Ⓑ Somewhat, but not always

Ⓒ My life has meaning to me, but hardly to anyone else.

Ⓓ I would like to find something meaningful, but so far I haven't been successful.

Ⓔ Hardly; I could drop off the planet tomorrow and no one would notice.

Score: Ⓐ 100 Ⓑ 70 Ⓒ 50 Ⓓ 30 Ⓔ 0

YOUR SCORE _____

■ **60. If you were a stranger in a strange land and suddenly passed out on the sidewalk, how would the medical emergency people find the information that just might save your life? (Circle *best* answer.)**

Ⓐ They would know who I am from my driver's license or other basic information that I carry in my purse or wallet— and they could take it from there.

ⓑ There is a medical-response card in my purse or wallet that includes the name and phone number of my doctor and whom to contact in case of emergency.

ⓒ My medical information is all online, and I carry a card in my purse or wallet that explains how to access my files.

ⓓ My medical information is all online, and I wear an ID bracelet or necklace that explains who I am and how to access my files.

ⓔ My medical information is contained on a miniature flash drive (thumb drive) that will plug into any Windows-based computer; it is with me at all times and clearly labeled.

ⓕ I would basically be screwed.

Score: ⓐ 20 ⓑ 50 ⓒ 80 ⓓ 100 ⓔ 100 ⓕ 0

YOUR SCORE _____

▪ **61. How would you describe your relationship with your primary doctor? (Circle *best* answer.)**

ⓐ I hardly ever see my doctor, and when I do, my doctor is tremendously busy running from treatment room to treatment room.

ⓑ My doctor and I work together as a team; we communicate frequently, and I'm very happy with the arrangement.

ⓒ My doctor is great when I go in; however, it is difficult to communicate with my doctor outside the office.

ⓓ I ain't got no stinking doctor.

Score: ⓐ 20 ⓑ 100 ⓒ 50 ⓓ 0

YOUR SCORE _____

▪ **62. When is the last time you had a blood test? (Circle *best* answer.)**

ⓐ Less than a year ago

ⓑ Within the last three years

© More than three years ago, less than five years

© I have never had one of these.

© It's been more than five years.

© When I was busted by an undercover narcotics officer.

Score: Ⓐ 100 Ⓑ 70 Ⓒ 30 Ⓓ 0 Ⓔ 10 Ⓕ 0

YOUR SCORE _____

■ **63. What is your total cholesterol count?**

Ⓐ Less than 180 ml/dL (excellent)

Ⓑ 200 ml/dL or less (good)

Ⓒ In the range of 200 to 240 ml/dL (moderate risk)

Ⓓ Over 240 ml/dL (high risk)

Ⓔ Don't know

Score: Ⓐ 100 Ⓑ 90 Ⓒ 50 Ⓓ 10 Ⓔ 0

YOUR SCORE _____

■ **64. How's your triglyceride level (amount of body fat in the bloodstream)?**

Ⓐ My fasting triglyceride level is less than 150 mg/dL (very good).

Ⓑ Over 150 mg/dL, less than 500 mg/dL (not great, but not terrible)

Ⓒ Over 500 mg/dL and less than 1,000 mg/dL (not good)

Ⓓ Over 1,000 mg/dL (alarmingly high)

Ⓔ I do not know.

Score: Ⓐ 100 Ⓑ 50 Ⓒ 10 Ⓓ 0 Ⓔ 0

YOUR SCORE _____

▪ **65. How many days during an average year would you say you are unable to work or leave your residence because of illness such as a severe cold or the flu? (Circle *best* answer.)**

Ⓐ Almost never
Ⓑ Less than 3 days
Ⓒ 4 to 7 days
Ⓓ 8 to 12 days
Ⓔ More than 12 days

Score: Ⓐ 100 Ⓑ 90 Ⓒ 50 Ⓓ 20 Ⓔ 0

YOUR SCORE _____

▪ **66. What is the size (circumference) of your waist? (For the most accurate measurement, place a tape measure around your bare abdomen just above your hip bone. In general, your waist is the narrowest part of your body, about one inch above your belly button. Make the tape snug and parallel to the floor, but do not squeeze. Relax, exhale, and measure your waist.)**

Ⓐ I am male; my waistline is less than 32 inches.
Ⓑ I am male; my waistline is between 32 inches and 36 inches.
Ⓒ I am male; my waistline is more than 36 inches and less than 40 inches.
Ⓓ I am male; my waistline is 40 inches or more.
Ⓔ I am female; my waistline is less than 28 inches.
Ⓕ I am female; my waistline is between 28 inches and 32 inches.
Ⓖ I am female; my waistline is between 32 inches and 35 inches.
Ⓗ I am female; my waistline is more than 35 inches.

Score: Ⓐ 100 Ⓑ 90 Ⓒ 40 Ⓓ 10 Ⓔ 100 Ⓕ 90 Ⓖ 40 Ⓗ 10

YOUR SCORE _____

■ **67. How much more do you weigh today than you did at age 20? (Circle *most accurate* answer.)**

- **Ⓐ** I actually weigh less today.
- **Ⓑ** About the same
- **Ⓒ** 10 pounds more
- **Ⓓ** 20 pounds more
- **Ⓔ** 30 pounds more
- **Ⓕ** 40 pounds more
- **Ⓖ** 40 to 50 pounds more
- **Ⓗ** More than 50 pounds, less than 1,000

Score: Ⓐ 100 Ⓑ 100 Ⓒ 90 Ⓓ 80 Ⓔ 40 Ⓕ 20 Ⓖ 10 Ⓗ 0

YOUR SCORE _____

■ **68. How would you rate your health compared with other people your age and sex? (Circle *most correct* answer.)**

- **Ⓐ** I am way healthier than my peers.
- **Ⓑ** Somewhat healthier
- **Ⓒ** About the same
- **Ⓓ** Slightly less healthy
- **Ⓔ** I am very unhealthy compared with other people my age and sex.

Score: Ⓐ 100 Ⓑ 80 Ⓒ 50 Ⓓ 20 Ⓔ 0

YOUR SCORE _____

■ **69. Are you diabetic or prediabetic? (Circle *one*.)**

- **Ⓐ** My doctor says I am prediabetic, and I am following my doctor's advice to deal with this (including taking any medications, if prescribed).
- **Ⓑ** My doctor says I am prediabetic and I should watch what I'm eating, but that's about it.

⊙ Yes, I'm diabetic, but I don't want to take any medications, so I'm trying to control it with diet and exercise.
⊙ Yes, I'm diabetic and taking medication.
⊜ Yes, and I use insulin therapy.
⊜ No, I am not.

Score: Ⓐ 90 Ⓑ 40 ⊙ 10 ⓓ 60 ⊜ 60 Ⓕ 100

YOUR SCORE _____

■ **70. Have you been diagnosed with heart disease?**

Ⓐ Heck no.
Ⓑ Yes, but that was years ago, and I'm making fantastic progress.
⊙ Yes, and I'm following a rehabilitation program.
ⓓ Yes, but I'm not doing much about it now.

Score: Ⓐ 100 Ⓑ 80 ⊙ 70 ⓓ 10

YOUR SCORE _____

■ **71. How's your blood pressure? (Circle *best* answer.)**

Ⓐ Below 120 over 80—very good.
Ⓑ Above 120 over 80, but below 140 over 90; I do not take blood pressure medication.
⊙ Above 120 over 80, but below 140 over 90; my doctor says I have prehypertension and has put me on a prescription drug.
ⓓ Above 140 over 90, but I control it with a blood pressure medication.
⊜ Above 140 over 90—no meds.

Score: Ⓐ 100 Ⓑ 50 ⊙ 90 ⓓ 80 ⊜ 10

YOUR SCORE _____

▪ **72. When did you last have a colonoscopy, if ever? (Circle *best* answer.)**

Ⓐ I am 50 or older and have never had one of these.

Ⓑ I am 50 or older and had a colonoscopy within the past two years.

Ⓒ I'm 50 or older, and my last one was more than two years ago.

Ⓓ I'm under 50, and I'm really looking forward to having my first colonoscopy when the time comes.

Ⓔ I'm under 50, and I have actually had a colonoscopy.

Score: Ⓐ 0 Ⓑ 100 Ⓒ 70 Ⓓ 70 Ⓔ 100

YOUR SCORE _____

▪ **73. *Women only*: What, if anything, are you doing to detect early signs of breast cancer? (Circle *closest* answer.)**

Ⓐ I regularly self-examine my breasts for lumps, and I routinely have a mammogram or other test (such as a digital tomosynthesis) as recommended by my doctor.

Ⓑ I regularly self-examine my breasts for lumps but have been lax about getting mammograms.

Ⓒ I don't self-examine my breast, or at least not on a regular basis, but I do follow my doctor's advice about mammograms.

Ⓓ I don't check myself or get mammograms.

Ⓔ I have been diagnosed with breast cancer, and I'm successfully dealing with it.

Score: Ⓐ 100 Ⓑ 40 Ⓒ 70 Ⓓ 0 Ⓔ 50

YOUR SCORE _____

■ **74.** *Men only*: **What, if anything, are you doing to check for early signs of prostate cancer? (Circle one.)**

Ⓐ I'm 50 or older, and my doctor does an annual rectal exam to check my prostate and also sends me to a lab for a prostate-specific antigen (PSA) blood test.

Ⓑ I'm 50 or older, and my doctor does an annual rectal exam to check my prostate, but my doctor doesn't recommend regular PSA blood tests, as they don't really work to detect cancer.

Ⓒ I'm under 50, and I have had a baseline PSA test, plus my doctor does the usual rectal exam when I go in for a checkup.

Ⓓ I'm under 50, and I'm not doing much about it.

Ⓔ I'm over 50, and I'm not doing much about this.

Score: Ⓐ 80 Ⓑ 80 Ⓒ 90 Ⓓ 50 Ⓔ 30

YOUR SCORE _____

■ **75. How often do you have your eyes examined? (Circle *best* answer.)**

Ⓐ I'm between the ages of 40 and 60, and I have my eyes examined every two years by an ophthalmologist.

Ⓑ I'm under 40 years old, and I have my eyes examined by an ophthalmologist every five years.

Ⓒ I'm over 60, and my ophthalmologist sees me once a year.

Ⓓ I have my eyes examined by an optometrist on a regular basis.

Ⓔ I'm over 40 and have great eyesight, so I don't need to bother with this.

Ⓕ I'm over 40, and I have had my eyes examined by an ophthalmologist, but not every two years.

Ⓖ None of the above for me.

Score: Ⓐ 100 Ⓑ 100 Ⓒ 100 Ⓓ 0 Ⓔ 0 Ⓕ 60 Ⓖ 0

YOUR SCORE _____

■ **76. What do you do to prevent and to detect skin cancer? (Circle *all* that apply.)**

Ⓐ If I'm going to be out in the sun for more than 15 or 20 minutes, I wear sunscreen.
Ⓑ When I'm out in the sun, I always wear a hat.
Ⓒ I am 40 or older and have an annual skin exam by a dermatologist.
Ⓓ I bake myself at the beach.
Ⓔ I regularly check my skin for any suspicious growths or changes in any moles I might have.
Ⓕ I stay inside and never go out into the sun.

Score: Ⓐ 30 Ⓑ 20 Ⓒ 50 Ⓓ 0 Ⓔ 20 Ⓕ 0

YOUR SCORE _____

■ **77. Who in your family has lived past age 85? (Circle *all* that apply.)**

Ⓐ Mother
Ⓑ Dad
Ⓒ One of my grandmothers
Ⓓ My other grandmother
Ⓔ One of my grandfathers
Ⓕ My other grandfather
Ⓖ One of my aunts or uncles
Ⓗ More than one of my aunts or uncles
Ⓘ One or more of my great-grandparents
Ⓙ One or more of my siblings

Score: 10 points for each

YOUR SCORE _____

■ **78. Does anyone in your family have Alzheimer's disease, or has anyone died from Alzheimer's disease? (Circle *all* that apply.)**

Ⓐ Mother

Ⓑ Dad

Ⓒ One of my grandmothers

Ⓓ My other grandmother

Ⓔ One of my grandfathers

Ⓕ My other grandfather

Ⓖ One of my aunts or uncles

Ⓗ More than one of my aunts or uncles

Ⓘ One or more of my great-grandparents

Ⓙ One or more of my siblings

Ⓚ No one that I know of

Score: Ⓐ through Ⓙ 0; Ⓚ 100

YOUR SCORE _____

YOUR FINAL SCORE

Using a calculator, if you have one handy, add up the scores you earned from each question. If you don't have a calculator, sorry—you'll just have to add it up the old-fashioned way.

Total score _____

What Your Score Means

The highest score is 7,900. We don't think it is possible for anyone to achieve this, but please let us know if you do, because we'd like to support your petition to the Vatican for sainthood. A "passing score" is 3,830. At this level you're not doing enough positive things to counter the aging process, but you're not speeding it up, either. To begin to count down your age, you have to score higher.

From our research and experience, we believe you can count down your age by 20 years if you achieve a near perfect score. Based on this, we have devised an algorithm for computing the number of years you can count down your age based on our test. The following tabulation shows you how many years you can count down your age:

Count Down Your Age Scorecard

Your Score	Number of Years You Can Count Down Your Age
3,630–3,820	0 Years
3,830–4,020	1
4,030–4,220	2
4,230–4,420	3
4,430–4,610	4
4,620–4,810	5
4,820–5,010	6
5,020–5,210	7
5,220–5,410	8
5,420–5,610	9
5,620–5,810	10
5,820–6,020	11
6,030–6,210	12
6,220–6,400	13
6,410–6,590	14
6,600–6,790	15
6,800–6,990	16
7,000–7,190	17
7,200–7,390	18
7,400–7,590	19
7,600–7,900	20

8 4 3
5 2
6
3 7
1
6 3
5
2
8

2

Live Better, Live Longer Lifestyle Plan

Sleep, Have Sex, and Laugh Your Way to the Fountain of Youth

In this chapter we are going to be really preachy and tell you how to live your life. To be honest, neither of us is a Goody Two-shoes, and we don't like sanctimonious people telling us how to live. Neither should you—and we'd be ashamed to even begin if we both hadn't learned the value of a healthy lifestyle the hard way.

Dave was recently at a health conference where a well-known antiaging doctor commented that he had eaten at McDonald's only once; he said he took one bite of a Big Mac and spit it out into a napkin. "I never went back," he claimed. Whether this is true or not, it reminded Dave of Bill Clinton's statement about smoking marijuana: "I never inhaled." Dave would have liked the doctor more if he had said, "I used to scarf down Big Macs morning, noon, and night," and he would have liked Clinton better if he'd said, "It was heavy, man; I got totally wasted."

No matter what condition your life (and your body) may be in, it is not too late to turn things around. Start now, and you can get healthier and happier and live a more rewarding, fulfilling life.

An unhealthy lifestyle can bring you down, but a healthy one can provide miraculous restoration. We are both prime examples.

We want you to know our *true* Long Lifestyle stories.

THE PRESTIGIOUS HEART SURGEON

Dr. Frederic J. Vagnini, a.k.a. "Dr. V," was one of the world's most successful and highly regarded heart surgeons. A flashy dresser, he wore hand-tailored suits, drove fancy cars, and for recreation went sportfishing off the coast of Florida on his own yacht. He operated on thousands of people with heart and blood vessel disease. Dr. V knew the consequences of unhealthy living, yet he smoked cigarettes, drank more than he should, had a horrible diet, and, other than the fishing, got no exercise. "I was really down the drain," he says.

When he opened his first private practice on Long Island, Dr. V was a handsome, six-foot-five, slightly built man who seemed to have it all. Happily married, he settled into his comfortable life and looked forward to raising a family. Gradually, he started to put on the pounds, and when his wife was pregnant with their first child, he discovered snack food. He recalls, "When my wife ate some ice cream in the evening, she would be satisfied with just a few bites. However, when I joined her, it triggered my cravings."

The cravings got so severe that Dr. V started going to bed with two sandwiches. One he would eat while watching the late-night show. The other he saved for when he woke up in the middle of the night.

Smoking got to be a serious problem, too; he started using an inhaler to continue his tobacco habit. Smoking was also "tearing up my stomach," he says, "yet I kept right on smoking." For this problem, Dr. V started taking Zantac.

In those days, breakfast was pretty simple: a cigarette and some black coffee with an artificial sweetener. Lunch at the office was a sandwich, some potato chips, and a Coca-Cola or, if he went out for lunch, a plate of bow-tie pasta, plenty of bread and butter, and a martini. Not the greatest diet, for sure, but not a huge number of calories either—not enough to explain how he got to weigh well over 300 pounds. Dr. V started buying his suits at the big and tall men's store.

After the birth of his first daughter, Dr. V fulfilled a promise to his wife and stopped smoking. Ultimately, this was a huge health step, but its immediate impact wasn't so great. He explains: "I replaced the cigarettes with sugar. I drank more alcohol, and I ate all kinds of cakes and pies, often with ice cream. And then, I started eating Doritos at night." He quickly added on another 40 pounds.

"It was the Doritos," he says. "You can actually become addicted to them, and I was." Dr. V ate Doritos all day long. We now know that eating carbohydrates such as Doritos quickly raises insulin levels, which subsequently lowers blood sugar levels, which causes a craving for more carbohydrates. Thus, Dr. V's addiction was very real.

Dr. V still managed to convince himself that he could bring his eating and weight under control if he just tried a little harder. But given his obvious lack of success, he felt a tad uncomfortable advising patients on weight loss. As do many other doctors, he simply handed out the typical diet sheets, knowing his patient wouldn't follow them anyway.

Looking in the mirror, Dr. V saw yellow, fatty spots appearing on his eyelids—a condition called *xanthelasma*, that results from high cholesterol. When he took his infant daughter out in the stroller, he found himself so out of breath that he had to stop and rest on a bench. Dr. V ordered blood tests for himself.

Dr. V's office assistant placed the test results on his desk along with a stack of other paperwork, so he didn't see them right away. Then, late one evening, when he was the last person in the office, he absentmindedly picked up the lab sheet and started reading it without realizing that it was *his* test. "Oh, my," Dr. V thought, "this patient is in serious trouble." Wondering who it was, he looked up at the name and was shocked. It was his.

Dr. V's lifestyle didn't change much at first; that took an act of "divine intervention," triggered by one of his patients. Appearing at the office for a routine physical, this middle-aged man was dramatically healthier than he had been for years. His weight was down, his blood pressure was normal, and he seemed happy—not his usual grumpy self. The patient smiled mischievously as he explained the basis of his newfound health and handed Dr. V a copy of the book *The Carbohydrate Addict's Diet*, by Dr. Richard Heller and Dr. Rachael Heller.

Clearly visible on the book cover, the words *carbohydrate addict* screamed out at him. "That's me," he thought. "I'm addicted to carbohydrates." Dr. V threw out his remaining packages of Doritos. He read the book, changed his diet, and even sought out the authors and started working with them on a program for heart disease prevention and restoration. Dr. V became the coauthor of their sequel, *The Carbohydrate Addict's Healthy Heart Program*. Over the next few months, he lost 90 pounds, regained his strength, and built a powerful-looking physique. He studied to become a nutri-

Americans Are Fatter than Reported

Researchers at the Harvard School of Public Health were somewhat dumbfounded when they discovered that the obesity levels of Americans were far worse than had been previously reported. The problem was that people often provided incorrect information about their weight and height, particularly in telephone surveys, and as a consequence, the researchers found that estimates of obesity have been too low by more than 50 percent.

Women underestimate their weight more than men do; however, men tend to overestimate their height. The researchers calculated the corrected prevalence of obesity in the United States at 28.7 percent for adult men and 34.5 percent for adult women—more than 50 percent higher than previously estimated.

tionist and an antiaging doctor, stopped doing surgery, and opened his own wellness center. Dr. V reinvented himself.

Today Dr. V eats a very healthy diet, following the guidelines of the Long Life Eating Plan, and he works out regularly. His weekly radio programs, heard around the country, focus on the latest health and longevity developments. Dr. V has also learned how to drastically reduce the stress in his life through "stress awareness," meditation, and prayer and by regularly getting a good night's sleep. He's still a great cook, only his favorite cookbook is no longer *The Meat Lover's Cookbook*, but rather *The Slow Mediterranean Kitchen*.

COMPUTER PUBLISHING MOGUL

Founder of computer magazine blockbusters *PC*, *PC World*, and *Macworld*, Dave Bunnell had it made in the shade. Chairman and CEO of a booming media company, he was making great money and lived in a large California ranch-style house in the wealthy suburb of Hillsborough, California, with a second home in the Colorado Rockies.

Unlike Dr. V, Dave knew about good nutrition and living a healthy lifestyle. His inspirational grandmother, Sadie Taylor, was one of the first Americans to practice yoga and advocate eating organic fruits and vegetables. She carried copies of Adelle Davis's book *Let's Eat Right to Keep Fit*, handing them out for free to anyone who would listen to her mildly scolding lectures. People thought of her as a "health nut," but she was very special to Dave, and he took her message to heart. The only problem was that he didn't practice what he knew.

Dave decided that someday he would really be healthy, just not now. He was too busy with his magazines and coping with the enormous stress of running a large company.

"My day started with a glass of fresh-squeezed orange juice (160 calories, 20 grams of sugar) that I would make myself, followed by a large cup of espresso with milk. On my way to work, I almost always took two or three hits of marijuana from one of the joints that I always seemed to find in my ashtray," Dave says. "This is where the trouble with my diet began."

The drive to work was about 40 minutes. By the time he got close to the office, the munchies set in. Two nearby choices appealed to him: Noah's Bagels and McDonald's. If he stopped at Noah's, he would have one of the large onion bagels, slathered with extra sun-dried tomato smear (512 calories, 30 grams of fat); if it was McDonald's, he just had to have the Sausage McMuffin with cheese (560 calories, 32 grams of fat), washed down with another orange juice.

Dave didn't snack in the morning, but he drank about five cups of coffee with half-and-half to keep going until lunchtime. By noon he was famished. One of his favorite lunch spots was a nearby barbeque restaurant.

"On my way to lunch, unless I was with someone who wasn't 'cool,' I'd have another hit or two of marijuana, just to wake up the ole taste buds," he says. Dave's favorite sandwich was the one piled high with two meats, brisket and pulled pork, on a large sour roll, with extra sauce and spicy fries (approximately 1,200 calories, 32 grams of fat). Usually he drank iced tea, but sometimes he'd have a pint of beer.

No matter how much he ate for lunch, by midafternoon Dave would always be tired and hungry and ready to crash. It was time to send his assistant out for the Ben & Jerry's large coffee-flavored milk shake (520 calories, 24 grams of fat).

After work, Dave hopped back into his 12-cyclinder "Lister" Jaguar, lit up one of the fine cigars he was fond of smoking (Montecristo No. 2 Habano was his favorite), and drove about halfway home before stopping at the sports bar, where he liked to unwind with a couple gin martinis. Somehow he made it home, where he'd take a brief dip in his backyard pool or occasionally ride his bicycle around the neighborhood (so he could "stay in shape"). Dave had a complete gym set up in his house, which included $50,000 worth of resistance machines, free weights, and aerobic equipment, but he seldom bothered with this.

If Dave wasn't cooking in his gourmet kitchen, where he was a whiz with homemade pastas and all sorts of fruit tarts, he liked

Long Lifestyle Things *Not* to Do

We don't want to spend too much time telling you not to smoke or close down the neighborhood bar every evening, because if you did these things, you probably wouldn't pick up our book in the first place. However, our Long Life Program would be incomplete without a list of no-no's.

1. **Don't smoke anything.** This includes pipes and cigars as well as cigarettes—marijuana as well as crack cocaine. Anyone who tells you marijuana is safe is ignorant of the fact that both long- and shorter-term marijuana users perform more poorly on tests of memory, attention, and mental-processing speed than nonusers.
2. **Stop drinking.** If you can't have just one or two drinks and stop, then you need to get off the sauce completely.
3. **Don't be reckless.** No point in taking great care of yourself only to get killed because you didn't wear a seat belt or you were blabbing away on your cell phone while driving.
4. **Protect your hearing.** Avoid exposure to loud music. Take earplugs if your grandson insists that you come along to the next Cradle of Filth concert.
5. **Don't be bored.** Boredom leads to depression and a whole lot of negative energy, which is not good for you.
6. **Don't kick the dog.** If you can't manage your anger—seek help.
7. **Don't fool yourself.** Honestly assess your health, habits, and disposition, as well as the effect you have on people around you. Change begins with self-realization.

to go out for steak or chops. He loved the 16-ounce porterhouse cut (1,200 calories, 60 grams of fat) with grilled onions, mashed potatoes, and—remembering the wise words of his grandmother—spinach. Of course, dinner always included two or three glasses of red wine. He would eat dessert only if he was with his wife and she wanted to share something—he needed to cut back somewhere, he thought.

"To speak the bitter truth," Dave says, "I was out of control. The pot smoking and the drinking stimulated my appetite. There were days when I ate massive amounts of food." Compounding this, Dave stayed up past midnight, watching movies from his extensive collection, smoking more pot, drinking rare single-malt Scotch whiskey, and, more often than not, devouring an entire pint of Häagen-Dazs vanilla ice cream (1,040 calories, 60 grams of fat). "Once you pop off the lid of a Häagen-Dazs and start eating, it is hard to stop," he says.

Dave never went to see his doctor. He didn't have one. Head firmly buried in the sand, he lived this way year in and year out until a series of personal tragedies, including the death of his 26-year-old son and the dot-com bust, finally got him to look into the mirror and realize he needed to change his act before it was too late. "My wife told me that our son had appeared to her in a dream," he says, "and he wanted me to take care of myself."

For the first time in 20 years, Dave went to see a doctor for a checkup. What do you know: he had high blood pressure, high LDL (low-density lipoprotein) cholesterol, a very high homocysteine level, and a high level of triglycerides, and he was 60 pounds overweight. The doctor put him on a blood pressure medication, the prediabetic drug metformin, and told him to exercise more. She also suggested he see a nutritionist, but since Dave already knew all about that, he didn't bother.

Realizing how foolish it must be for a 50-year-old man to smoke pot, he simply stopped. It amazed him how easy this was, so he also cut way back on the drinking and started swimming on a regular basis. Dave bought a more sensible car, and since he didn't want it to smell like cigar smoke, he stopped smoking cigars. One day while he was swimming, he started thinking about his grandmother and how she made it her mission to spread the good news about exercise, organic food, and maintaining a healthy lifestyle. Lying on his back looking at the sky, he saw the epiphany that would change his life flash before his eyes: utilizing what he knew about media he could take on Grandma Sadie's mission and reach thousands, if not millions, of people. Having eaten lunch that day at a Chinese restaurant named Long Life Veggie House, he decided right then and there to start the LongLifeClub (longlifeclub.com)—an online resource for boomers like himself who wanted to be healthier and live longer.

The psychology of Dave's decision worked to his advantage. Always the overachiever, he realized he couldn't be the founder of the "LongLifeClub" and not be dedicated to his own healthy lifestyle. Redoubling his exercise efforts, Dave added cycling, weight lifting, and rowing to his routine. He volunteered to be the basketball coach at his granddaughters' all-girls school.

The absolute hardest change for Dave was cutting back on meat consumption. While growing up in Nebraska, he learned to love not only great steaks but also great hamburgers, ribs, lunch meat, sausage, and even meat loaf. Dave ate meat at lunch and dinner and often at breakfast. No wonder his LDL cholesterol was so high. He gradually accomplished this change—currently he eats meat about once a week—but it took several months of cutting back. At first he substituted chicken for the hamburgers he liked to eat for lunch, and he started eating more fish at dinner. One happy day, Dave discovered he could actually eat a vegetarian meal now and again *without losing his manhood.* These days he almost always eats salad for lunch and, two or three times a week, has a veggie dinner.

PULL OUT OF YOUR BRAIN FOG

We are convinced that a large percentage of middle-aged and older people live in a perpetual "brain fog." When Dr. V was fat, he didn't really think he was fat, even though he kept buying larger suits. For years, Dave kept telling himself he could stop drinking and smoking pot anytime he wanted.

The time to clear the fog is now. Changing your lifestyle can add 10 or more productive years to your life. If you can't figure out what to do with this health bonus, get involved in the world outside your doorstep and dedicate yourself to a cause in which you believe. Become an environmentalist or a missionary—we don't care which; just do something radically different. Get more involved with your grandkids or with your neighborhood church. Start an e-Bay business, travel to Africa, learn a new language, take up the violin, learn how to hang glide—let your imagination be your guide.

GET SOME SLEEP!

Believe it or not, a healthy lifestyle starts with sleep. Once you understand that we live in what Dr. William C. Dement, the father of sleep medicine, calls a "sleep-sick society," you'll get the picture and join us in making sleep a priority. Odds are better than 90 percent that you are not getting enough on a consistent basis. Changing this will profoundly enhance your mood, cognitive capability, productivity, communication skills, and overall health, including your gastrointestinal system, cardiovascular functioning, and immune systems.

If, like more than 50 percent of the adults living in the industrialized world, you are chronically sleep deprived, not addressing this problem can kill you. You might also take out a few innocent bystanders. In a National Sleep Foundation survey, 23 percent of the people polled admitted to having fallen asleep while driving in the past year, and more than 30 percent said they'd fallen asleep at the wheel at least once in their lifetime. Sleep deprivation plays a major role in most accidents labeled "cause unknown." Twenty-four thousand people die each year in North America and Europe in accidents caused by falling asleep at the wheel. And this is only the tip of the iceberg. Literally hundreds of thousands of people worldwide are dying each year because of undiagnosed and untreated sleep disorders. If you know someone who had a heart attack, chances are that an undiagnosed sleep disorder contributed to the problem.

Lack of sleep also contributes to weight gain. "There are a number of research studies that all support the thesis that too little sleep leads to weight gain," says J. Catesby Ware, director of the Sleep Disorder Center at Sentara Norfolk General Hospital, in Norfolk, Virginia. "How that happens is still somewhat unclear, but there are hormonal secretions that are affected with sleep loss that apparently affect appetite and eating."

Millions of people are fatigued and exhausted every day because they don't manage their sleep. On average, adults today sleep one and a half fewer hours each night than their great-grandparents. People are staggering through their lives in a stupor, not comprehending the cause of their endless sleepiness. Do you know anyone who is apathetic, run-down, glum? A few really good nights' sleep could be just what the doctored ordered.

Doctors once failed to understand how lack of sleep contributes so mightily to the ailments of their patients; today perhaps they understand it all too well. Many doctors and their patients have turned to the quick-fix solution—sleeping pills. More than 40 million prescriptions are written every year in the United States, and this number has been rising steadily over the past 10 years.

We're not 100 percent opposed to prescription sleeping pills, as newer drugs don't carry the same risk of dependence as older ones such as barbiturates. However, they don't provide a real long-term solution to sleep deprivation, often mask treatable causes, and have serious side effects, as in the case of Ambien. The most common side effect is grogginess the following day, but more serious side effects include sleepwalking and impaired consciousness, judgment, memory, and intelligence. Sleeping pills *do not* improve daytime function or performance. The kind of sleep you need to operate at optimum levels of energy ("quality sleep") is not provided by sleeping pills.

Your Nightly Sleep Cycle

We sleep because our primitive ancestors needed to avoid the dangers of wandering around in the dark, right? Until German physiatrist Hans Berger came along in 1929 and started measuring brain-wave activity by attaching small electrodes to the scalp, that was pretty much what we knew about sleep.

Thanks to Berger's invention of electroencephalograms (EEGs) we now know that sleep can be divided into five distinct stages of brain-wave activity that unfold within an hour from drowsiness to shallow sleep to deep sleep to rapid eye movement (REM) sleep and then, except for the first stage, repeat themselves. Each of these stages is vital to our mental and physical health; collectively, they form a sleep cycle that repeats itself every 90 to 110 minutes.

The deepest stage—stage four, or slow-wave sleep—lasts only 30 to 40 minutes. It is very important because it is a time of body recovery, during which the blood supply to your muscles is increased; body temperature is turned down to conserve energy; metabolic activity is lowered; and secretion of growth hormone, which also repairs the tissues, reaches its 24-hour daily peak.

The final stage is REM sleep. You experience the first dreams of the night when REM sleep begins, respiration and blood pressure increase and become somewhat irregular, and your brain emits theta waves. You are so relaxed that you are unable to move, literally paralyzed. Why? Well, sleep scientists think this is a mechanism to protect yourself and your bed partner from injury, because if you could move, you would "act out" your dreams. Some men have a defect that impairs the brain from stopping motor cortex impulses during REM sleep, and they have indeed caused serious injury to themselves and others. (Dreams occur during all stages of sleep, but they occur more frequently during REM sleep and are more vivid and emotional.)

Your body might be completely still during REM sleep, but your mind is active. As the blood flow increases to your brain, your eyes dart about rapidly, and neuronal stimulation skyrockets. All the ideas and information your brain has stored during the daytime is reorganized, edited, and filed away. Without REM sleep, your brain's ability to transfer short-term memory into long-term memory is impaired, and you become mentally dysfunctional.

REM sleep has an interesting side effect, namely erections in men and increased vaginal engorgement and lubrication in women. You may be surprised to know that this happens 95 percent of the time during REM sleep and has nothing at all to do with your dreams. Rather, it is nature's way of replenishing your sexual organs with oxygen and nutrients to help maintain healthy sexual functioning.

REM typically lasts only about 10 minutes per sleep cycle. However, it increases if you spend some of your daylight hours intensively learning new things. Researchers have shown that college students have a dramatic increase of REM sleep for several days after they study for a final exam. A significant increase in REM sleep will strengthen your memory circuits in the same way that lifting weights can strengthen your muscles. The more REM sleep you get, the better your short-term memory and cognitive performance.

Turn Off That Squawk Box!

One solution to sleep problems is to turn off the TV so you don't see those sleeping pill commercials! We live in a 24/7 culture that discourages us from sleeping too much, and TV is a big part of this. Way too many of us stay up late watching David Letterman or a movie or sporting event—perhaps because we want to talk about it at work the next day so we'll seem to be in the know. Seriously, though, if you have a television in your bedroom and you care one iota about the state of your health, get rid of it as soon as possible. Lying in bed while watching TV is one of the most common and most preventable causes of sleep deprivation.

Your ancestors didn't have late-night TV, all-night diners or movie theaters, Jack-in-the-Box open-'til-midnight drive-up windows, 24-hour Safeways, baseball under the lights, or after-hours clubs. Not so long ago, they didn't even have electric lights.

How Much Sleep Do *You* Need?

If you never yawn or feel fatigued during the day and you fall asleep at night in about 20 minutes, wake up "naturally" in the morning without the aid of an alarm clock, and repeat this pattern day after day, you are getting enough sleep and can skip to the next section of the book.

After believing for years that the average person can get by on 7 or 8 hours of sleep a night, sleep researchers are increasingly coming around to the conclusion that we really need the same amount of sleep our ancestors got—10 hours. This isn't making them very popular, as many people think of sleep as a waste of time. We live in a culture that frowns on people who "sleep too much." We see them as lazy and unproductive. True, our sleep needs are not all the same—there are people who can get by on as little as 3 hours of sleep a night, but this is rare. According to Dr. William Dement, "No one who is an unusually short sleeper has been studied in a way that absolutely proves the claim." Thomas Edison thought that people got twice as much sleep as they needed and that this extra sleep made them "unhealthy and inefficient." He boasted that he slept only 4 hours a night, but there is strong anecdotal evidence that he was a prodigious daytime napper whose total sleep was closer to 8 hours.

Also, our biological clocks change over time. Many people find themselves going to bed earlier than they used to and rising in the early-morning hours. Sleep researchers refer to this as changing from an "owl" to a "lark," and it is perfectly normal. Problems are created, however, when you resist the changes in your biological clock. If you can learn to understand what your body is trying to tell you and simply go with the flow, your sleep will improve automatically. Both Dave and Dr. V used to stay up past midnight, but now they both typically go to bed before 10 P.M. and rise around 6 A.M. A few years from now, it would not be surprising if one or both went to bed as early as 8 P.M. and got up at 4 A.M.

Many older people who have difficulty maintaining sleep resort to napping, which is fine, except that the quality of their sleep is also an issue. As we age, the amount of stage three, stage four, and REM sleep tends to decline, and we are stuck mostly in stage one and stage two. How much of this is "natural" and how much can be attributed to other factors is difficult to determine. Psychiatric disorders (particularly depression), the use of psychoactive drugs, and medical disorders (notably coronary heart disease and hypertension) are associated with the incidence and persistence of disturbed sleep.

There is no exact scientific way to determine how much sleep you need, but you can learn a lot about your biological clock by keeping a "sleep diary" for a week or two. The Count Down Your Age Sleep Diary will show some patterns to help you address sleep. If, for example, you always score low the hour after lunch, you might consider arranging to take a short nap (no more than 20 minutes) during lunchtime, or you might go to bed earlier and see how much difference this makes. We encourage you to experiment. If it turns out you feel more rested after nine hours of sleep than after eight hours, then you know you need nine hours.

Your Sleep-Conducive Bedroom

You'll never get a good night's sleep if you don't have a great place to sleep that isn't cluttered with lots of distractions. This means a bedroom limited to three basic functions: getting dressed and undressed, sleeping, and sex. Likewise, your bed should be limited to bedtime reading, sleeping, and sex.

The best bedrooms are quiet, dark, and cool. Any sound that exceeds 70 decibels can stimulate your nervous system enough to keep you awake—so, for heaven's sake, fix that dripping faucet in the nearby bathroom, and if your alarm clock goes tick-tick-tick too loudly, get a new one. Some sounds are hard to control, including barking dogs, car alarms, noisy radiators, late-night revelers,

Countdown Your Age Sleep Diary

Date _____

Complete in the morning

Time you went to bed _____

Time you fell asleep _____

Time you woke up _____

Number of times awakened during the night _____

Amount of time awake during the night _____

Total nighttime sleep _____

Describe the quality of your sleep_____

Were you groggy when you woke up? Yes _____ No _____

If yes, how long? _____

Complete before going to bed

Did you take any naps today? Yes _____ No _____

If yes, estimate your total nap time _____

Describe the quality of your naps _____

   Using the following Long Life Scale, note how alert you were during the day:

   1. Vital, alert, full of piss and vinegar
   2. Great, but not at my absolute best
   3. Relaxed, not fully alert, but functioning OK
   4. Slow, a little fuzzy, mellow, not active
   5. Dragging my butt, maybe depressed
   6. Sleepy, prefer to be lying down
   7. Extremely hard to stay awake

In the early morning, after waking up, I would rank myself (1 to 7)

_____

A couple hours after waking up _____

Late morning _____

Lunchtime _____

An hour after lunch _____

Midafternoon _____
Late afternoon _____
Dinnertime _____
An hour after dinner _____
Late evening _____
Using this scale, rate your overall sleepiness/alertness today _____

If you are not scoring 1 or 2 on the overall question, you need more sleep. We urge you to add some hours to your sleep schedule to see how much of a difference this might make. If you feel better but still aren't scoring as high as you'd like, chances are you are carrying a large sleep debt. In this case, we recommend that you add a regular nap to your daily routine, and if this still doesn't do the trick, add two naps.

---

your deaf neighbor's blaring TV, cats in heat, and sirens. If these or other nuisances bother you, get a "white noise" machine such as SleepMate, which masks out disturbances with a low-level, soothing sound. Try earplugs like the ones they sometimes give you on airplanes. If you're a helpless tightwad, tune your FM radio to a neutral spot between two channels and leave it on at a low volume; the "pseudo white noise" really works—you could become addicted to it.

Humans were designed to sleep in darkness; you really want your bedroom to be dark. When you get ready to go to bed, pull the curtains and shut the door. If you can't get the room near a pitch-black state, use eyeshades. Dave uses them every night and swears by them. In fact, tired of the cheap eyeshades sold at airports, he sought out a better pair, which he found at a high-end travel store.

Keep the temperature in your bedroom in the range of 60 to 65 degrees. If it is any warmer than this, or if you sleep with too many blankets and bedclothes, you're much more likely to have nightmares or wake up in a sweat. Some people like fresh air when they sleep, which is fine, but it is not a prerequisite. If your bedroom air is dry, a humidifier will also help.

A sleep-conducive bedroom is neat and tidy. Piles of laundry and stacks of unpaid bills, reports, and half-finished manuscripts will only serve to distract you; you'll wind up lying in bed all night thinking you should have, could have, would have, but didn't do this thing or that thing.

Invest in your bedding! Clean, good-quality sheets and pillow-cases, especially those made of linen, create a soothing feeling and make a difference in how quickly you lapse into a really deep sleep. A good pillow and a firm mattress give you the support you need in the right places and will keep you from developing neck or back pain. Neck-roll and contour pillows provide excellent cervical support and also are highly recommended.

12 Strategic Sleeping Tips

The International Classification of Sleep Disorders, Diagnostic and Coding Manual, published by the American Sleep Disorders Association, recognized 78 sleep disorders, some of which are too serious to be treated without the assistance of a doctor or sleep specialist. The next section of this chapter offers suggestions regarding what to say to your doctor to get the help you need, if you need it. Before pursuing that course, you can employ some very effective strategies to get a better night's sleep.

1. Make sleep a priority in your life. When you are out at night, don't be afraid to say, "Sorry, good buddy, I've got to go home and get my beauty rest."

2. Establish a regular sleep cycle. Your body has biorhythms that are day-to-day consistent, and the more consistent you are about sleeping, the easier it will be for you to get the rest you need. Don't deprive yourself of a night out to the movies, but otherwise, stick to the schedule, *even on the weekends.*

3. Let the evening wind down. As bedtime draws nearer, detach yourself from the stressful concerns of daily life. Quit thinking about work or about things you have to do. Relax by watching TV, reading, playing cards, or whatever else you can do to eliminate disturbing thoughts. Unplug the phone.

4. Meditate. If you have difficulty unwinding, try this:
- Find a quiet place with dim light where you can lie on the floor and close your eyes.
- Breathe slowly and deeply through your nose until your lungs are completely full, and then exhale slowly.
- Focus on your toes—totally relax them. Next, focus on your feet, relaxing them as well. Move progressively up your body: lower legs, thighs, stomach, chest, arms, neck, head, and finally, your face.
- Completely relaxed and breathing slowly, remain for a minimum of 5 minutes and a maximum of 20 minutes. If your mind wanders too much, try saying a single, one-syllable word to yourself each time you exhale. "Om" works well, but if this is just too corny for you, use a different word.
- When you finish with this exercise, if you're not yet ready for bed, spend the rest of the evening doing something quiet, such as reading or listening to soothing music. No TV.

5. Don't smoke anything! If you regularly smoke cigarettes, pipes, or cigars, don't smoke for two or three hours before going to bed. Nicotine stimulates brain-wave activity and increases both your blood pressure and your pulse. Marijuana also stimulates brain-wave activity and increases blood pressure and pulse rates.

6. No booze near bedtime. Alcohol will sometimes make you fall asleep quickly, but the quality of your sleep will be poor and disturbed. Within three or four hours, you are likely to wake up and have a hard time going back to sleep. The best rule is to not drink alcohol three hours before bed.

7. No caffeine. Starting in the late afternoon, avoid drinking coffee or any other beverage that has caffeine, including tea and soft drinks. If you eat chocolate at night, have only a tiny bit, as it contains a small amount of caffeine. Caffeine is the enemy of sleep. If you don't believe this, have a double espresso at Starbucks around 9 P.M.; you'll be sorry.

8. Unwind in a hot tub or in a warm bath or shower before bed. Warm water tends to pull blood to the surface of your skin and away from your brain, helping you relax and become drowsy.

9. Avoid bedtime arguments or stressful conversations. Have an agreement with your domestic partner, your wife, your lover, your roommate, or the servant who sleeps at the foot of your bed that neither of you will initiate any type of anxiety-inducing arguments or discussions in the bedroom.

10. Establish a bedtime ritual. Do a few gentle stretches before climbing into the sack. Turn off the overhead light, and use a reading lamp to read an enjoyable novel or magazine (nothing work related). Listen to some mellow music. If you are religious, say your prayers—only make them prayers of thanks and not urgent pleas for divine intervention. Create a bedtime routine that works for you, and stick to it. You'll find yourself looking forward to this special time of the day. Your routine will help you clear your mind of the day's worries.

11. Have some hot sex. Endorphins released by having sex with your partner or yourself can promote the onset of sleep and enhance the quality of your sleep. However, avoid sexual experiences that make you feel anxious, dissatisfied, or disgusted with yourself—you'll lie awake at night wondering, "What the hell is wrong with me?"

12. Try melatonin. Melatonin is a natural hormone made by your body's pea-sized pineal gland that induces sleep, among other things. During the day, the pineal is inactive, but when the sun goes down and darkness occurs, the pineal is "turned on" and begins to actively produce melatonin. As a result, melatonin levels in the blood rise sharply, and you begin to feel less alert, making sleep more inviting.

As we age, the pineal gland produces less and less melatonin. Fortunately for many people, synthetic melatonin is available as a supplement in doses as small as 1 milligram up to 5 milligrams. The research on melatonin is mixed, with some studies concluding that it is no more effective than a placebo and other studies saying it is effective, particularly for people suffering from jet lag or any prolonged period of sleep deprivation. Our personal experience is that melatonin, correctly used, works incredibly well. Dave takes it on a nightly basis, and Dr. V recommends it to some of his patients.

The biggest problem with melatonin is that the dosage required varies from person to person, and for most people it is very small—much smaller than the pills you buy at the drugstore. If you're not taking melatonin, Dr. V recommends you start with the 1 milligram size and take half or less. If this doesn't work, keep taking a bit more until it works. You can take up to 10 milligrams, and some people require this much. Other than the grogginess, there are no known side effects.

Are You *Sure* You Don't Have Sleep Apnea?

If you have a good bedroom for sleeping and a cooperative sleeping mate (or none at all), and you've tried our 12 Strategic Sleeping Tips, but you still can't seem to get the sleep you need, you may very well have a sleeping disorder that requires medical intervention. Call your doctor for an appointment—and when you go in, make it clear that sleep deprivation is *the reason* you are there. Don't make it secondary by saying something like, "By the way, Doc, I know I'm here about that little itchy thing, but I thought I'd mention I haven't got a good night's sleep for 10 or 12 years." Doctors are often distracted by their heavy patient loads and will focus on your primary complaint—essentially ignoring anything else. If your doctor doesn't seem concerned or simply says "Ah-huh" and writes you a prescription, ask for a referral to a sleep specialist.

We specifically want you to rule out any possibility that you have an extremely underdiagnosed condition called sleep apnea. Sometimes called the "disease of the 21st century," sleep apnea can lead to obesity, heart disease, diabetes, strokes, and heart attacks, to say nothing of fatal automobile accidents. An estimated 30 million Americans and more than 100 million people worldwide have undiagnosed sleep apnea.

Do you sometimes doze off during the day because your sleep the night before was restless? Do you snore? Frequently feel tired and sometimes irritable? People with undiagnosed sleep apnea often try various forms of sleep therapy and medications, or they just accept being tired and miserable. Many times, it is the complaints about loud snoring from spouses or bed partners that provide the key to a belated diagnosis. If you say to your doctor, "My wife says I have to do something about my snoring," your doctor might suspect sleep apnea. If you say, "I'm having a hard time sleeping," the easy thing to do is prescribe a "sleep aid" like Ambien or Lunesta.

What the Heck Is Sleep Apnea? The word *apnea* comes from the Greek word meaning "without breath," and there couldn't be a better description, because people with this condition literally stop breathing. It is not uncommon for someone with apnea to stop breathing 700 or more times in one night. Muscles that normally keep the throat open during wakefulness relax and allow the throat to narrow. The result is that air is restricted or cannot pass through.

What happens when you stop breathing in your sleep? Well, your brain wakes up so that your body can breathe again, and then you quickly go back to sleep. This happens so fast and frequently that most sufferers aren't even aware of it. The result is predictable: you never really get a deep sleep but instead experience a shallow, fragmented sleep that leaves you tired and often grumpy during the day.

To learn more about sleep apnea, and how to diagnose and treat it, we suggest you look up the website sleepquest.com. Sleep Quest is a commercial company, but it provides some great information about sleep apnea, including a test to determine if you are a likely candidate. If appropriate, it offers a home diagnostic test instead of requiring that you go to a "sleep laboratory." This is hugely important because sleeping in a lab with all sorts of wires attached to your body is not something many people want to do, but until recently, it was the only way to diagnose sleep apnea.

HAVE A LONG LIFE SEX LIFE

Not much question about it, sex is good for your health. According to the *British Medical Journal*, men who have an orgasm more often than twice a week are 50 percent less likely to die prematurely than men who have an orgasm less often than once a month, and they are three times less likely to have a heart attack. Of course, if you think about it, men who have an orgasm only once a month tops are probably not very healthy in the first place. So, you may wonder, does sex really make you healthier, or does good health make you sexier? Does it matter?

The picture with women is a bit clearer. Researchers at Duke University's Center on Aging found that the enjoyment of sex is a powerful predictor of reduced mortality in women. No matter how many times a woman has sex, if she is happy with the quality of her sex life, she is likely to live longer than if she is dissatisfied.

No matter how *old* you think you are, there are many important health benefits of maintaining an active sex life. Among these are the following:

▪ **Reduced risk of prostate cancer.** A U.S. study that followed 30,000 men over eight years showed that those who ejaculated most frequently—21 times per month—were a third less likely to develop prostate cancer than those who ejaculated far less frequently (four to seven times a month). Moreover, those ejaculations don't have to involve a partner. Masturbation is just as effective.

▪ **Increased hormone levels.** Sexual activity boosts testosterone and estrogen levels in men and women. For both, increased testosterone fortifies bones and muscles. For women, increased estrogen levels keep vaginal tissues suppler and protect against heart disease.

▪ **Increased blood flow.** The faster heart rate and deep breathing associated with sex improve the flow of blood to your brain and other organs.

▪ **Stress reduction and better sleep.** You know it is true—after sex you are more relaxed, and it is easier for you to sleep. Just don't have one of those after-sex cigarettes as they sometimes show in the movies. Cigarette smoking will speed up your pulse and restrict your blood flow, thereby negating the positive effects you got from getting laid in the first place.

▪ **Pain relief.** Sex causes the release of endorphins, natural opiates that elevate your pain threshold, offering relief for conditions such as arthritis, whiplash, and headaches.

▪ **Vitamin T.** Unless you are having sex only with yourself, the intimacy of sex, especially when love is involved, is very healing. Caressing, hugging, stroking, cuddling—what we call Vitamin T (for Tenderness)—promotes physical and emotional healing. Dr. Dean Ornish, in his book *Love and Survival: The Scientific Basis for the Healing Power of Intimacy*, writes that "an open heart can lead to the most joyful and ecstatic sex." His research indicates that if you have someone in your life for whom you really care, and he or she really cares for you in return, you may have three to five times less risk of premature death and disease from all causes. Count down your age!

Sex and Your Doctor

Your doctor should ask you about your sex life. If not, you might bring up the subject, as this exchange could show that you have the wrong doctor. Doctors are like everybody else—mostly shy about discussing intimate matters. This is an important medical question, and the answer can indicate the state of your physiological or mental health. If you have any sexual dysfunction, there is usually a simple solution. There's no reason for natural, age-related changes to permanently suppress desire or inhibit good lovemaking.

When it comes to sexuality, men and women are very different. ("No, duh," you say.) The peak of a man's sexual functionality occurs around age 18 (what a waste!), while a woman doesn't normally hit her peak until age 35 to 40. Teenage boys can have as many as 10 or 12 erections followed by ejaculations during a single night, whereas men past 50 often feel lucky if it happens once. A woman's ability to achieve orgasm also decreases with age; however, a woman's interest in sex and her ability to enjoy it persist.

Dr. V had an 86-year-old patient who said the sex she was having with a much younger man of 55 was being curtailed because vaginal dryness was making her sore, and she could no longer make love in the mornings. "I can only do it at night," she said. Dr. V gave her a prescription for estrogen cream to restore her vaginal strength and recommended a water-based lubricant before sex. A few weeks later, she reported back to him that she had broken with the 55-year-old man to take on an even younger lover!

LAUGH YOUR HEAD OFF?

"These guys must be nuts," you might be thinking. "First they want me to sleep a lot, and then have sex a lot, and now they want me to laugh a lot." So, what's this got to do with "lifestyle"? The answer is everything.

Laughing might not be as important as sleeping and getting enough sex, but it is very close. People with heart disease are much less likely to laugh in a variety of situations compared with people of the same age without heart disease, according to a study by researchers at the University of Maryland Medical Center. Michael Miller, M.D., who directed this study, said, "The ability to laugh— either naturally or as learned behavior—may have important implications in societies where heart disease remains the number one killer. We know that exercising, not smoking, and eating foods low in saturated fats will reduce the risk of heart disease. Perhaps regular, hearty laughter should be added to the list." We agree.

Norman Cousins, the famous peace activist and former editor of the *Saturday Review*, was one of the first to discover the healing powers of laughter. He watched old Marx Brothers movies as part of his self-devised "humor strategy" to recover from ankylosing spondylitis, a painful and deadly form of arthritis that causes the vertebrae to grow together, making the body stiff and inflexible. Given a 1-in-500 chance of recovery, Cousins famously defied the medical odds and recovered fully.

Just 15 minutes of laughter allowed Cousins to sleep pain-free for two hours. And indeed, blood samples taken at the time showed that his inflammation level was lowered after the laughter treatments. Published in the *New England Journal of Medicine* in 1979, this was the first documentation showing that humor positively affects disease.

Count Down Your Age Laugh Test

To test your ability to see the lighter side, we've devised this short test. (Circle the best answer for each question.)

■ 1. An old friend you haven't heard from in years calls you at 3 A.M. just to chat. How do you respond?

- Ⓐ I slam down the phone immediately and unplug it.
- Ⓑ I politely say, "It's 3 A.M. here. Please call me back during a more decent hour, you moron!"

Ⓒ I talk to my friend in a matter-of-fact voice and get it over with as quickly as possible.

Ⓓ I find something to smile about and have a brief but pleasant conversation with my old buddy.

Ⓔ I'd say to myself, "What the hell" and have a lengthy, friendly talk, during which there is much giggling and hearty laughter.

Score: Ⓐ 0 Ⓑ 1 Ⓒ 2 Ⓓ 3 Ⓔ 4

YOUR SCORE _____

■ **2. You dress to the nines for a special event. When you arrive, one of your friends is wearing the identical outfit. What do you do?**

Ⓐ I walk up and slap her (or him) in the face.

Ⓑ I avoid being too close so other people won't notice.

Ⓒ I find it mildly amusing but don't mention it to my friend or anyone else.

Ⓓ I laugh out loud, and if people ask me why, I tell them.

Ⓔ I walk up to my friend and have a wonderful conversation, during which we point fingers at each other and laugh our fannies off.

Score: Ⓐ 0 Ⓑ 1 Ⓒ 2 Ⓓ 3 Ⓔ 4

YOUR SCORE _____

■ **3. You're at the movies, and one of the characters says something hilarious. You start laughing loudly, but then you notice that no one else is laughing. In fact, some of the people in front of you have turned in their seats and are looking at you. At this point . . .**

Ⓐ I glare back at the people who are looking at me. I hiss loudly.

Ⓑ I clam up and slink down into my seat.

Ⓒ Amused at myself, I stop laughing, but I don't let it bug me.

Ⓓ I let my laughing complete its natural course and pay no
attention to what other people are doing.

Ⓔ The fact that no one else got the joke makes it even funnier;
I laugh a little louder.

Score: Ⓐ 0 Ⓑ 1 Ⓒ 2 Ⓓ 3 Ⓔ 4

YOUR SCORE _____

Total score

A score of 25 or more means you have laugh protection against
heart disease and other stress-related illnesses. *Just kidding!* You
need only 8 points or more to rate this extra insurance. If you score
fewer than 4 points, you are a miserable old dog.

Today humor is broadly accepted for its therapeutic value.
Many hospitals and wellness centers have both formal and infor-
mal laughter-therapy programs. In India, laughing clubs, where
people gather in the early morning to laugh, are growing faster
than Internet social networking sites.

"Ha-ha, where's the scientific evidence?" you may respond.
Well, researchers at the University of Maryland School of Medicine found that laughter significantly increases blood flow by causing the tissue that forms the inner lining of blood vessels—the
endothelium—to expand. The endothelium has a powerful effect
on blood vessel tone and not only regulates blood flow but also
adjusts coagulation and blood thickening, along with secreting
chemicals and other substances in response to wounds, infections,
or irritation.

In the study, a group of 20 healthy men and women first watched
a graphically violent battle scene from the war movie *Saving Private Ryan* and then watched a funny scene from the comedy *King-
pin*. The researchers describe the results as being "dramatic": after
viewing the battle scene, subjects had significantly reduced blood

flow averaging 35 percent; however, after viewing the funny scene, they had significantly increased blood flow averaging 22 percent. This increase is similar to results you'd expect after a 15- to 30-minute workout! The effect of the increased or decreased vasodilation lasted about two hours.

We don't think it necessary to join a laughing club or take laugh therapy to get the benefits from laughter. As a first step, make comedy a regular part of your experience by watching a comedy show on television, going to a funny movie, or reading a funny book. Dave regularly watches the "Daily Show" on the Comedy Central network, and Dr. V has a collection of "I Love Lucy" reruns he likes to watch whenever he's in a sour mood.

The more difficult challenge is to learn how to see humor in stressful situations as a tool for managing anger and controlling unhealthy impulses. This takes some time, but you can do it. Just think back on some recent stressful situation, perhaps a driving-related incident, and think about how ridiculous it was and how you might have dealt with it differently. Dave used to regularly "flip the bird" at inconsiderate drivers and even yell out epithets, but these days he just smiles or laughs at them—and they often return the favor. Dr. V is fortunate in that he's never really been an angry person, but he could be a little thin-skinned; over the years he's learned to set his ego aside enough to laugh at himself. For both of us, humor is the salve for irritations, big and small.

LEAVE THE MOMENT

Laughing isn't the only tool available for reducing the mind-boggling stress of modern life. There's also meditation and an abbreviated form of meditation we call "leaving the moment."

At any point in your day when you feel extra tension or tiredness, you can quickly escape, or leave the moment, by simply focusing on your breathing and taking a few deep breaths. This remarkably effective tool is so darn easy that we're amazed that more people aren't hip to it. Next time you are in a horrendous traffic jam and freaked out about whether you'll make it to work or to the ballpark on time, breathe deeply. Get into the habit of doing this, and you'll too be amazed—amazed at how much easier it is to cope with everyday annoyances so you can concentrate on things that matter.

Another great technique is to focus on areas of tension and allow the corresponding muscles to relax. Try this with the small muscles around your eyes—you can do this right now. Let the muscles relax. Try the same thing with your forehead and then your jaw. Incredible, isn't it? Add your shoulders and the muscles in your belly, and you've pretty much covered the areas in your body where you carry a lot of tension.

By combining relaxation techniques with deep breathing, you can learn to induce a meditative state, which is sometimes called the "relaxation response." Coined by Dr. Herbert Benson, a professor at the Harvard Medical School and president of the Mind Body Medical Institute (mbmi.org), the relaxation response is the body's counterbalance to stress. Stress initiates the fight-or-flight response, in which perceived dangers cause an increase in your heart rate, breathing, and blood flow. In today's modern society, except for relatively rare cases of road rage and the like, we hardly ever fight or run away. Instead, our response causes anxiety, depression, cardiac arrhythmia, and a lowered pain threshold, all related to insomnia, decreased sperm count and sexual response in men, and increased hot flashes, PMS, and infertility in women.

During meditative states, Dr. Benson discovered, breathing slows, heart rate and blood pressure drop, pain threshold increases, a sense of serenity replaces anxiety, hot flashes go away, and sperm count goes up. People who meditate on a regular basis have been able to lower their blood pressure and keep it under control without the use of medications.

Maharishi Mahesh Yogi, who gained fame by hanging out with the Beatles and then established the Transcendental Meditation movement, says that your body is like an ocean. When you stand on the beach and look out at the ocean, you see only the sur-

Count Down Your Age Simple Meditation

Find a quiet place to sit, on the floor or in a comfortable chair. If you are in a chair, your feet should touch the ground. Put your hands in your lap, close your eyes, and pause for a moment. Focus attention on your breathing.

- Slowly and deeply inhale, using your diaphragm to draw air into your lungs.
- As you breathe in, say to yourself, "Count down my age."
- Hold your breath for a second or two.
- Slowly exhale, using your diaphragm to push all the air out of your lungs. Repeat the phrase "Count down my age" as you breathe out.
- Hold your breath for a second or two.
- Repeat the process, only more slowly if possible.
- Stay focused on your breathing as you feel your body relax; you may even have the sensation that it is getting heavier.
- When your mind wanders, return to consciously paying attention to your breathing.

Continue for a few minutes or as long as you can—15 minutes or longer. You will feel refreshed—charged up and ready to face more of the daily battle. During the day, remember how good you felt during your meditation. This is a "starter meditation" that may or may not last you for the rest of your life. There are literally hundreds of more advanced forms of meditations, which you can research on the Internet.

face activity (a few surfers, a boat or two), and you hear the sound of waves crashing to shore; what you don't see is the vast world beneath. Meditation is a journey away from the surface of your mind into the deepest depths. Should you decide to make meditation a serious part of your everyday life, we advise you to go to a meditation center where you can get some guidance. Otherwise, do what we do: when things get hectic, breathe deeply so you can leave the moment and occasionally practice the Count Down Your Age Meditation.

CHERISH YOUR RELATIONSHIPS

Isolation leads to an early grave. You don't have to be married or have a significant other to extend your health span (though it helps), but you need to have an active social network. According to a host of studies, people who are married or have strong social support have less heart disease and lower blood pressure, live longer, and are likely to be happier (less depression) than people who don't.

You may be surprised to learn that the "marriage benefit" is more substantial for men than women. According to a study published in the *American Journal of Sociology*, 88 percent of married men live to the age of 65, while only 63 percent of never-married men, 65 percent of divorced men, and 69 percent of widowed men live to that age. Among women, 92 percent of married, 81 percent of never-married, 82 percent of divorced, and 90 percent of widowed women live to the age of 65. We think the reason for this is twofold: first, single men are much more likely to engage in self-destructive behavior (drinking, smoking, and carousing) than single women, and single women are more likely to have a good network of reliable friends.

If you simply live with someone, there is a greater likelihood you'll get loving care in times of illness. Having a spouse or significant other tends to promote good habits and discourage bad ones. If you are married and have an extended family, you may have more reason to take care of yourself because others depend upon you. The odds are you will be more likely to exercise, eat healthy foods, and keep up with your medical checkups—and less likely to drown your sorrows in alcohol (among other things).

Additionally, married people live longer because they tend to have higher incomes, save more, and get a larger Social Security check when they retire. Doesn't seem fair, but wealthier people have more access to health care and information, and they are less likely to smoke, drink, eat poorly, and be sedentary. They can afford to travel, join health clubs, eat organic foods, take expensive supplements or prescription medicines not covered by health insurance, seek out the best doctors, hire personal trainers, and pursue many other health-related activities. If you're not yet a multimillionaire, don't despair; there are plenty of superhealthy poor people and plenty of extremely sick rich people. You don't have to be rich to exercise, eat healthy foods, and maintain a healthy lifestyle.

And being married isn't *always* good for people, either. Staying in a *bad* marriage, according to studies published in the *Archives of Internal Medicine* and in *Health Psychology*, is associated with an increase in blood pressure as well as other cardiovascular risks. Bad marriages are also associated with depression and mental illness. When you hear someone say, "My mate is driving me crazy!" it might be a literal statement. Your priest or rabbi might say differently, but if you are in a bad marriage and have already sought counseling to no avail, we say, "Slip out the back, Jack! Make a new plan, Stan!"

As editor of the LongLifeClub, Dave has had the opportunity to interview dozens of centenarians and has read about many more, and one characteristic they *always* seem to have in common is a strong social network. If they're not married, they maintain close ties with family members and friends and get out into the community. They are actively involved in their churches or temples or in community organizations, and even though they are more than 100 years old, they have a sense of purpose.

Dr. V firmly endorses this last point: *a sense of purpose* is crucial to health and longevity. Otherwise, you just don't have as much of a reason to work so damn hard to maintain your vitality. Why go out and walk 10 miles if you don't believe your life is somehow making a difference in the lives of others? Being selfish in the sense of taking care of yourself is important, but when you believe you have a cause or meaning to your existence, guess what: you have a powerful motivation to live long. So, if you are actively involved in the outside world, find a calling in which you can believe and pour your heart and soul into it. It could be a religious endeavor, political, environmental—as long as it is positive, you should go for it. We think this alone will add five great years to your life.

A final observation on centenarians: no matter what they've lived through—and some of them have amazing stories—they are universally optimistic. Might seem simplistic, but a sense of optimism goes hand in hand with a strong social network. A positive outlook, the ability to see the bright side of even the direst situations, is another absolutely essential characteristic of people who live long and live well. If you are a grumpy old fart, a mean old bitch, or simply a dour sour-face, get some help! It could be that you are depressed, or it could be you are suffering from an overactive or underactive thyroid or a hormonal imbalance. See your doctor; get some counseling; try some mood-enhancing supplements such as Saint-John's-wort, SAMe, or HTTP-5; or talk frankly to your friends or your spiritual adviser.

3

The Rest-of-Your-Life Nutrition Plan

Maximize Your Health, Stabilize Your Weight, and Count Down Your Age

Eating the right amount of nutritional foods while avoiding foods that are bad for you can provide tremendous health benefits, but you don't need to be on a diet to do this. In our minds, the very word *diet* implies restrictions, and our nutrition plan will *expand* your culinary experience. We say, you don't need to be on a diet to count down your age. With very few exceptions, the only proven benefit of dieting is *temporary* weight loss. Everyone seems to know this, and yet, for some unfathomable reason, millions of people keeping trying. The worldwide sales of diet products and books are estimated to be more than $100 billion annually, even though two-thirds of dieters who lose weight gain it back within one year, and 97 percent regain it within five years.

As we see it, the diet industry and the "prison industry" are the only major growth industries in the world in which the vast majority of the customers or inmates fail over and over. Like crack cocaine, dieting must be extremely addictive. How else can you explain why very few dieters give up on the practice? Instead, like repeat offenders, they move from one fad diet to another. We don't want you to waste your valuable time and money contributing to this folly. In designing our "Rest-of-Your-Life Nutrition Plan," we blended scientifically proven ideas, based on the best available evidence from studies conducted around the world, for promoting good health, maintaining positive body size, and extending life, with our experiences and those of Dr. V's patients. We also sought guidance from nutritionists, psychologists, and other health advocates.

Instead of a diet, we propose a "way of eating" full of wholesome foods and endless culinary discoveries. The Rest-of-Your-Life Nutrition Plan is a specific set of carefully chosen "smart eating concepts" that will make your body strong and resistant to disease. We have faith in you: once you are familiar with these concepts and the reasons we've included them, you'll be more health-conscious about what you eat. Our simple idea is to arm you with knowledge so you can make your own decisions based on your own perceptions and needs.

Fantastic, life-changing efforts start with great attitudes, so we want to give you a boost in this department by first telling you to toss your scale (if you have one) into the trash or stash it deep inside a closet where retrieving it will be too damn much trouble. You won't need it. Weighing yourself on a daily or frequent basis can be misleading and depressing. There are many reasons why our bodies gain a pound or lose a pound here and there. Sustained weight loss takes time. It is the long haul that matters, losing weight and keeping it off forever.

Suppose it's Friday morning. On Thursday, you ate modestly, avoided all snacks, and walked 5 miles; yet, now when you stand on the scale, you are shocked and dismayed because you have gained two pounds! What do you do? Rush down to Denny's and have the "Grand Slam" breakfast (665 calories, 49 grams of fat, and 1,106 mega grams salt)—or redouble your efforts, eat a carrot for lunch, and walk 10 miles? Either way, your self-esteem is down the drain.

"I must really suck," you say to yourself.

Calories fuel the body, and unused calories are stored as fat. The American Dietetic Association, the U.S. Department of Agri-

Smart Eating Concepts

1. Fall madly in love with food.
2. Get your fiber.
3. Distinguish good carbs from bad carbs.
4. Eat the right breakfast.
5. Make yogurt part of your world.
6. Drink tons of water.
7. Avoid sugar like the plague.
8. Know your fats.
9. Eat lots and lots of fruits and veggies.
10. Make your plate colorful.
11. Eat less meat!
12. Eat more fish!
13. Add longevity foods.
14. Learn to eat less.
15. Take your supplements.

culture, and the National Institutes of Health all say the best way to shed pounds is to cut back on calories and increase your physical activity. We tell you how to do this, by focusing on how many calories you eat and, just as important, how many calories you burn through exercise and other physical activities.

The Rest-of-Your-Life Nutrition Plan is not a quick fix, but it is powerful—so powerful that it will halt and even reverse the aging process. For the time being, we grant you permission not to worry about how many pounds you weigh. Don't even think about it! When you get your annual checkup, you can let the doctor weigh you, and if you've been following our advice, your doctor will say something complimentary to you like, "This is fantastic. You must be on a diet."

SMART EATING CONCEPT #1: FALL MADLY IN LOVE WITH FOOD

We love food, and we want you to love food. We love trying out new restaurants, shopping at farmers' markets, discovering the cuisines of different cultures, and taking on the challenge of cooking new recipes. We both have extensive cookbook collections, and when we get together, food is one of our favorite topics.

You can love food and at the same time learn to discern between foods that promote health and foods that don't. Some foods pack a tremendous amount of nutrition in a small volume (sometimes referred to as "nutritional density"), and others yield much less, if any. One of the simple concepts of long-term weight loss and stabilization is to eat more nutritionally dense calories while eating fewer calories.

Fresh food contains nutrients that energize your body and reinforce its ability to fight disease. Unfortunately, modern food technology has transformed slow-digesting grains into snack foods made of pulverized starches that quickly raise blood sugar levels and promote

Hidden Sources of Sodium

You probably know that eating too much salt is linked to high blood pressure. But, are you aware of the high levels of sodium in processed foods and restaurant cuisine? The average American consumes 4,000 milligrams of salt a day—2,500 more than necessary. The American Medical Association says any food with more than 480 milligrams should be considered a high-sodium food and avoided. A Starbucks Cheese Danish contains 750 milligrams, while a can of Campbell's Chunky Chicken soup has 889 milligrams. Many of the dishes from Weight Watchers and Lean Cuisine have more than 600 milligrams of salt. The lesson is to avoid canned and prepackaged food and be careful what you eat when you go out.

insulin resistance and weight gain. When food is processed, over-cooked, oversalted, preserved with chemicals, flavored with additives, or sweetened with corn syrup, it looses this ability and can turn into something poisonous. Instead of building you up, it tears you down.

One popular diet book we read while researching had a recipe for black bean soup that made us laugh and cry at the same time. You dump a can of black beans and a can of chicken stock into a bowl with some salsa from a jar and pop the resulting mixture into the microwave for two minutes! This is disrespectful of food and completely ignorant of the value it can bring to our lives.

Because we respect the things we love, the more we learn, the stronger our commitment is to eating fresh, whole foods. Locally grown and seasonal organic foods are on the top of our list, but we don't limit ourselves, since an astonishing variety of great produce and other food is available from around the world. If you are lucky enough to have a farmers' market nearby, we urge you to become a regular customer. Talk to the people behind the booths; many of them are the actual farmers or producers, and they tend to be passionate and knowledgeable about the foods they are selling. You'll be amazed at what you'll learn about local growing conditions and techniques for raising produce without the use of pesticides, herbicides, or fungicides, or for humanely raising chickens and other animals without growth hormones and antibiotics.

Test Your Food-Buying IQ

■ **1. If you don't want to buy conventional meat, there are three other choices: natural, organic, and grass-fed. Which of the following statements are true?**

- **A** Only organic farms are inspected for compliance by a qualified person certified by a federal or state agency.
- **B** Unless otherwise stated, natural meat can be produced exactly the same way as conventional meat.

⊙ "Grass-fed" on the label means the animal has been fed only grass and not feed grains or the by-products of other animals.

⊙ Regardless of the label, all meat products come from animals that have been treated with antibiotics or hormones.

⊙ Organic animals spend most of their lives outdoors in pastures.

The true statements are Ⓐ and Ⓑ. Natural meat is often raised using higher standards than conventional, but this is totally up to the producer. Grass-fed meat can be from animals that have eaten only grass, but no laws or standards say this has to be the case. Organic meat comes from animals that are not treated with antibiotics or hormones—and they must have "access" to the outdoors, which could mean they get outside for a few minutes here and there.

■ **2. When buying eggs, which of the following statements should you consider?**

Ⓐ Fresh eggs that you might be able to buy at the farmers' market taste better than conventional eggs from the grocery store.

Ⓑ It is always better to buy the large or jumbo-size eggs.

Ⓒ Brown eggs are nutritionally better than white eggs.

Ⓓ Certified organic eggs come from hens that eat organic feed, are allowed access to the outdoors and sunlight, and are inspected to make sure the rules are followed.

Ⓔ Conventional eggs are more likely to be contaminated with salmonella.

Statements Ⓐ, Ⓓ, and Ⓔ are true. Because eggs contain more cholesterol than any other food, it is better to buy the smaller ones. Brown eggs and white eggs have the identical nutritional value.

■ **3. When you're reading food labels, which of the following guidelines pertain?**

Ⓐ The stated amount of calories and other nutritional ingredients on food labels refers to the amount in a "serving size," which can be quite small. This is the first thing you should check when reading a label.

Ⓑ The "Percent Daily Value" listing is based on either a 2,000-calorie or a 2,500-calorie diet. The label will tell you which one.

Ⓒ The total amount of carbohydrates on a label includes "good" carbs, such as those from whole grain, and "bad" ones, such as those from added refined grains. The Food and Drug Administration (FDA) doesn't distinguish one from the other.

Ⓓ The ingredients are listed in order of their volume—the most abundant one being first.

Ⓔ The FDA considers a food to be low in a particular nutrient if it contains 5 percent of the daily value or less, and high if it contains 20 percent or more.

True answers: Ⓐ, Ⓑ, Ⓒ, Ⓓ, and Ⓔ

Score: Give yourself 10 points for each correct answer. If you score 100, you are a genius! A score of 50 or more is all it takes to have an average or better food-buying IQ.

SMART EATING CONCEPT #2: GET YOUR FIBER

Fiber is the foundation of our Rest-of-Your-Life Nutrition Plan. Fiber cannot be digested and passes through your system virtually intact. Seems counterintuitive, but fiber is the basis of a long, healthy life, and most people do not eat nearly enough of it. (And it is so cheap!)

Eat enough fiber and you will reap many rewards—particularly, improved "intestinal function," a euphemism for unpleasant-sounding but vital functions such as healthier stools, more frequent bowel movements, and less constipation. But this is only the beginning. When fiber pulls water from your body into your intestines to keep things moving along, it also tends to gather up nasty chemicals, some of which might be carcinogenic. Because fiber in your diet makes you digest food more slowly and tends to fill you up, eating lots of fiber will help you control your weight. People on a high-fiber diet can maintain their weight, or even lose some weight, while consuming more calories than people on a low-fiber diet. And fiber does wonders for your cardiovascular system by lowering cholesterol levels, triglyceride levels, and blood pressure. This adds up to a reduced risk of heart disease, heart attacks, and strokes. Fiber also increases insulin sensitivity and thereby helps prevent or control diabetes. It has also been shown to reduce the risk of colon cancer and breast cancer for women and prostate cancer for men.

The China Study, a significant analysis of the dietary habits of 6,500 adults living in 130 rural Chinese villages, found that high-fiber intake was consistently associated with lower rates of cancers of the rectum and colon. Harvard University published a study on fiber showing that the risk of colon cancer is reduced by as much as 40 percent in people who eat the recommended amount of fiber. Earlier, a 1992 study of 32,208 Seventh-Day Adventists found that those who ate whole wheat bread versus white bread had an impressive 50 percent reduced risk of heart disease (whole wheat bread has three times the fiber of white bread). Other studies have shown that fiber reduces the risk of diabetes, intestinal problems, heart disease, and prostate and breast cancer. It is even good for your teeth. Researchers from Canada who collected diet information from 34,000 men over a 14-year period discovered that the men who ate the most brown rice, dark breads, and other whole grains were 23 percent less likely to develop periodontitis than those who reported eating less than one daily serving of whole grains.

Fantastic Fiber Factoids

1. Whole wheat bread and pasta have three times as much fiber as bread and pasta made from white flour.
2. When you eat fruit, eat the skin, which has more fiber.
3. Fruit juice has no fiber and is loaded with sugar. People who line up at Jamba Juice are fooling themselves, we fear: downing large juice drinks is a surefire prescription for obesity and related diseases. Might as well drink Pepsi.
4. Beans, on the other hand, are loaded with fiber. One-half cup of kidney beans has 7.5 grams. Beans rule!
5. Broccoli has more fiber than other vegetables. One cup has as much as two slices of whole wheat bread (4.5 grams).
6. To increase fiber, add wheat germ to your cereal or try a supplement, such as FiberChoice (fiberchoice.com).

To get the benefits of fiber, you need to eat about twice as much of it on a daily basis as the average person eats. The Institute of Medicine recommends that adult men under the age of 50 consume 38 grams of fiber. For adult women under 50, the magic number is 25 grams. If you are male and over 50, it is somewhat less: 30 grams. Female and over 50: 21 grams. To help you calculate how much this is, consider that an ounce equals 28 grams, so 30 grams would add up to only 1.2 ounces. Not much, but we are talking about the weight of the fiber, not the food itself.

Dave recently bought a loaf of Vital Vittles 12 Grain bread, which weighs two pounds (908 grams). According to the label, a slice of this bread weighs 47 grams and has 3 grams of dietary fiber. For comparison, regular whole wheat bread has approximately 2 grams of fiber per slice. To get his daily minimum of 30 grams of fiber from this Vital Vittles 12 Grain bread alone, Dave would have to eat 10 slices—not likely. If Dave ate 2 slices, then he would still need to get 24 grams elsewhere.

What foods have the most fiber? The answer is whole grains, fruits, vegetables, nuts, and seeds. Here's an example of the type and amount of fiber-rich foods you would need to eat on an average day to get 30 grams of fiber:

- One bowl of oatmeal = 6 grams of fiber
- Two slices of whole wheat bread = 4 grams
- One apple = 3 grams
- 1 cup of broccoli = 4.5 grams
- ½ cup of spinach = 2 grams
- ½ cup of pinto beans = 7.5 grams
- One handful of walnuts = 1.5 grams
- One orange = 3 grams

Total: 30.5 grams of fiber
To learn more, see Appendix A, "Fiber Content of Basic Foods."

Some Pretty Amazing Benefits

Fiber does not provide vitamins, minerals, or calories—but when you eat it, you are eating whole grains, vegetables, fruits, and beans. Because of this, fiber-rich foods are rich in disease-preventing "phytonutrients," including antioxidants and flavonoids.

Phytonutrient is a broad term covering a variety of nutritional compounds in plants that act on human cells and genes to reinforce our natural defenses against illness. Since 1986, when the ability of phytonutrients to stop cancer in test tubes was first discovered, our knowledge of these active compounds has exploded. We now know that they play a role in preventing all major diseases.

Antioxidants are a type of phytonutrient. The more familiar ones, including vitamins E and C, are colorless, while the less familiar ones, called flavonoids, are red, purple, orange, and other colors (the darker the color, the greater the potency). There are thousands of these little chemical substances. All are indirectly derived from photosynthesis, the process by which plants turn sunlight into simple sugars, complex carbohydrates, fats, and proteins.

Energy in plants and animals is driven by the exchange of electrons between molecules. As photosynthesis takes place, billions of electrons get all "excited" and zoom around like crazy. Most go where they are supposed to go, but a significant number stray off course, turning into free radicals. Free radicals cause plants to get sick and die. Phytonutrients protect plants against free radicals by intercepting and sponging up electrons that have strayed off course.

In humans, free radicals damage cells and accelerate the progression of all age-related diseases. Since our bodies don't engage in photosynthesis, we have no way of creating our own supply, so we must rely on getting them from our diet or supplements. The more fiber-rich grains, fruits, and vegetables we eat, the more disease resistant we become.

SMART EATING CONCEPT #3: DISTINGUISH GOOD CARBS FROM BAD CARBS

Some carbohydrates ("bad" ones) digest rapidly and literally dump sugar into your bloodstream. You feel full and energetic for about an hour, before your blood sugar level plummets, leaving you tired and hungry. Other carbohydrates ("good" ones) raise blood sugar slowly and steadily, so you feel full longer and have continuous energy. An overwhelming amount of research demonstrates that different carbohydrate foods have dramatically different effects on glucose levels, and these differences have huge health implications.

A simple measure of carbohydrate quality is the glycemic index, or GI. Simple sugars (yes, sugars are carbohydrates) with the highest GI score become glucose almost instantly. Starches such as potatoes and rice, as well as foods made from refined white flour, including pasta, bread, bagels, and pastries, also have a high GI. Beans and whole grains have a low GI. Scientists have tested the glycemic index of hundreds of foods and carried out long-term studies on its potential to improve diabetes control, resolve the symptoms of metabolic syndrome, and reduce heart disease and even the onset of dementia.

Eating bad carbohydrates causes the glucose level of your blood to soar, and your pancreas produces a large spike of insulin. Insulin helps move the glucose out of your blood and into your cells. This system works well for a while but breaks down over time. High levels of insulin overshoot the mark, driving your glucose levels too low, which makes you crave more high-GI foods. This is also why you might find yourself tired in the middle of the morning if you had pancakes and syrup for breakfast.

Many people with poor eating habits get midmorning or midafternoon blahs, and they often eat candy such as a Snickers bar or a few jelly beans. A vicious cycle ensues. Eating large amounts of high-GI food leads to a quick spike of insulin, which leads to insufficient glucose levels, which makes you hungry for more high-GI food. Tragically, cells develop a lower sensitivity to insulin—known as insulin resistance—and this can result in a major health problem called *metabolic syndrome*, which in turn accelerates atherosclerosis and other aging processes. Or, worse, it leads to type 2 diabetes.

The glycemic index ranges from 0 to 100, with glucose (straight, no chasers) on the top. Carbohydrates with a "high" rating are those ranked 70 and above; "moderate" is between 55 and 70; and "low" is below 55. It's even possible, though rare, for a food to rank higher than glucose: an example is dried dates from Australia, which have a GI of 104. Paradoxically, even though fruit is loaded with sugar, most fruits have a low GI. Fruit contains a fair amount of fiber, but not enough to explain the phenomenon. Fructose, the predominant sugar in fruit, has a surprisingly low GI value, measuring in with a 20. Our interpretation: God wants us to eat fruit!

The 10 Lowest-GI Fruits
1. Cherries (GI value of 22)
2. Grapefruit (25). The low GI of grapefruit may be due to its high acid content, which slows absorption from the stomach.
3. Pears (32)
4. *Dried* apricots (32). An excellent source of beta-carotene and potassium, dried apricots are a wonderful fruit for anyone worried about insulin sensitivity. Fresh ones aren't that bad either, with a GI of 57.
5. Apples (38)
6. Plums (39)
7. Apple juice (40). Take away the fiber, leaving only the juice, and apples still have a low GI because the sugar in apples is mainly fructose. However, beware: apple juice is high in calories.
8. Oranges (42)
9. Peaches (42). Most of the sugar in peaches is sucrose. (A high fiber content and acidity account for this low value.)
10. Grapes (46)

Amount Matters

When you eat carbohydrates, your blood glucose levels rise and fall. The extent to which blood glucose rises and remains high is critically important to your health and depends upon two things: the nature of the carbohydrates (GI value) and the amount. Just choosing a carbohydrate with a low GI value doesn't mean you can stuff yourself without consequences. And conversely, a small amount of a carb with a high GI value isn't going to do much damage.

It doesn't take much brainpower to realize you are better off eating foods such as nuts, beans, lentils, carrots, brown rice, and whole grains instead of white potatoes, white rice, pasta, candy, most ready-to-eat breakfast cereal, cakes, and white bread. As you become more familiar with what is healthy for your body and eat more of these foods, you will discover that they make you feel better.

You can reverse the vicious cycle. Eat moderate amounts of high-fiber carbohydrates; your digestive system will gradually release glucose into your blood, causing a mild production of insulin, which will help maintain your insulin sensitivity. You'll have steady energy, and you won't be hungry for several hours. And when you eat again, you won't feel so ravenous that you overeat.

SMART EATING CONCEPT #4: EAT THE RIGHT BREAKFAST

Breakfast is still the most important meal. Eating breakfast stabilizes your blood sugar levels, which regulate appetite and energy. People who eat breakfast are less likely to be hungry during the rest of the day—and less likely to overeat. Typically, when you wake up, you haven't eaten for eight or more hours; the time span between dinner and breakfast is the longest between-meal period. While you are sleeping, your body actually uses up a lot of energy just to keep your heart beating, your brain functioning, nerves transmitting, and so forth. This energy comes from glucose stored in your blood.

Come morning, your body is in fasting mode—and if you don't break this fast until lunch, your supply of glucose will be depleted. You'll find yourself tremendously hungry. Most likely, you'll also be tired and irritable. Around 11 A.M. your performance level will suddenly drop. You'll be virtually worthless to yourself and the people around you. By lunchtime, you'll be hungry as a horse, and you'll eat way too much food to compensate. If you keep this up, you'll get fat, develop diabetes and heart disease, and die a much too early death!

Don't believe this? Well, a major study at Harvard University of 2,831 participants found that people who ate breakfast every day were a third less likely to be obese and half less likely to have blood sugar problems than those who skipped breakfast. Another recent study, this one dealing with teenage girls, published in the *Journal of the American Dietetic Association*, found that those who ate cereal for breakfast at least three times a week were more likely to maintain a healthy body mass index (BMI, a ratio of weight to height) over a 10-year span. Hey, if it works for teenage girls, it should work for you.

Make It a "Proper" Breakfast

Of course, just eating breakfast is not enough—you need to eat a proper breakfast. And by that we don't mean huge. Breakfast should be the smallest meal of the day.

Your breakfast should also be low in fat, high in fiber content, and low in sugar and should include a small amount of protein and calcium, which you can get from yogurt or nonfat milk on your cereal or from nonfat milk in your coffee. If you are lactose intolerant or just want to avoid dairy, you have plenty of good alternatives. One of them is soy milk, and another is delicious milk made from almonds or cashews.

Eat a small amount of fruit every morning. Eat it raw, and—unless it's a banana or papaya, or some other fruit with inedible skin—for heaven's sake, eat the skin. The skins of apples, apricots, blueberries, figs, grapes, pears, plums, strawberries, and the like, are the place where the fruit interacts with sunlight and forms a variety of colored pigments, including flavonoids. Fruit also contains sugar, of course, so you don't want to eat too much. However, the more fiber there is in the fruit you select, the longer the sugar will take to metabolize.

One fruit you shouldn't eat is raisins. Made by dehydrating grapes, they have a heavy concentration of sugar. In fact, a handful of raisins (¼ cup) weighs 36 grams and has 24 grams of sugar; in other words, two-thirds of every raisin is sugar. If you are diabetic or predisposed to being diabetic, you should most definitely avoid raisins. Watch out for them in cereals and salads.

Do *Not* Drink Your Fruit

One whole orange has 62 calories and 12 grams of sugar—and it has a wealth of nutrients, including beta-carotene, calcium, vitamin C, vitamin A, and folate. Meanwhile, a six-ounce glass of orange juice has 248 calories and contains 48 grams of sugar, no fiber, and almost no nutrients.

High-Fiber Cereal

In combination with whole fruit, the absolute best breakfast food is high-fiber cereal, particularly if it has little or no sugar. Dave lives in Berkeley, which abounds with suppliers of organic and so-called natural foods, yet finding a good breakfast cereal or granola *without sugar* is nearly impossible. Stores such as Whole Foods and the famous Berkeley Bowl carry literally dozens of granolas, none of which is truly sugar free.

Check it out for yourself. If a package of cereal or granola doesn't specify "sugar" on the label, it instead has one or more of the following: fructose, corn syrup, barley malt, cane-juice, caramel, dextran, dextrose, fruit juice, glucose, lactose, honey, molasses, maltose, malt syrup, sucrose, or white grape juice. And to add to this, many of these cereals are packed with little carbohydrate bombs called raisins that burst into sugar when chewed.

One of the best breakfast alternatives is cooked oatmeal, particularly if you take the time to prepare the "steel-cut" variety, which has more fiber—and you don't smother it with honey or maple syrup and raisins. We eat oatmeal about twice a week. Dave eats his with blueberries, while Dr. V likes his with low-fat milk.

Dave was eating Grape Nuts until he figured out that the "malted barley flour" listed as one of its ingredients is an insidious form of sugar. One so-called serving, which is only ½ cup, contains five grams of sugar as well as 310 milligrams of salt. Your blood glucose level could go through the ceiling after you eat a bowl of this stuff. Why are the sugar and salt there? Our guess: without them, Grape Nuts would taste like the cardboard box it comes in.

Dave also tried Uncle Sam's brand whole-wheat cereal, which likewise contains "malted" barley and plenty of salt. And he tried eating plain wheat germ with nonfat milk. You can get wheat germ that doesn't have additives, but it tastes best combined with a grainier cereal. Still, it didn't rate a thumbs-up.

We're both leery of wheat, as Dr. V sees more and more patients who are intolerant to gluten, which is a protein in wheat, rye, and barley. (An extreme form of gluten intolerance called *celiac disease* is a common genetic disorder. People with this condition suffer joint pains, depression, irritability, and fatigue—and it is often not diagnosed.) We prefer oats to wheat because oats have very little gluten, are high in fiber, and have more protein. Oats also contain saponin, a phytonutrient that works like little sponges to literally soak up cholesterol in the digestive tract. Research shows that if you eat enough oats, you can actually reduce your LDL cholesterol by 20 to 30 percent.

Out of frustration with this situation, Dave started to make his own breakfast cereal. The ingredients come from the bulk food bins at Berkeley Bowl, his favorite grocery store. He combines organic rolled oats with crushed almonds and walnuts, coconut flakes, pumpkin seeds, oat bran, and ground flaxseeds. He doesn't bother to toast the oats, though you could easily do this. Dave eats his homemade cereal with fresh berries (usually blueberries), soy milk, and sometimes low-fat yogurt.

Dave's Totally Awesome Breakfast Cereal (One-Week Supply)

- About 6 cups rolled oats
- ½ cup crushed almonds
- ½ cup crushed walnuts
- ½ cup coconut flakes
- ½ cup toasted sunflower seeds or pumpkin seeds (no salt)
- ¼ cup oat bran
- ¼ cup ground flaxseed (if available)

Combine all ingredients thoroughly. Transfer the mix to a plastic bag, and store it in the refrigerator. Serve with a handful of fresh blueberries (if available), a tablespoon or two of nonfat plain yogurt, and soy milk or nonfat milk. Delicious!

Experiment with substitutes or additional ingredients for variety or for individual taste. Some possibilities are pistachio nuts, wheat germ, oat bran, triticale (a cross between wheat and rye that has less gluten than wheat), spelt (an ancient, tasty grain with 25 percent more protein than wheat), and even bits of dark chocolate (cocoa content of 65 percent or higher). If blueberries aren't available, try strawberries, sliced bananas, raspberries, or blackberries.

If you don't want to make your own cereal, find a cereal you like that is low in sugar and high in fiber content. There are more than 250 brands, which can make your trip down the cereal aisle confusing. We suggest you select only those that have at least six grams of fiber, no artificial sweeteners, less than three grams of fat, and no more than five grams of sugar (per serving). A whole wheat cereal that is sweetened with apple juice or cane sugar is not great, but it's much better than eating cereal that contains fructose. Make cereal a part of your breakfast at least four days a week.

Other Great Breakfast Foods

OK, you might find it boring to eat cereal with blueberries and yogurt every day, and we promised you "endless culinary discoveries." Once or twice a month, Dave goes out for a Tex-Mex style breakfast called "Huevos de la Casa," which features two eggs with cheese and shredded chicken breast on top of a corn tortilla, smothered with fresh grilled peppers and onions, which Dave tops with "salsa fresca," plus a side of pinto beans and rice. The salsa fresca is made with fresh chopped tomatoes, onions, and cilantro. This breakfast is packed with nutrition, fiber, fresh vegetables, and even fruit (tomato). To prove the point, let's look more closely at each:

▪ **Peppers (red, green, orange, and yellow).** Peppers are high in fiber, vitamin C, and carotenoids. Eating peppers helps to prevent or minimize the impact of diseases related to high cholesterol.

▪ **Onions.** Glucose-tolerance tests show that eating onions can decrease fasting blood glucose levels, improve glucose tolerance, and decrease triglyceride levels, while increasing levels of HDL ("good") cholesterol. If this isn't enough, eating onions two or more times a week has been associated with reduced risk of colon cancer.

▪ **Tomatoes.** These "berries" are famous for their high concentration of a phytonutrient called *lycopene*, which has been shown in human studies to be protective against a growing list of cancers, including colorectal, prostate, breast, endometrial, lung, and pancreatic. An analysis of 21 studies found that men who ate the highest amounts of raw tomatoes had an 11 percent reduction in risk for prostate cancer. Eating cooked tomatoes was even better, as the amount of lycopene is higher than it is in raw tomatoes: the reduction was 19 percent. Tomatoes are also high in fiber and jam-packed with vitamins C and A. The cup of chopped tomatoes Dave eats with his Huevos de la Casa provides him with 57 percent of his daily need for vitamin C, 23 percent of his vitamin A, and 8 percent of his fiber.

▪ **Cilantro.** Known for its remarkable ability to aid digestion, cilantro packs so many nutrients that you may be incredulous when we mention them. However, we'll chance it—minerals calcium, iron, magnesium, phosphorus, potassium, zinc, and manganese; vitamins C, B_6, E, B_1, B_2 (niacin), and folic acid; plus the phytonutrients carvone, caryophyllene, limonese, 1,8-cineole, alpha-pinese apigenin, beta-carotene, beta-sitosterol, caffeic acid, myristicin, psoralen, quercetin, rutin, scopoletin, tannin, umbelliferone, and vanillic acid!

▪ **Pinto beans.** As great as the foregoing foods are, when it comes to fiber content, none of them can hold a candle to pinto beans. Huevos de la Casa has approximately 1½ cups of pinto beans, which provides Dave with 22 grams of fiber, more than two-thirds of his daily requirement. Pinto beans lower cholesterol, and when combined with rice, they provide a virtually fat-free protein. They also provide an excellent supply of magnesium and potassium. Researchers have found that people who eat diets higher in potassium-rich foods, as well as foods high in magnesium, have a substantially reduced risk of stroke. Pinto beans are fine right out of the can, as long as an excessive amount of salt hasn't been added; you don't have to go through the process of soaking the dry ones.

▪ **Eggs.** Much maligned because of their high cholesterol content, eggs have received a bum rap. Nutritionists who once steered people away from eggs now know that "dietary cholesterol" has very little impact on the blood cholesterol levels of humans. What influences blood cholesterol the most is saturated fat and trans fat.

Some research suggests that eating eggs can improve your cholesterol profile. A study by the Food and Nutrition Database Research Center at Michigan State University of more than 27,000 subjects showed that the risk of cardiovascular disease in men and women did not increase if they ate more eggs. In fact, it did the opposite. The people who ate eggs had lower overall cholesterol levels than those who didn't eat eggs at all. While men who ate two or three eggs per week had slightly lower levels than men who consumed four or more eggs per week, both groups had lower levels than those who abstained completely. In women, those who ate four or more eggs per week had the lowest levels of all!

Meanwhile, the two eggs in Huevos de la Casa provide Dave with 11 grams of high-quality protein, some healthy polyunsaturated fat, folic acid, vitamins A and E, and a nice big dose of choline. A key component of cell membranes, choline is an important molecule for brain function and for some of the critical chemical processes used to send messages between nerves and muscles.

Two Kinds of Cholesterol

Cholesterol is made naturally in the bodies of all animals and humans. Necessary for the production of hormones and vitamin D, and for keeping cell walls healthy, cholesterol needed by humans is made in the liver. This kind of cholesterol is called "serum" cholesterol.

The cholesterol in eggs and in other animal foods such as meat, fish, poultry, and dairy products is "dietary" cholesterol. As you probably already know, there are two main types of serum cholesterol: HDL (high-density lipoprotein) and LDL (low-density lipoprotein). HDL can reduce the plaque on artery walls and is associated with reduced risk of heart disease, which is why it is commonly referred to as the "good" cholesterol. "Bad" cholesterol, LDL, does the opposite. It contributes to buildup of plaque and is linked to heart disease.

Dietary cholesterol does not automatically become blood cholesterol when eaten. But this doesn't mean you should stop worrying about it. Both the American Heart Association and the National Cholesterol Education Program say healthy people should limit dietary cholesterol to an average of 300 milligrams a day; if you already have heart disease, the limit is 200 milligrams.

Still, Dave and Dr. V suggest that you don't go hog wild and eat eggs every day. When Dr. V makes an omelet, he uses one whole egg and three additional egg whites, since the yoke is where most of the cholesterol resides. They both eat eggs about once a week.

■ **Chicken.** Add in the chicken, and Huevos de la Casa covers Dave's protein needs for the whole day. The two ounces or so of boiled, skinless chicken breast has less than half the saturated fat found in an equal amount of beef and delivers a whopping 17 grams of protein. It also provides 35 percent of the daily value for niacin, which is a cancer-protective B vitamin, and 20 percent of the daily value of selenium, a cancer-protective antioxidant.

The Downside

If there is a downside to the Huevos de la Casa, it is the cheese, the rice, and, to a lesser extent, the tortilla. Although cheese is a good source of protein, calcium, iodine, and selenium, it contains a substantial amount of saturated fat, which Dave tries to avoid. And while the corn in the tortilla is high in fiber, making this a much better choice than flour tortillas, it has probably been fried in a polyunsaturated fat such as, well, corn oil. The rice in Huevos de la Casa is particularly problematic because it is white rice, converted from brown rice in a process of milling and polishing that destroys most of its nutritional value. White rice winds up being not much more than starch, which is linked to weight gain and an increased risk of insulin resistance.

Dave avoids these problems by not eating the rice and by eating only a bite or two of the cheese and corn tortilla. A remaining concern, though, is that Huevos de la Casa makes for a substantial breakfast, one reason to eat this only once in a while. Adding up the calories (chicken 110, cheese 150, beans 235, eggs 136, tomatoes 37, peppers 24, one-half tortilla 20) yields a total of 712, which is a lot if you are trying to keep your total daily calorie count under 2,500, or even 3,000. For this reason, Dave considers this meal more of a brunch than breakfast; he eats very little until dinner.

In number of calories, Huevos de la Casa is similar to a McDonald's breakfast of orange juice and a bagel with ham, egg, and cheese, which has 795. However, the McDonald's breakfast contains only 2 grams of dietary fiber (as compared with 20 grams), and it includes 21 grams of saturated fat (compared with 8.7 grams), 50 grams of sugar (compared with none), and a whopping 1,460 milligrams of salt. When you eat Huevos de la Casa, you control the saltshaker.

Thanks to the beans, with a little help from the corn tortilla, the Huevos de la Casa breakfast is digested slowly and provides a prolonged release of energy, whereas the McDonald's breakfast creates a sudden blood sugar spike followed by an equally sudden drop-off. One hour later, you will either fall asleep or find yourself craving a midmorning snack.

Dr. V's Simple Breakfast

Dr. V's simple breakfast consists of one piece of multigrain toast with olive oil instead of butter, a cup of nonfat yogurt, a handful of almonds or cashews, and a cup of black coffee. This provides him with enough low-glycemic calories, fiber, and protein (from the yogurt) to get him safely to his early lunch without hunger pangs. For a busy doctor who still sees 30 to 40 patients a day in addition to managing two wellness centers, writing books and articles, producing his own radio show, and so forth, this is a great way to start the day. What about fruit, you ask? Dr. V eats two servings of fruit in the evening for dessert.

Our point is this: breakfast can be simple or complex and still meet the requirements for a proper balance that includes ample fiber and ample nutrients. And it doesn't have to send your blood sugar to the moon and back.

SMART EATING CONCEPT #5: MAKE YOGURT PART OF YOUR WORLD

Did you know that your body contains approximately 400 types of bacteria, weighing approximately 3.5 pounds? In terms of individual microorganisms, the number is thousands of billions. Most reside in your gastrointestinal system, where they are vital for metabolizing your food. Less than 1 percent can be pathogenic or toxic, yet these have the potential to multiply into overwhelming numbers that can defeat "friendly" bacteria and cause disease and even death. Good health depends on maintaining a critical balance between various groups of bacteria—a proper "intestinal flora." Stress, the onset of disease, ingestion of antibiotics, alcohol, improper food, or lack of sleep can throw off this balance. Harmful environmental conditions, including exposure to mercury or lead, can have the same consequences.

The friendly bacteria in yogurt are sometimes referred to as *probiotics*, a term first used by the Nobel Prize–winning Russian scientist Ilya Ilich Metchnikoff, who devoted the last decade of his life to the study of lactic-acid-producing bacteria as a means of increasing human longevity. He was a big fan of yogurt and attributed the longevity of Bulgarians (many of whom live to beyond the age of 100) to their propensity to eat vast quantities on a daily basis.

Interest in probiotics waned after Metchnikoff's death in 1916, but in modern times these friendly bacteria have become the basis of a serious field of scientific and nutritional research. Benefits attributed to probiotics include the ability to alleviate anxiety, assist digestion and absorption of fats and carbohydrates, increase lactose tolerance, fight and prevent bacterial infections, improve HDL/LDL ratios, inhibit food pathogens, provide anticarcinogenic properties, fight fungal and candida infections, aid liver function, prevent osteoporosis, boost the immune system, promote longevity, and even prevent bad breath!

The evidence varies from anecdotal accounts to rigid, double-blind, placebo-controlled studies. In the latter category, Swedish researchers examined the ability of probiotics to reduce short-term illnesses, including colds. At TetraPak International (manufacturers of food-packaging equipment), 262 workers were randomized in a double-blind fashion to receive a daily dose of either 8 billion units of probiotics or a placebo for 80 days. Results were impressive: those who took probiotics had 60 percent fewer colds and used less than half the number of sick days. In this study and others, only the daily digestion of probiotics has proved to be an effective method for reducing the severity of colds and, in some cases, preventing them in the first place.

The easiest way to get probiotics into your diet is by eating yogurt, but you have to make sure it contains living cultures and is not pasteurized. Other foods with probiotics include kifir and yogurt drinks such as DanActive. Supplements are available in freeze-dried, powdered, capsule, wafer, and liquid form. Of these, capsules are probably the best, being the least likely to degrade from oxidation. Whatever form you use, the product must be kept refrigerated to preserve its potency.

Advocates of probiotics usually recommend that adults ingest between 5 billion and 10 billion cultures per day; for children it's 2 to 4 billion. This makes it somewhat difficult to get enough by eating yogurt alone, but not impossible. We try to eat unpasteurized yogurt every day, and when we can't, we take a probiotic supplement (available wherever supplements are sold). Our suggestion is that you do the same. The amount of cultures in yogurt can vary—look for the National Yogurt Association's "Live and Active Cultures" seal on the yogurt you buy. Yogurt with this seal has a minimum of 2.4 billion cultures per cup. For more information, see aboutyogurt.com.

SMART EATING CONCEPT #6: DRINK TONS OF WATER

Drinking water is probably the most important factor in controlling your weight. If you are overweight, it can help in both losing pounds and, better yet, keeping them off. It does this by suppressing your appetite and by aiding the "metabolization" of stored fat. Drink more water and the fat deposits in your body decrease. Drink less and the fat deposits increase.

The reason for water's impact on fat deposits is rather mechanical. Your kidneys need plenty of water to function properly, and when they don't get enough, they off-load some of their work to your liver. The more work your liver has to do, the less capacity it has for performing its primary functions, which include metabolizing stored fat and turning it into energy. The less fat the liver gets around to metabolizing, the more stored fat you retain in your body, and guess what: you gain weight.

Many people do not drink enough water. Instead, they drink soda, which is loaded with sugars or artificial sweeteners, and coffee or tea. For the most part, these liquids are diuretic, meaning they cause your body to discharge more urine and actually dehydrate you. The more soda, coffee, and tea you drink, the more water you need. Also, the bigger (or fatter) you are, the more water your body needs, because larger people have greater metabolic needs.

Many aspects of water are counterintuitive. For example, if you suffer from excess water in your body (water retention), the solution is to drink *more* water. When you do not get enough water, your body reacts by trying to hold all the water it can. It starts storing it in extracellular spaces; thus, you get swollen feet, legs, and hands.

Water is essential for proper muscle tone, providing the lubrication muscles need to maintain their ability to contract correctly. Water also prevents your skin from sagging when you lose a substantial amount of weight. It does this by plumping up the cells to keep them healthy and resilient. If you want younger-looking skin, drink more water.

According to research, people who drink only two 8-ounce glasses or less of water a day have approximately 50 percent more heart attacks and strokes than people who drink five or more glasses. Another study concludes that people who drink only two to four glasses of water a day are five times more likely to come down with a cold and twice as likely to suffer from headaches, versus people who drink six to eight glasses. Drinking enough water can also reduce the risk of bladder cancer and even breast cancer. One study suggests that drinking eight to ten glasses of water a day could significantly ease back and joint pain for up to 80 percent of sufferers.

So, how much should you drink? The most common number cited by medical professionals is eight glasses a day. According to a 2001 survey of 1,000 adults nationwide, people are more likely to check the weather (69 percent) or have a caffeinated beverage (58 percent) than drink eight glasses of water a day (40 percent). Yet, more than a third of Americans choose "drinking more water" as the easiest health-improving lifestyle change they could make.

For people who exercise every day or who are simply trying to lose weight, eight glasses is probably not enough. The operative question should be, How can I be as healthy as possible without doing things that are inconvenient, extreme, overly expensive, or plain ridiculous? Therefore, we recommend that you drink ten or more glasses of water every day. Sounds like a lot, but what could be simpler? Water is convenient, cheap, and portable, and it is everywhere.

Tips for Getting Enough Water
- Take water with you in your car, backpack, or briefcase and drink while you are commuting to and from work.
- Get into it. Be a water snob; there are many outstanding bottled waters on the market, and some are delicious.
- Try not to go more than two hours without a glass of water. Always have a bottle or pitcher on your desk.
- Drink water before and after you exercise.
- Have a glass before you eat a meal. It will help fill you up, so you eat less.
- If you drink wine, coffee, or tea, always drink some water afterward to counteract the diuretic effects.
- Drink plenty of water in the evening while you are reading or watching TV. This may mean that you will find yourself getting up at 2 A.M. to go to the bathroom, but so what? You'll get used to it. Go to the bathroom, and then drink another glass of water before you go back to bed.

Finally, what kind of water? Sadly, tap water is often contaminated with impurities that may include inorganic poisons and pathogens such as fungi, bacteria, and viruses. The Natural Resources Defense Council (NRDC) tested the tap water in 19 major American cities and found that while a few cities, including Chicago, have excellent or good tap water, many do not. Contaminants that the NRDC identified in some samples included lead, arsenic, germs, pesticides, and even rocket fuel. So, unless you live in Chicago or you know something about the quality of the water in your town and you feel good about it, we recommend that you don't drink tap water.

One of the best solutions (and most economical) is to use a filtering device to remove impurities. It should include an ultraviolet light system to destroy pathogens; better yet is a system that also alkalinizes water to help maintain a proper pH of between 9.5 and 10. The reason for alkalinizing water is that most diets are acidic. Soft drinks, fast foods, and processed foods deposit acid waste in your body, which builds up over time, creating an ideal environment for the propagation of diseases and cancer cells. The accumulation of acidic by-products in the body is believed to be a rapid accelerator of aging. You can learn more about alkaline water purifiers and compare models at ionizers.org.

Another solution is to drink bottled water. Here, though, caution is in order. While many of the bottled waters on the market are excellent, some are *more* polluted than tap water. One problem: the FDA requires state or local approval of bottled water sources, but there is no federal definition of what constitutes a bottled water source. This FDA requirement is sometimes called a "regulatory mirage," since the actual source could be almost anything—even a pond next to a nuclear power plant.

The NRDC has also tested 103 brands of bottled water and reports that two-thirds are of good or excellent quality, but about a third contain "significant contamination." So, we suggest that in choosing bottled water, you get one that is "purified," meaning it has been produced by distillation, deionization, or reverse osmosis, or one that comes from a "natural spring" or "artesian well." Skip mineral water and carbonated water, as they are exempt from FDA regulations. Then, once you have selected safe, delicious-tasting water, drink tons of it!

What About the Ice?

You plop down two bucks for a nice bottle of pure springwater, and then you cool it down with . . . ordinary cubes of ice made from tap water. Enter, AquaICE, prepackaged ice-cube trays containing purified water and costing $5 for 50 cubes. No one knows how many of the 16 million annual cases of gastrointestinal illness attributed to tap water in the United States resulted from tainted ice, but no doubt this does happen. Perhaps you should switch to AquaICE, or start using Evian in your ice trays—and ask about the ice when you're at your favorite bar or restaurant.

SMART EATING CONCEPT #7: AVOID SUGAR LIKE THE PLAGUE

Sugar is the enemy of a healthy lifestyle. It appears in almost every prepackaged food in your grocery store—often disguised. An estimated 17 million Americans have type 2 diabetes (100 million worldwide), making it the seventh leading cause of death overall. Eating sugar causes your body to increase its insulin production, and over time this causes insulin resistance, which in turn leads to diabetes. Studies have shown that sugar is actually an addictive drug. In addition to diabetes, eating sugar leads to high blood pressure, high cholesterol, heart disease, weight gain and obesity, depression, allergies, and premature aging. The more sugar you eat, the more you can count *up* your age.

Everyone needs to get smart about how to detect sugar. The food-processing industry has come up with dozens of ways to add sugar without using the actual word on the food labels. Ingredients such as fructose, corn syrup, barley malt, cane-juice crystals, caramel, dextran, dextrose, fruit juice, fruit juice concentrates, glucose, lactose, honey, molasses, maltose, malt syrup, and sucrose are nothing more than buzz words for sugar.

All sugar is bad for you. Some nutritionists advise people to avoid "refined" sugar, such as sugar refined from cane or beet juice. The idea is that complex sugars, such as those in honey or fruit juice, are natural and thus are better for you. Well, maybe they don't metabolize quite as fast, but once sugar is processed by your body, its effects are pretty much the same.

Think of it this way: on a scale of 1 to 100, with 100 being the most harmful, refined sugar is 100 and honey is 97. There is even one sugar substance that, in our opinion, is *100-plus*, namely high-fructose corn syrup. The processed-foods industry loves this stuff, which representatives endearingly call "HFCS." Made from cornstarch by converting it to glucose, it is cheaper and tastes slightly sweeter than sugar, and when used in baked goods, it helps to keep products moist.

High-fructose corn syrup is the most insidious of all sugars and is contained in a vast array of packaged foods and beverages. The introduction of HFCS into U.S. food in the early 1970s and its subsequent rapid acceptance ramp up suspiciously close to the explosive growth of diabetes and obesity. If you look at the ingredients listed on labels, you may be taken aback to find HFCS in ketchup, jams, crackers, high-end soft drinks, and lunch meats, not to mention many so-called natural or health foods. It is even in most mass-produced breads.

More jolting to learn is that some HFCS-injected products are endorsed by the American Heart Association and carry its seal of approval logo with the message, "Meets American Heart Association food criteria for saturated fat and cholesterol for healthy people over age 2." Two examples are Kellogg's Smart Start cereals and Nutri-Grain cereal bars.

Fructose is not just a substitute for sugar; it stimulates less insulin secretion and is excluded from entering brain cells. The latter means excessive fructose ingestion may result in blunting the body's ability to recognize when it is full, so you tend to eat more.

While you can totally avoid HFCS by carefully reading the labels, we want to be realistic. No one *totally* avoids sugar, and it would be hypocritical of us to expect you to do this. We admit it: we *occasionally* eat sugar. Please don't spend the rest of your life not eating one more bite of ice cream or a small piece of chocolate cake. Simply cut back, and be diligent; your very health and longevity depend upon it.

SMART EATING CONCEPT #8: KNOW YOUR FATS

Fat is bad, right? Well, not necessarily. Some fats are actually good for you. The main form of fat in our bodies is called triglycerides. Your body can both store and manufacture these fats. The manufactured ones are mostly created out of carbohydrates, which is why eating pasta makes you fat.

Ninety-five percent of body fat is triglycerides, with the other 5 percent being phospholipids and sterols. Phospholipids, found in practically every cell of the body, are essential to brain health. Although present in many foods, phospholipids appear in higher concentrations in soy, eggs, and the brain tissue of animals—which may provide a biochemical rationale for the folk wisdom that says eating brain food makes one smarter. Sterols, however, are a different matter. The best known is chole*sterol*, a type of fat that attaches itself to protein molecules to be carried through your blood vessels.

As discussed earlier in the chapter, cholesterol is good news and bad news: the bad type is LDL cholesterol, while the good stuff is HDL. An excess of LDL can lead to the buildup of plaque in your arteries and actually kill you. Meanwhile, HDL fights back by carrying LDL to your liver, where it can be processed and actually excreted from your body.

Food does not contain either HDL or LDL—food contains various forms of triglycerides. Some triglycerides are good for you because they lower LDL, some may be good for you because they lower *both* LDL and HDL, and the rest are definitely really, really bad for you because they raise LDL.

The Good Fats

Conventional wisdom says that all fat is bad for you—but this is not true. The two fats discussed here are really good.

Monounsaturated Fats. Found in olive oil, grape seed oil, hazelnuts, almonds, Brazil nuts, cashews, avocados, sesame seeds, and pumpkin seeds, these fats lower LDL cholesterol while leaving your HDL at the same level. The high consumption of olive oil in Mediterranean countries is one significant reason why Mediterranean people have lower levels of heart disease.

Omega-3 Fatty Acids. These are the oils in fish and in supplements including cod liver oil. Your body utilizes omega-3s in the formation of cell walls, making the walls supple and flexible, which improves circulation and oxygen uptake. Thus, omega-3 is important to good cardiovascular health. Consuming it regularly will lower your LDL cholesterol and total serum triglyceride levels. It can also reduce blood pressure.

The association between omega-3s and human health was first observed by scientists who found it puzzling that the Inuit (Eskimo) people living in Greenland suffer very little heart disease, rheumatoid arthritis, diabetes, and psoriasis, even though their diets are alarmingly high in fat from whale, seal, and salmon meat. Eventually the scientists figured it out: these foods are very high in a type of fat (omega-3 fatty acids) that must be really good for you.

The American Heart Association recommends eating fish at least twice a week to maintain a desired amount of omega-3s in your system. Many people exceed that minimum by taking daily supplements and/or eating fish more regularly. Omega-3s have been shown to reduce the inflammation associated with arthritis and psoriasis and may even reduce the odds of your getting dementia or Alzheimer's disease.

The two forms of omega-3 supplements that are most beneficial are eicosapentaenoic acid (EPA) and docosahexaenoic acid (DHA).

On to the "Iffy" Fats

Some fats are difficult to label either "good" or "bad." We call them the "iffy" fats.

Alpha Linolenic Acid. This is actually an omega-3 found in flax-seed oil and in some other foods. Alpha linolenic acid (ALA) is converted by your body into EPA and DHA. The American Heart Association recommends eating ALA-rich foods, including soy-beans and canola, walnut, and flaxseed oils. However, the extent to which your body converts ALA to EPA and DHA is limited. Moreover, some studies have linked alpha linolenic acid with rapidly progressing prostate cancer and macular degeneration, which is why we put this omega-3 on the "iffy" list.

Omega-6 Fatty Acids. Omega-6s are "essential" fatty acids, meaning your body cannot manufacture them and therefore must obtain them from food. Dietary sources include cereals, whole grain breads, most vegetable oils, most baked goods, eggs, and poultry. There is supposed to be a balance between omega-6s and omega-3s—the ratio should be 1:1 and no more than 4:1 (four times

Fat Has More Calories

All fats contain the same amount of calories. A gram of fat, whether it is a trans fat or a monounsaturated fat, has nine calories. Meanwhile, a gram of protein or a gram of carbohydrate has only four calories (a gram of alcohol, which is also a carbohydrate, has seven). For this reason, it is a good idea to eat less fat. The rule of thumb is that fat shouldn't be more than 30 percent of your diet. We think you can do better than this, though. While we don't expect you to take daily measurements, we think you can count down your age two years by keeping the fat content of the food you eat under 25 percent.

as much omega-6). The average North American diet provides 10 times the necessary amount of omega-6, making the average ratio about 15:1. This imbalance contributes to the development of long-term diseases such as heart disease, cancer, asthma, arthritis, and depression and is one reason we recommend eating fish and taking an omega-3 supplement.

Polyunsaturated Fats. Most vegetable oils, including safflower oil, canola oil, sunflower oil, and corn oil, are polyunsaturated fat. They tend to lower *both* LDL and HDL cholesterol levels; on this score they are definitely a mixed bag. Like monounsaturated fats, they are liquid at room temperature.

It is probably a huge mistake to use these oils for cooking. A toxin associated with heart disease and neurological disorders referred to as 4-hydroxy-trans-2-normal (HNE) forms in high amounts in these oils when they are cooked. HNE has been linked in numerous studies with all sorts of nasty things, including heart disease, stroke, Parkinson's disease, Alzheimer's disease, Huntington's disease, liver ailments, and cancer.

These oils are fine for salads, though olive oil is better. Beware: polyunsaturated oils are used in most baked goods.

The Really "Bad" Fats

The remaining fats on our list are absolutely, completely horrible. They include the following.

Saturated Fats. Solid at room temperature, saturated fats are considered by the traditional medical establishment to be the most detrimental of all the fats. They trail only smoking, alcohol dependence, and high-fructose corn syrup as public enemy number one.

Derived from animal products, saturated fats include butter, cheese, cream, and the fat in milk and meats. Eating these fats will raise your LDL cholesterol and serum triglyceride levels and, as the saying goes, harden your arteries. They are strongly correlated to heart disease. In recent years, however, this iron-clad concept has got more than a bit rusty. First, there was Dr. Atkins, who proved you could lose weight by eating a diet high in saturated fats but low in carbohydrates. Then along came the South Beach Diet, which says it's not *all* the carbohydrates that are bad for you, just the simple ones (as compared with complex carbs). And finally, there's the Women's Health Initiative's Low Fat Diet Study, which showed that saturated fats do raise your LDL levels, but not as much as previously thought.

Tips for Eating Less Saturated Fat

- Eat less dairy. Choose low-fat or nonfat milk and cheese. Try milk substitutes such as soy milk or almond milk.
- Trim all visible fat from meat before and after cooking.
- Give up on fried food.
- Don't eat chicken skin or salmon skin.
- Eat less meat.
- Prepare soups and stews ahead of time so you can refrigerate them to let the fat harden. Remove the hardened fat and reheat.
- Use corn tortillas—never flour tortillas.
- Use olive oil instead of butter. Olive oil is great to cook with and great on toast.
- Forget store-bought salad dressings. Make your own vinaigrette by mixing extra-virgin olive oil with a delicious vinegar (balsamic, champagne, raspberry, red wine)—always checking the label to make sure no added sugar has been slipped in. Chop up some scallions or garlic for added flavor.
- Eat oat bran daily. Oat bran has been shown to lower LDL cholesterol while raising HDL cholesterol, thus counteracting some of the saturated fat you eat.
- Learn to love fat-free, sugar-free spicing condiments and sauces, including salsa, Tabasco, picante, ginger, adobo, chipotle, and the many Asian hot sauces. Substitute these for the fat-laden stuff such as ketchup and mayo.

So, are saturated fats still bad? Well, a study of 447 dieters in Switzerland, in which one group ate a low-carbohydrate diet while the other group ate a low-fat diet, found that after a year, weight loss for each group was about the same. However, low-fat dieters experienced a drop of about 10 percent in their LDL and overall cholesterol levels, whereas the low-carb dieters experienced about a 10 percent increase.

We strongly believe it makes good sense to keep saturated fats in check. If you feel you are eating too much saturated fat, the best solution is to gradually reduce the amount and keep reducing it; if you can eliminate saturated fats altogether, that would be great. Our theory is: a diet too high in saturated fats will still eventually kill you—just not quite as quickly as we once thought.

Hydrogenated (and Partially Hydrogenated) Fats—a.k.a. Trans Fats. Purely an invention of the processed-foods industry, these fats are polyunsaturated fats that have been turned from a liquid to a solid or semisolid form through a chemical process that should make you think twice: particles of nickel or copper are added to a polyunsaturated fat (usually corn oil) and heated to an extremely high temperature under pressure for up to eight hours while hydrogen gas is injected. The hydrogenated process destroys the essential fatty acids in polyunsaturated fat and replaces them with a deformity called trans-fatty acids. Because your body's digestive system is the result of thousands of years of evolution, it's not equipped to process these "Frankenfats." The result is an imbalance throughout your metabolism and fatty deposits in your arteries.

You probably think hydrogenated fats are a fairly new invention, but the first one was Crisco, which was introduced by Procter & Gamble in 1911. Today hydrogenated and partially hydrogenated fats are in almost every processed food from soups to chips, margarine, vegetable shortening, crackers, cookies, pastries, and mixes of all kinds, even some pasta and rice mixes. They can also turn up in frozen food, including pizza and potpie, and, of course, they are widely used in deep-fried food, including french fries.

More than any other fats, hydrogenated, partially hydrogenated, and trans fats raise LDL levels, and there is little doubt they cause obesity, diabetes, and heart disease. You should simply avoid them at all costs.

SMART EATING CONCEPT #9: EAT LOTS AND LOTS OF FRUITS AND VEGGIES

There is a striking inverse relationship between consumption of fruits and vegetables and disease. In short, the more daily servings of fruits and vegetables you eat, the less likely you are to develop a chronic disease. Research into this phenomenon found that people who consume at least seven to ten servings a day get the most benefit. The Rest-of-Your-Life Nutrition Plan emphasizes fruits and vegetables.

To accommodate that many servings, some of us have to rethink the concept that an animal protein (meat, fish, chicken, or pork) has to be the most substantial part of our meals. It is very hard to eat a big piece of meat for lunch and dinner and still get enough vegetables. Something has to give.

A sad fact of modern life is that the average person gets more antioxidants from drinking coffee than any other source. This is because our diets are so lacking in fruits and vegetables—not because coffee is so great.

In 1997, the American Institute for Cancer Research reported that "diets containing substantial and varied amounts of fruits and vegetables could prevent 20 percent or more of all cases of cancer." We believe that you need to eat two to three servings a day of fruit and five to seven servings of vegetables. And since we emphasize fruit in the morning with your breakfast, you need to eat veggies for lunch because it is highly unlikely that you will eat enough of them at dinner. Vegetables are a great source of fiber and phytonutrients.

A minor hitch is that most of the literature about this topic fails to specify how much a "serving" is. A serving can't be quantified for all-purpose use because it depends on the fruit or vegetable and how it's prepared. A serving of apple, for example, equals an apple (medium size), whereas a serving of cooked greens is ½ cup, compared with a serving of raw greens, which is a whole cup. It is not important to know *exactly* what a serving is, but it is good to have an adequate approximation.

Fruit or Vegetable	Serving Size
Raw fruit or vegetable, chopped	½ cup
Apple, orange, banana, or pear	One medium
Berries of all kinds	¾ cup
Melon of all kinds	1 cup chopped
Grapes	17
Baby carrots	Six to seven
Celery	Two to three stalks
Cooked vegetables	½ cup
Dried fruit	¼ cup

Should You Be a Vegetarian?

If vegetables are so damn good for you, you might be asking yourself, why not simply be a vegetarian? If you are a vegetarian, we applaud you; if you aren't but are considering it, we encourage you. The same goes for vegans, people who don't eat meat *or* dairy.

Most vegetarians (and particularly, vegans) eat less saturated fat than carnivores and thus have a lower incidence of heart disease, obesity, and diabetes. Studies show that vegetarians are more insulin sensitive and can dispose of glucose better than meat eaters. A large study of 30,000 Seventh-Day Adventists living in California found that vegetarians live about two years longer than meat eaters. Those who also eat nuts twice a week, exercise regularly and vigorously, maintain a healthy body weight, and have never smoked *live 10 years longer.*

What About Protein? Animal protein is a "complete" protein, and your body needs this stuff. It manufactures some 10,000 types of its own protein daily. Hair, skin, muscles, oxygen-carrying hemoglobin in your blood, and the multitude of enzymes that keep you alive and humming are mostly protein. Without it, you would slowly disintegrate.

Proteins are constructed from 20 basic building blocks called amino acids. Eight of these are called "essential"—again, because your body cannot synthesize them and must get them from food. Some dietary proteins are complete, meaning they contain all the essential amino acids; the others are not and are called "incomplete." (Dave is always impressed when science is straightforward and not ridiculously obtuse.)

Poultry, fish, eggs, and dairy products—like meat—contain complete proteins, while vegetables contain incomplete protein. However, eating a broad variety of vegetables makes this fact less of a concern. If not eating animal-based protein were really a serious problem, there wouldn't be so much evidence that vegetarians and vegans have fewer life-threatening diseases than carnivores.

The famous Oxford Vegetarian Study of 6,000 vegetarians and 5,000 nonvegetarians found vegetarians to have a 20 percent lower death rate from all causes than meat eaters. Amy Joy Lanou, a nutrition scientist with the Physicians Committee for Responsible Medicine, thinks patients hospitalized with life-threatening cardiac conditions should be told by their doctors to switch to a low-fat, *vegetarian* diet if they want to avoid another heart attack. Even though cardiologists know about these lifesaving advantages, they often don't recommend the diet because they don't think their patients will follow it.

What do you think? If a vegetarian diet could extend your life, would you switch?

There is little doubt that vegetarians are healthier overall than carnivores. Both of us enjoy eating meat, chicken, and fish and have no immediate plans to change, and we don't think most other carnivores will make the leap either. Our Rest-of-Your-Life Nutrition Plan is flexible: as long as you understand the pitfalls of eating meat (such as consuming too much saturated fat) as well as the shortcomings of eating just vegetables (such as the need to get plenty of protein from alternative sources and take vitamin B_{12}), in our view, you'll do well.

SMART EATING CONCEPT #10: MAKE YOUR PLATE COLORFUL

The best age-defying lunch you can eat is a salad. Dave's favorite salad comes from a grocery store—well, not any grocery store. He often drives all the way across Berkeley to eat a salad from the remarkable Whole Foods store on Telegraph Avenue. The salad bar at Whole Foods contains a vast assortment of fresh organic veggies, including lettuces, spinach, sprouts, broccoli, cauliflowers, beets, carrots, sunflowers, tomatoes, red and yellow peppers, and onions, along with tuna, chicken, and cheese—and this description hardly does it justice. Dave can put together a great salad with lots of color, and the combinations are endless, so each salad is unique.

Color is the key when it comes to veggies. The more colorful your plate, the more nutrients you are getting. Pigments in fruits and vegetables contain phytonutrients that play a role in the prevention of cancer and heart disease and also delay cellular aging.

How many colors are there? Seven:

- **Red/purple:** Grapes, grape products (red wine, grape juice), prunes, cranberries, blueberries, blackberries, strawberries, red peppers, plums, cherries, eggplant, red beets, raisins, red apples, red pears
- **Red:** Tomatoes, tomato products (pasta sauce, tomato soup, tomato-based juices, ketchup), pink grapefruit, watermelon
- **Orange:** Carrots, mangoes, apricots, cantaloupes, pumpkins, acorn squashes, winter squashes, sweet potatoes

- **Orange/yellow:** Orange juice, oranges, tangerines, yellow grapefruit, lemons, limes, peaches, papayas, pineapples, nectarines
- **Yellow/green:** Spinach, collards, mustard greens, turnip greens, yellow corn, avocados, green peas, green beans, green peppers, yellow peppers, cucumbers, kiwifruits, romaine lettuce, zucchini, honeydew melon, cantaloupes
- **Green:** Broccoli, brussels sprouts, cabbages, Chinese cabbages, bok choy, kale
- **White/green:** Garlic, onions, leeks, celery, cauliflower, asparagus, artichokes, endive, chives, mushrooms

Red foods (tomatoes, pink grapefruit, watermelon, and so forth) contain the awesomely powerful carotenoid called *lycopene.* Red and purple foods, including blueberries, strawberries, eggplants, plums, and red peppers, contain antioxidants known as *anthocyanins,* which are believed to delay cellular aging and promote heart health. Orange and yellow vegetables have a number of antioxidants, including carotenoids that give yellow peppers and carrots their color. Another carotene, *lutein,* is found in many yellow and green vegetables.

A food's phytonutrients are contained in the colorful part. The healthiest part is in the purple skin, as opposed to the white-greenish flesh inside. So, eat the skin. The same holds for the red skins on apples and some potatoes, as well as the skins on peaches and other fruits and vegetables.

We don't want to mislead you with this discussion of salad into thinking your veggies have to be raw to have great nutritional value. A Europe-wide study concluded that the body can absorb more nutrients from cooked vegetables than from raw ones—particularly carrots, broccoli, and spinach. If you don't eat a salad for lunch, have some cooked vegetables or some raw ones on the side. Chicken or fish and a small salad, or soup and salad, makes for a great lunch. Ideally, the volume of the veggies will be more than half of your meal.

SMART EATING CONCEPT #11: EAT LESS MEAT!

Both of us love a good steak. If it weren't for health concerns, a big fat juicy rib eye with grilled onions, some french fries, and a few shots of bourbon would make us both happy. Unfortunately, eating too much meat is an express ticket to the other side. You can still enjoy it, but to stay healthy and live longer, you need to eat less.

Excessive consumption of red meat, pork, and even chicken if it is fried, all of which are loaded with saturated fat, is first and foremost a major factor in cardiovascular disease. It is associated with high blood pressure, high cholesterol, and high rates of homocysteine, an amino acid in our blood that is created by the complex chemical processes of digesting meat. High levels of homocysteine are in turn linked to heart attacks, strokes, and atherosclerosis. If this weren't bad enough, eating meat is also a factor in colon cancer and pancreatic cancer.

After following the eating patterns of 150,000 people, the American Cancer Society reported that those who ate the most meat were 30 percent more likely to develop colon cancer than those who ate the least. For people eating a lot of processed meat (ham, bacon, sausages, hot dogs, lunch meat, and so forth), the number jumps to 50 percent. An even larger study of 200,000 men and women from five ethnic or racial groups found that those who consumed the greatest amount of processed meat had a 67 percent increase in the risk of pancreatic cancer.

An occasional hot dog at the ole ball game isn't going to make any difference whatsoever, but on the whole, we think any sane person who knows the statistics on pancreatic cancer will quit eating processed meat, or eat it only rarely.

What Is a Lot?

For the studies just discussed, "a lot" of meat isn't really that much—about the equivalent of the amount of hamburger in a Big Mac every day over an extended period. The people in these studies were followed for 10 years. Many Americans eat much more beef than this, of course. The National Cattlemen's Beef Association *proudly* says that America's per capita beef consumption is 66 pounds. U.S. consumer spending on beef was $71 billion in 2005, up $20 billion since the turn of the century. The average American, according to this industry group, eats meat, pork, or chicken 2.2 times a day!

Another problem is that while the meat you eat is being digested, acid is dumped into your blood (not just homocysteine). Acid taxes your kidneys, and as you age, your kidneys start to loose their functionality. The result of all this is that your body starts to draw upon skeletal calcium to neutralize the acid buildup in your blood. An excess amount of meat in the diet of older people is associated with bone loss, osteoporosis, and hip fractures.

Endocrinologist Deborah E. Sellmeyer, director of the Mount Zion Osteoporosis Center at the University of California, San Francisco, computed the bone loss of 750 elderly women over a seven-year period. Her findings are telling: women eating the most animal protein lost nearly 1 percent of the bone in their hips *annually*—four times the bone loss in women who ate equal parts animal and vegetable protein.

Enough Already

We could dig up more dirt on meat, but we think the case for avoidance is clear—so, why do we still eat it? We eat meat because we love it and because, frankly, we've been eating meat our whole lives and it is hard to give it up. But we both have gradually cut and now indulge about once a week. We both eat chicken once or twice a week and eat fish three or more times.

If you are going to eat meat, organic or grass-fed beef is best. Cows (also pigs, chickens, ducks, and so forth) that are raised to be organic or grass fed aren't pumped up with antibiotics, and they eat organic feed (no pesticides). Organic beef can still be fed corn,

---

Where Do All the Antibiotics Go?

According to the Union of Concerned Scientists, more than 70 percent of all antibiotic production in the United States goes to feed cows, chickens, and pigs. Much of this is given to animals not only to prevent them from getting sick but also to improve weight gain so producers can spend less money on food. A chief objection is that regular exposure to antibiotics favors hardier strains of bacteria, which pass on their resistance to successive generations. In Europe, all growth-promoting antibiotics have been banned, but we still use them in the United States.

---

however; in fact, the marbling of fat prized by steak lovers, including Dave and Dr. V, is dependent on corn.

What's wrong with cows eating corn? Well, God did not engineer cows to eat corn; they are ruminants, a class of animals whose digestive systems are specifically designed to eat grass. Eating corn causes cows to have excessive acid, which can lead to a host of ailments ranging from simple heartburn to ulcers and even liver disease. It changes the composition of the cow's meat so it has a lot more saturated fat and a lot less omega-3 fat and conjugated linoleic acid (CLA), an essential omega-6 fat.

If you can find it, grass-fed beef is your best choice by far, as it obviously contains less saturated fat and more omega-3 and CLA. Eating CLA reverses some of the otherwise negative aspects of beef. It is associated with increased metabolism, loss of abdominal fat, increased muscle density, lower insulin resistance, and even lower cholesterol levels.

Dave sometimes uses grass-fed beef to make hamburgers for his grandchildren. To add back in a little "good" fat, he cooks the burgers in olive oil. The kids love the taste, but it is a struggle to get them to eat whole grain hamburger buns.

We Like Chicken

Chicken, the world's number-one source of protein, is also the world's most versatile food. There are more than 10 million chicken recipes on the Internet. Four ounces of chicken has enough protein, 68 grams, to meet most people's needs. A skinless chicken breast has half the saturated fat of a choice-grade T-bone steak of comparable size. With the skin, the fraction rises to four-fifths.

Oh, what a shame, as chicken definitely tastes better with the skin. No problem, though, if you eat only one skin-on chicken breast and you consume no meat and not much dairy that day.

Chicken is an excellent source of the B vitamin niacin and the trace mineral selenium. We frequently eat chicken, but only the organic or free-range variety, as conventional chicken—like conventional beef—is raised in concentration camp–like conditions and must be fed a steady diet of antibiotics.

Pork, Too?

Sad to say, the "production" of pork has succumbed to the same type of industrial practices as their beef and chicken cousins. The vast majority of pigs spend most of their lives standing in their own feces. Mostly confined indoors, many of them live in a small pen and are not able to even turn around. Pigs have been bred over the years to produce more meat in relationship to the amount of feed they eat, and as a consequence, conventional pork has lost much of the flavor that old-fashioned farmed pork had.

We love good pork when we can find it, which is not often.

Dinner with Dr. V

Dr. V eats a modified low-carbohydrate, Mediterranean type of diet. He abstains completely from alcohol. Because his family has a history of diabetes and he has had mildly elevated blood glucose levels in the past, he avoids starches and keeps his total carbohydrate consumption low.

For dinner, he likes to start with a mixed green salad with olive oil–based vinaigrette and about half of an unbuttered whole wheat roll. For the main course, he likes to have some fish (rarely swordfish or tuna) or chicken, along with one or two vegetables, including spinach or another leafy dark green. Once a week, he'll have a steak or roast beef. Dr. V avoids dessert, but later he'll often have one or two pieces of fruit, a pear or plum or other fruits, depending on the season.

This shifting of protein source—eating more fiber, vegetables, and fruit—is the core of our plan.

SMART EATING CONCEPT #12: EAT MORE FISH!

Don't freak out about mercury poisoning. We think fish is fantastic, and, unless you're a vegetarian, you should eat more of it. Fish is good for your circulation, your heart, and your brain—and even improves your mood. Dozens of studies have concluded that the omega-3 fats in fish have a protective effect on the cardiovascular system. Eating fish can prevent hardening of the arteries, improve the viscosity of blood (the rate at which it flows), help control blood pressure, increase the levels of HDL cholesterol in the blood, and reduce irregular heartbeats (arrhythmias).

While eating fish, you are upgrading both your cardiovascular system and your brain. For a long time, scientists have known omega-3 is essential for neuron-cognitive development and normal brain functioning. Recently, however, they've discovered that older people who eat fish twice a week or more reduce their amount of cognitive decline and lower their risk of dementia and stroke.

As part of the ongoing Chicago Health and Aging Project, researchers tracked the diets of 6,158 people 65 and older for six years, periodically testing their cognitive skills. One finding was conclusive: the rate of decline among those who ate fish twice or more a week compared with those who ate fish less than once a

> **Eating Fish Helps Your Heart Regulate Electrical Activity**
>
> The federally funded Cardiovascular Heart Study has found that eating fish rich in omega-3 fatty acids is associated with a lower heart rate and a lower likelihood that the heart will take a long time to reset its electrical system after a beat. These findings "support studies suggesting that fish intake reduces the risk of sudden death," said lead study author Dr. Dariush Mozaffarian, a cardiologist at Women's Hospital, in Boston. The study also found that the more fish you consume, the greater the benefits.

week was 13 percent less *per year*. Researchers wrote, "The rate reduction is the equivalent of being three to four years younger." Count down your age!

Coming to Grips with Mercury

A scourge, a plague, a disaster—however you describe it, mercury contamination of fish sucks. The good news is mercury doesn't affect all species equally. If you're smart about fish, you can eat all you want.

Mercury is a potent neurotoxin that can cause nerve and brain damage. While most of the alarm raised about mercury contamination focuses on fetuses, infants, and young children, it is naive to think mercury doesn't damage adults as well. Mercury poisoning is a known factor in short-term memory loss, fatigue, and headaches.

How do fish get contaminated? Big fish eat little fish. Really big fish eat a whole lot of little fish. Because mercury, which largely originates from coal-burning power plants, bio-accumulates, really big fish are much more contaminated than smaller fish. Tuna, shark, swordfish, king mackerel, pike, Atlantic halibut, and tilefish contain the most mercury, and you should avoid these except on rare occasions.

FDA figures show that expensive canned albacore tuna has on average 0.358 parts of mercury per million, while cheaper light tuna has only 0.123 parts per million. The reason for this differential is that the expensive tuna tends to be larger and older. A 132-pound person who eats two cans of albacore tuna per week would take in three times the Environmental Protection Agency's recommended limit of one-tenth of a microgram of mercury per kilo (2.2 pounds) of body weight. For crying out loud—if you must have a tuna sandwich or tuna salad, use the cheaper version.

What fish can you eat? The organicconsumers.org site has a "Guide to Which Fish Are Safe to Eat" that is constantly updated to reflect changes in climate and pollution levels. Among the safe fish are Dungeness crabs, Alaskan halibut, black cod, blue (Gulf Coast) crabs, cod, oysters, mussels, anchovies, arctic char, crayfish, scallops, Pacific sole, clams, striped bass, and sturgeons. Atlantic cod, Atlantic sole, Chilean sea bass, monkfish, orange roughy, shrimp, and snapper are also good, but some people avoid these for environmental reasons. The Monterey Bay Aquarium website (mbayaq.org) has a handy series of downloadable pocket guides to seafood.

If you want to know how mercury contamination in specific fish can affect a person of your body weight, an environmental organization called Got Mercury can tell you. It offers a fantastic online mercury fish calculator at gotmercury.com. Dave tried it out and found he could eat endless amounts of wild salmon without worrying about mercury; however, sea bass was a different matter—the calculator recommended he not eat this more than twice a month.

Wild salmon is the best fish, as it has the highest concentration of omega-3s and is one of the cleanest fish when it comes to mercury and other pollutants, including persistent organic pollutants (POPs) and polychlorinated biphenyls (PCBs). POPs include pesticides, lubricants, coolants, incinerated plastics, and the like, that are in polluted waters. The chemical PCB has been banned throughout most of the world but still pollutes the oceans and some freshwater lakes and streams.

Farmed salmon is another story. The "Atlantic" salmon you see in the grocery store is farm raised—just so happens the "farms" are in the ocean. We strongly advise you to avoid this product. You'd think farm-raised fish would be contaminant free, but don't be fooled. Vaccinated soon after birth, a farmed salmon spends its days lazily swimming around a disease-infested oceanic feedlot. Lacking krill in their diets, farm-raised salmon would be an unappetizing, pale gray color if not for the chemicals (canthaxanthin and astaxanthin) that growers add to their "salmon chow," a ground-up mixture of fish parts and oil. Some grocery chains, including Safeway, Kroger, and Albertson's, label their farm-raised salmon as being artificially colored.

How Much Fish Should You Eat?

We suggest you eat fish two to four times a week, being careful to avoid fish with high mercury levels.

If you like sushi, be aware that sushi-grade tuna is the oldest (and fattest) tuna—and thus has had more time to bio-accumulate mercury. Much of the "fresh" fish in sushi restaurants has been previously frozen, but this is perfectly fine with us. In fact, fish that is frozen soon after it is caught (often on the boat) is safer and even "fresher" than fish in the case at your grocery store. We dig frozen fish—but not the heavily breaded, microwavable kind.

One more note: heart health is also linked to the differences in how fish is cooked. Boston scientists reported in the *American Journal of Cardiology* that they found broiled or baked fish to be strongly associated with a lower heart rate, lower blood pressure, and increased blood output per beat (a.k.a. stroke volume). Fried fish is also linked to these good things, but much less so, and has been linked to higher resistance in the peripheral circulation (not good). In other words, baked or broiled fish is great for your heart, whereas fried is not nearly as good and could even be harmful.

SMART EATING CONCEPT #13: ADD LONGEVITY FOODS

Having read this far, you've probably surmised that some foods are so packed with nutritional value that they not only provide short-term energy but also provide tremendous long-term benefits. These foods, which we call "longevity foods," have anti-inflammatory properties that build up the body's ability to fight off diseases, including cancers. They give you energy all the way down to the cellular level and slow down the inevitable aging process. The more longevity foods you eat, the healthier you'll be and the more you can count down your age. Study our list of the "20 Greatest Longevity Foods," and incorporate these into your diet.

20 Greatest Longevity Foods

There are hundreds of healthy foods but very few that can actually enhance your longevity. After considerable debate, we've come up with the following list of foods we think you should be eating.

Blueberries. The U.S. Department of Agriculture, in a comparison of 100 foods, lists the blueberry as the best fruit source for antioxidants. Many studies indicate the blueberry's possible role in fighting such maladies as memory loss, high cholesterol, diabetes, and strokes. Eating blueberries improves the blood flow through your body, which keeps both your brain and your heart healthier. Blueberries contain a compound called *pterostilbene*, which has been shown to be effective in reducing LDL cholesterol. It's no wonder that blueberries have such an attraction as a health food: a mere ½-cup serving has as much antioxidant power as five servings of other fruits and vegetables.

We eat blueberries year-round. They are great with yogurt or on cereal, and they make a great snack. When they are not in season, they can be expensive, but you can seek out less-expensive dried blueberries or even pure blueberry juice (no added sugar). We mix the juice with water before drinking it or add a bit of undiluted juice to our cereal.

Grapefruit. Over the years, many studies have associated eating grapefruit with weight reduction. At the Scripps Clinic in San Diego, researchers divided 100 obese men and women into four groups. One group received grapefruit extract, another drank grapefruit juice with each meal, a third group ate half a grapefruit with each meal, and the fourth received a placebo. At the end of 12 weeks, the placebo group lost on average just under half a pound, the extract group 2.4 pounds, the grapefruit juice group 3.3 pounds, and the fresh grapefruit group 3.5 pounds (they ate one and a half grapefruit a day).

Grapefruit (particularly red grapefruit) can also significantly decrease cholesterol and fight heart disease. Eating one *red* grapefruit a day for 30 days has been shown to reduce cholesterol by 15 percent and triglycerides by 17 percent. Separate the fruit from the skin before eating it—you'll get more fiber and more antioxidants. One concern is that grapefruit can have an accelerating and dangerous effect on some prescription drugs. Check the label on any prescription drugs you are taking before you eat grapefruit.

Almonds. A true superfood, almonds are a fantastic source of protein, fiber, and minerals, including calcium, magnesium, iron, potassium, and zinc. They are high in vitamin E and contain monounsaturated fats, which can help to keep arteries supple. Stick to the raw, unsalted nuts for maximum benefit.

Apples. We grew up hearing "an apple a day keeps the doctor away." By golly, it's true. Apples contain the phytonutrient quercetin, which prevents oxidation (damage) of LDL cholesterol, thus lowering the risk of damage to our arteries and, in turn, the risk of heart disease. They also contain pectin, a soluble fiber that seems to be effective in lowering levels of blood cholesterol.

Avocados. Pound for pound, avocados provide more heart-healthy monounsaturated fat, fiber, vitamin E, folic acid, and potassium than any other fruit. They are the number-one source of beta-sitosterol, a substance that can reduce total cholesterol, and lutein, an antioxidant that protects people from getting cataracts and lowers the risk of prostate cancer.

Beets. Low in calories but packed full of nutrients, beets contain high levels of carotenoids and flavonoids that reduce the oxidation of LDL cholesterol, protecting artery walls and reducing the risk of heart disease and stroke. They are one of the richest sources of folic acid. The silica in beetroot helps the body utilize calcium and boost musculoskeletal health, reducing the risk of osteoporosis. Many people drink beetroot juice for its cleansing and detoxifying properties.

Broccoli. Here's a "mega-longevity" food if there ever was one. Researchers have identified a wealth of healthy compounds in this vegetable, including two powerful anticancer substances, sulforaphane and indole-3-carbinol. According to research at Johns Hopkins University, sulforaphane destroys ingested carcinogenic compounds and kills the bacteria *Helicobacter pylori*, which can cause stomach ulcers and greatly increase the risk of gastric cancers. Indole-3-carbinol metabolizes estrogen, potentially protecting against breast cancer. Broccoli is also a good source of beta-carotene and potassium. Many nutritionists suggest eating broccoli three times a week, and now we know why.

Flaxseeds. The absolute richest plant source of omega-3 fatty acids, flaxseeds reduce the risk of heart disease, strokes, and inflammatory diseases. They also contain high levels of lignin, thought to improve cholesterol profiles. Flaxseed is essential for vegetarians who cannot get their essential fatty acids from fish. It comes in seed or oil form, but make sure you refrigerate the oil, as it easily oxidizes.

Garlic. Numerous clinical trials have shown garlic to be an excellent cancer fighter. It has the ability to prevent development of cancers of the breast, colon, skin, prostate, stomach, and esophagus. Garlic stimulates the immune system by encouraging the growth of natural killer cells, which directly attack cancer cells. A study at the University of East London claims that garlic not only has the ability to kill many of the antibiotic resistant strains of methicillin resistant staphylococcus aureus (MRSA), the "hospital superbug," but also is able to destroy the newer super-superbugs that are resistant to the most powerful antibiotics used against MRSA.

Olive Oil. Packed with healthy monounsaturated fat as well as antioxidants, consumption of olive oil is the main reason people who eat a Mediterranean-style diet have very few heart attacks and live longer, healthier lives.

Oranges. Research published by the *American Journal of Clinical Nutrition* has connected a higher intake of hesperetin, the main flavonoid in oranges, with lower rates of heart disease. Hesperetin helps protect against inflammation. Oranges are a rich source of pectin, which lowers cholesterol; potassium, which reduces blood pressure; and folic acid, which lowers levels of homocysteine.

Wild Salmon. One of the best oily fish, wild salmon is an excellent source of omega-3 and has been linked with protecting against heart disease, breast cancer, and other cancers and relieving autoimmune diseases such as rheumatoid arthritis and asthma. It's good for your brain, too.

Soy. A nutritional powerhouse, soy is the only plant food that has all of the essential amino acids your body requires, making it a complete protein. Soy foods do not have any cholesterol, and most are high in fiber. Eating soy reduces artery-clogging plaque, improves blood pressure, and promotes healthy blood vessels, which protects the body from free-radical damage, boosts the immune system, and lowers the risk of atherosclerosis, heart disease, and hypertension. A ton of research links soy consumption with a reduction in breast cancer and prostate cancer.

Tea. Black, green, and now white teas have all been hailed for their antioxidant properties. According to epidemiological and animal evidence, green tea may inhibit breast, digestive, and lung cancer. The polyphenols in green tea are powerful antioxidants (100 times as effective as vitamin C) and may protect cells from free-radical damage. A study published by the *Archives of Internal Medicine* found that people who drank two or more cups of green or black tea per day for 10 years had enhanced bone density.

Tomatoes. Tomatoes contain high levels of lycopene, the consumption of which significantly reduces the risk of prostate, lung, and stomach cancer. It is best to cook your tomatoes before you eat them, as this makes the lycopene more easily absorbable. Tomatoes also contain potassium, vitamin C, and beta-carotene, which is essential for the immune system and helps keep skin healthy.

Whole Grains. People who consume large amounts of whole grains every day have a lower risk of heart disease. Whole grains include brown rice, millet, and oats, as well as whole grain bread. Population research also suggests that whole grains help prevent colon, breast, and prostate cancer. The complex carbohydrates and fiber slow the release of blood sugar, providing a great slow-energy source.

Beans. All beans (a.k.a. legumes), including those in Dave's Huevos de la Casa, are loaded with energizing complex carbohydrates, calcium, iron, folic acid, B vitamins, zinc, potassium, and magnesium. They contain large amounts of both soluble and insoluble fiber, more than any other plant. The soluble fiber helps to reduce blood cholesterol levels and normalize blood sugar. Insoluble fiber helps regulate bowel movements and may play a role in preventing colon cancer. Beans are cheap, too!

Sea Vegetables. No other type of food is as rich a source of minerals essential to maintaining and improving your health as sea vegetables, which ignorant Westerners disparagingly refer to as "seaweed." Because they don't have roots like other plants, sea vegetables must absorb nutrients from the ocean water. Dark sea vegetables, such as arame, wakame, hijiki, and certain varieties of kelp, contain sodium alginate, which converts the heavy metals in your body into harmless sea salt, which you subsequently expel when you urinate. Regular consumption of sea vegetables may account for the low rates of cancer in Japan. Sea vegetables also contain a high level of iodine, which aids in weight loss and can lower the amount of radioactive iodine absorbed by the thyroid by as much as 80 percent.

If you eat sushi, you are eating nori, which is a sea vegetable exceptionally high in protein and vitamin A, as well as other vitamins, including vitamin K, iodine, and potassium. Dried sea vegetables can be added to cooked foods to impart a salt flavor or eaten as a snack. Becoming familiar with sea vegetables and eating them every chance you get could add a few years to your life. "Seaweed" salad is delicious.

Cabbage. The medicinal qualities of cabbage are so significant that it is a wonder you don't need a prescription to buy one. Cabbage is high in fiber, vitamin A, and all the usual minerals. Eating cabbage stimulates the immune system, kills bacteria and viruses, inhibits the growth of cancerous cells, protects against tumors, helps control hormone levels, improves blood flow, and even boosts your sex drive. Eat enough and it will speed up the metabolism of estrogen and thereby reduce the risk of breast cancer and inhibit the growth of polyps in the colon. Studies have shown that eating cabbage once a week can reduce the risk of colon cancer by 60 percent. In its raw form, especially as a juice, cabbage contains ascorbigen—sometimes referred to as "vitamin U," in recognition of its ability to heal and protect against stomach ulcers.

Kale. Gee, did we save the best for last! Kale, the richest of all leafy greens, might even have more medicinal qualities than cabbage. As with cabbage, eating kale helps regulate estrogen and wards off many forms of cancer, including breast cancer, bowel cancer, bladder cancer, prostate cancer, and lung cancer. It also protects against heart disease and helps you regulate your blood pressure. The calcium in kale is more absorbable by the body than calcium in milk—and there is more of it. Kale is sometimes called the "wonder food" because eating enough of it protects against osteoporosis, arthritis, and bone loss.

More Longevity Foods

We encourage you to learn more about the vast world of healthy foods. Our list is only the beginning. It doesn't even include spinach, as we decided kale ranked higher as a longevity food, but not that much higher. Several excellent websites and books can help educate you on the medicinal and other benefits of food. One of the best websites is The World's Healthiest Foods, whfoods.com, which is published by the nonprofit George Mateljan Foundation, and one of the best books is *SuperFoods HealthStyle: Proven Strategies for Lifelong Health*, by Steven G. Pratt, M.D., and Kathy Matthews (William Morrow, 2006).

SMART EATING CONCEPT #14: LEARN TO EAT LESS

As you follow our Rest-of-Your-Life Nutrition Plan, the nutritional value of your meals steadily increases. You maintain a healthy, vibrant self while consuming fewer total calories. You become more energetic, and some very important, *measurable* effects kick in—lower LDL cholesterol, reduced blood pressure, and a drop in fasting blood sugar. Your resistance to inflammation and disease increases, there is a reduction in free-radical activity and oxidative damage, and you're less susceptible to cognitive decline and Alzheimer's disease. Chances are you'll live longer and better.

According to *Scientific American* (March 2006), restricting food intake is the only longevity strategy "absolutely proven to work." The article goes on to say that reducing food consumption by 30 percent can result in not just a longer life but also a *far healthier* one. But can you really learn to eat fewer calories? The answer to this is yes, but it won't happen overnight, and it shouldn't. As we stated at the beginning of this chapter, we don't think that you should starve yourself by going on a quick-solution, weight-loss diet. Learning to eat less is a skill, much like learning to ride a bicycle. It takes times and practice, but once you've got it down, you never forget how.

As usual, awareness is a good place to start. Our consumer society encourages you to pig out as much as possible. Americans are constantly bombarded with TV, radio, billboard, newspaper, and magazine advertisements depicting slim, happy people eating mostly bad food or drinking sodas and beer. You can't drive down a major street in any city without seeing dozens of fast-food

Fantastic Source for Nutritional Data

Many books and websites will give you the number of calories in food (and other nutritional data). One outstanding source is nutritiondata .com. Created by two of the giants of the fitness world, Ron and Lori Johnson, "as a way to give something back to the world that has treated us so well," this site has an immense database of nutritional information. It also has a useful "Daily Needs Calculator," which will calculate how many calories you burn on an average day based on your sex, age, height, weight, and exercise level. Great stuff!

restaurants. Many popular restaurants serve gigantic portions of food, and everywhere food has been supersized. Twenty years ago, the average soda was 8 ounces; today it is 32 ounces. We could rant about this for pages, but you already know these things.

The first step to eating less is to say no to the industrial food complex that is trying to fatten you up for the kill, and we're not kidding. Just say no to McDonald's and every other fast-food restaurant, no to canned food and prepackaged meals, no to soda pop and "sports" drinks, no to trans fat, and no to high-fructose corn syrup. You'll consume fewer calories and extend your life.

10 Little Tricks for Eating Less

The next step is to practice a few little tricks.

1. Learn that you are full before you stop eating. We all have a human survival gene, left over from more primitive days, called the "thrifty gene" that encourages us to keep on eating even when we are full. Stop before downing those last few bites of mashed potatoes, wait, and the desire to eat will go away.

2. Cut back on fat. Fat has nine calories per gram, as compared with four calories per gram for carbohydrates and protein. You can eat the same amount of food while automatically cutting back on calories.

3. Put less food on your plate. Researchers have found that people presented with large portions will eat up to 30 percent more than they would otherwise.

4. When you eat out, order two appetizers instead of an appetizer and a main dish, or simply order a main dish—skip the appetizer or share one. Skip the dessert or, if you must indulge, share it. If you aren't too embarrassed, ask for a doggie bag before you start eating, and put a portion of your meal in the bag ahead of time. Don't have any buttered bread or rolls before the meal. If the waiter asks if you want bread, stand up, throw your arms in the air, and yell, "Hell no!" (just kidding).

5. Have a light soup before your main meal. Or, better yet, have soup as the main meal. Soup makes you feel full on fewer calories.

6. Drink a large glass of water before you eat. You'll be less hungry.

7. For heaven's sake, slow down. Enjoy every single bite; chew it and savor it. To slow the pace even more, set your fork down between bites. Twenty minutes after your first bite of food, there will be sugar in your bloodstream; you'll feel full regardless of how much you've eaten.

8. Don't ever let yourself get extremely hungry. Another primitive instinct is to overeat when you are really hungry. Don't skip meals, and make it a point to eat healthful, low-calorie snacks between meals.

Mother's Little Helper

Some remarkable research reveals that pinolenic acid, which is derived from pine nuts, stimulates production of an important hunger-suppressing hormone known as cholecystokinin (CCK). A randomized, double-blind, placebo-controlled study of overweight women found that three grams of pinolenic acid consumed before breakfast reduced hunger by 29 percent and resulted in a 36 percent decrease in food intake. Four hours later, test subjects who took the supplement had 60 percent more CCK circulating in their blood. Pinolenic acid is safe and seems to be very effective.

9. Eat by yourself! After 30 years of research on overeating and obesity, psychologists at the University of Toronto have concluded that regardless of how hungry you are, social cues can dictate how much you eat—usually too much. In groups as small as two people, you will tend to eat 30 to 50 percent more than if you were alone. So, eat alone, or be more aware of how much you are eating when you are with others.

10. Notice when the flavor is gone, and stop eating. You'll be amazed that after a bite or two of ice cream, you really can't taste it anymore. Your taste buds are numb, but your stomach is on autopilot. Stop eating for a moment, and your desire will go numb as well.

Over time, these tricks work. As we did, you'll get valuable reinforcement from looking younger, feeling great, and receiving comments like, "You look wonderful!" and "Have you lost a lot of weight?" Dave estimates he has reduced his calorie intake from nearly 4,000 a day to less than 2,500, and he regularly burns off 100 to 500 calories a day through exercise. Dr. V, who is a much bigger man than Dave, has cut his calories to under 3,000.

If we can do it, you can too!

SMART EATING CONCEPT #15: TAKE YOUR SUPPLEMENTS

Supplements are a powerful addition to a nutritious diet. We agree with the premise that you should get your nutrients from food and not from pills; however, supplements aren't so much a substitute for food as a substitute for the *future use* of drugs. Used correctly, supplements help your body's natural defense mechanisms to function better and thereby resist diseases that may later require stronger and more destructive therapies.

For example, clinical research at Rush Institute for Healthy Aging, in Chicago, found that subjects in a study of more than

3,000 people aged 65 and older were *80 percent less likely* to develop Alzheimer's disease if they had a high level of niacin in their diets. Other studies have shown niacin's positive role in reducing LDL cholesterol and triglyceride levels. Because it is difficult to get enough niacin just from eating meat and dairy products, and most multivitamins have only a tiny amount of it, we recommend daily niacin supplements. Over the long term, taking niacin could help you avoid later taking memantine, an Alzheimer's drug that only slows the progression of the disease. Or it could help you avoid becoming diabetic and needing insulin injections.

There is conflicting information about supplements. While considerable science backs up claims that natural remedies are often at least as effective as medications, misleading headlines sometimes present a much different conclusion from what a reading of the actual study would show. The *New England Journal of Medicine* (February 2006) published a study comparing the use of the drug Celebrex with the combination of glucosamine and chondroitin. The subsequent headline in the *New York Times* said, "2 Top-Selling Arthritis Drugs Are Found to Be Ineffective." Leaving aside the fact that glucosamine-chondroitin is a supplement and not a drug, the headline implies that neither therapy (the drug or the supplements) was effective.

Upon reading the study, we learned that Celebrex was minimally more effective than the natural therapies for *mild* to *moderate* arthritis. For *moderate* to *severe* arthritis, glucosamine-chondroitin was much more effective. Overall, pain relief was greater from the natural remedies, and particularly when they were used in combination as opposed to using just glucosamine.

What's going on here is a lot of politics. Drug companies have a vested interest in your *getting sick*, and they don't have a vested interest in supplements that might prevent this. Supplement manufacturers have a vested interest in people's putting *too much* faith in supplements. Supplement studies are sometimes designed to create confusion.

We could write a whole book on the ongoing saga of the supplement world versus the prescription drug world. We are more interested in finding the right supplements that reduce free radicals and inflammation, stimulate blood flow, increase production of good hormones, and strengthen cell membranes and mitochondria.

What the Heck Are Supplements, Anyway?

Supplements are not regulated in the same way drugs are regulated. Manufacturers don't need the FDA to preapprove a supplement for it to be marketed. However, any health claims have to be approved, and the FDA has the power to remove supplements from the market if they prove to be dangerous.

There are thousands of different supplements, which can be divided into vitamins, minerals, amino acids, fatty acids, nutrients, hormones, and herbs—though a few defy categorization. Included are 13 essential vitamins, 17 essential minerals, and two essential fatty acids (*essential* meaning your body must get them from outside sources because it cannot manufacture them). The term *vitamins* is often misused to represent all supplements.

Based on research that concludes taking a multivitamin may help prevent a number of chronic diseases, including heart disease, some cancers, and osteoporosis, the American Medical Association recommends that all adults take a daily multivitamin. In 2006, however, a panel of scientists from the National Institutes of Health determined that more rigorous scientific research is needed on multivitamins before it could recommend them.

Reading the report, we found it ironic that the major stumbling block for the scientists was that people who take multivitamins tend to be the very same people who exercise regularly, eat fresh vegetables and fruits, and don't smoke. They live longer and have fewer major diseases, the report acknowledged, but can you attribute this to multivitamins or to the other factors, or what? Notwithstanding, the same NIH scientific panel recommended that all adults take the antioxidants zinc and beta-carotene to reduce the risk of macular degeneration and also recommended calcium, magnesium, and vitamin D for women in danger of developing osteoporosis. This panel convened for only two days; it likely would have made many more recommendations had the members stayed in session longer.

We strongly believe taking a daily multivitamin is a must; however, it is only the beginning. You need to be taking at least 12 additional supplements and, depending on personal health considerations, up to 20 more.

12 Top Longevity Supplements

In presenting our list of a dozen "longevity supplements" that we think you should be taking in addition to a multivitamin, we recommend dosages that are equivalent to the "optimal nutritional allowance" (ONA), as opposed to the "recommended daily allowance" (RDA). If you're taking a multivitamin that contains the ONA of any of these (which is unlikely), then you don't need to take the additional supplement.

1. Omega-3 (EPA/DHA Combination)—2,000 Milligrams After Meals.
Omega-3 oils promote cardiovascular health and prevent heart attacks by lowering blood pressure, maintaining arterial flexibility, and reducing triglycerides by up to 25 percent. Omega-3 oils also increase levels of HDL cholesterol. In a study published in the *American Journal of Clinical Nutrition* comparing fish oil with the drug Lipitor, only fish oil influenced HDL. Lipitor did not increase this effect when combined with the fish oils and did not produce a similar effect on its own. Omega-3 oils also lubricate joints and help alleviate the symptoms of arthritis, and they improve your mood. DHA is an essential structural component of brain cells, and deficiencies have been linked to cognitive decline and Alzheimer's disease. We strongly recommend this supplement; it is unlikely you can get enough omega-3 from just eating fish.

Make sure the brand you take is mercury free and not rancid (you can tell from the taste).

2. Vitamin B Complex. This cluster of related nutrients includes B_1 (thiamine), B_2 (riboflavin), B_3 (niacin), B_6 (pyridoxine), folic acid, B_{12}, pantothenic acid, and biotin. While each has unique therapeutic properties, they work together to produce energy by extracting fuel from the carbohydrates, proteins, and fats in food. Their unique properties and ONA are outlined here:

■ **B_1 (thiamine)—100 milligrams.** As you get older, it is harder for your body to metabolize the thiamine in food, and a lack of thiamine causes a loss of heart-muscle function. Drinking alcohol and using diuretic drugs to control blood pressure can deplete the body's supply of this vitamin. Most B-complex vitamins contain an adequate amount.

■ **B_2 (riboflavin)—50 milligrams.** Not a superstar vitamin by itself, riboflavin makes it possible for the other B vitamins to metabolize food, safeguard cells, and forestall deficiencies of other nutrients. Of particular importance, it accelerates conversion of vitamin B_6 to its active form in the body. Riboflavin works in concert with the antioxidant glutathione—a powerful, cancer-fighting amino acid.

■ **B_3 (niacin)—100 milligrams.** There are two forms of this nutrient—niacin and niacinamide. Niacin can help raise HDL cholesterol levels while lowering LDL cholesterol and triglycerides. Niacinamide, which acts differently, helps reduce the effects of osteoarthritis and may prevent diabetes. Both are useful in reducing the risk of Alzheimer's disease by up to 80 percent, as described earlier in this section. Most B-complex formulas contain niacinamide. If you want to reduce your cholesterol and triglyceride levels, you need to take an additional niacin supplement (the "no-flush" is best). Starting with 100 milligrams, you can gradually increase intake to 1,000 milligrams a day. There is a time-released, prescription-strength niacin supplement called Niaspan, which you may want to discuss with your doctor.

▪ **B$_6$ (pyridoxine)—100 milligrams.** Sometimes referred to as the "most essential vitamin," pyridoxine is integrally involved in maintenance of women's hormonal health, diabetes and heart disease prevention, reduction of colon cancer risk, arthritis treatment, and—especially important—immune system strength. A Harvard Medical School study found that B$_6$ may reduce the risk of colon cancer by 58 percent.

▪ **Folic acid—800 micrograms.** While folic acid deficiency is most commonly associated with birth defects, scientists have discovered that it is also associated with Alzheimer's disease, heart disease, arthritis, colitis, dementia, chronic fatigue, skin disorders, multiple sclerosis, menopausal symptoms, and postpartum depression. Folic acid may be the one vitamin we need more than any other, and yet the federal government imposes dosage limits of 800 micrograms on a single pill because too much folic acid given alone can mask vitamin B$_{12}$ deficiency (no worry if you are also taking B$_{12}$). Folic acid can reduce homocysteine levels, but for this, you need up to four milligrams daily (five 800-microgram pills).

▪ **Vitamin B$_{12}$—250 micrograms.** B$_{12}$ is the "vitality vitamin." It metabolizes food, helps the body manufacture red blood cells, guards against stroke and heart disease, fine-tunes the nervous system, and provides relief from disorders including asthma, bursitis, depression, low blood pressure, and multiple sclerosis. Along with folic acid and B$_6$, it also lowers homocysteine. People needing an energy boost often go to their doctors for a B$_{12}$ injection, which speeds up metabolism. For a once-a-week B$_{12}$ energy boost, consider the B$_{12}$ Patch—see b12patch.com for details. Note: Vegetarians are particularly susceptible to a B$_{12}$ deficiency because the dietary form comes only from consuming meat.

■ **Pantothenic acid (B₅)—100 milligrams.** Pantothenic acid is critical in the metabolism and synthesis of carbohydrates, proteins, and fats. Small quantities are present in nearly every food.

■ **Biotin (B₇)—100 micrograms.** Often recommended for strengthening hair and nails, biotin helps release energy from food.

3. Alpha Lipoic Acid—200 Milligrams Twice Daily, 400 Milligrams Total. Heralded as the "universal antioxidant" because it is readily absorbed into the body and has been shown to protect the integrity of cells in organs ranging from the brain to the liver, alpha lipoic acid, according to Nicholas Perricone, M.D., is "400 times more powerful than vitamin C and E combined." Alpha lipoic acid plays a central role in the body's defense network, cellular energy, and prevention and repair of collagen damage (which is why you see it in antioxidant skin creams). It helps control inflammation and converts dietary carbohydrates to energy in mitochondria (the energy-producing component of cells). Combined with acetyl-L-carnitine, it has been shown to repair mitochondria, which may be the key to extending life.

4. Acetyl-L-Carnitine—500 Milligrams Twice Daily, 1,000 Milligrams Total. Better absorbed and more active than the plain amino acid carnitine, acetyl-L-carnitine refreshes mental energy, improves mood, and slows the aging of cells—in particular, brain cells. It also might impede the development of Alzheimer's disease.

5. Curcumin—500 Milligrams. Derived from the Indian spice turmeric, curcumin is the plant pigment responsible for turmeric's characteristic canary-yellow color. It is a powerful anti-inflammatory agent that has been used for centuries to combat arthritis, ulcers, irritable bowel syndrome, and asthma. Scientists have discovered that curcumin provides protection against the multitude of mutagens in our modern environment. A mutagen is a toxic substance

Mitochondria: The Key to a Longer Life

Bruce Ames, a world-famous biochemist from Berkeley, has developed a supplement called Juvenon that "slows down the clock on aging cells" by repairing and strengthening the mitochondria.

Ames compares mitochondria to the internal combustion engine. Just as an automobile engine creates a small amount of black smoke, the mitochondria create a small amount of free radicals—and just as the engine emits more smoke as it gets older, the older the mitochondria get, the more free radicals they are likely to release.

"Ten percent of mitochondria is eaten up every day," Ames explains. "Your cells create new mitochondria but over time don't quite keep up." Each cell has 500 or more mitochondria. Brain cells have more than 1,000.

Juvenon is a combination of two supplements—the amino acid nutrient alpha acetyl-L-carnitine and the antioxidant lipoic acid. The formula in Juvenon is 200 milligrams alpha lipoic acid and 500 milligrams acetyl-L-carnitine per pill, taken twice daily. You can buy Juvenon at health stores that carry Dr. Andrew Weil's line of supplements or order it directly from juvenon.com. Or do as we do—take alpha lipoic acid and acetyl-L-carnitine supplements.

that causes a change or mutation in your body's DNA structure, which in turn often causes cancer.

6. Vitamin D—2,000 International Units. Twenty minutes of sunlight every day is a good prescription for most people because it enhances mood and provides much-needed vitamin D. Vitamin D is associated with a decreased risk of many common cancers, including colon, breast, prostate, and ovarian. It is critical for maintaining normal calcium in the blood and for bone health. We get our 20 minutes of sunshine or take the supplement every day, in part because *Cancer Research* concluded that men with the highest levels of vitamin D have up to 65 percent less incidence of prostate cancer. Research presented to the American Association for Cancer Research has found that women with the highest levels of vitamin D have a 50 percent reduced risk of breast cancer versus women with the lowest levels. This may explain why women who live at lower, sunnier latitudes have less breast cancer.

7. Vitamin E with Selenium—400 International Units Vitamin E, 200 Micrograms Selenium. We lump these two together because selenium has been observed to activate vitamin E and because together they have a protective effect against the toxicity of methylmercury, the mercury contaminant detected in fish and seafood.

Vitamin E is a potent antioxidant that improves blood viscosity, protects the heart, and may help reduce the risk of dementia. The famous Nurses' Health Study, involving more than 87,000 women, reported a 41 percent reduction in risk of heart disease among nurses who had taken vitamin E for more than two years. We prefer that you use natural, mixed "tocopherols" and not the cheaper and less-effective alpha-tocopherol. (Taking more than 100 international units of the latter may actually be harmful.)

Selenium is a powerful antioxidant with real cancer-fighting properties. The results of a major (more than 1,300 participants) double-blind, placebo-controlled trial showed that selenium cut cancer occurrences by almost 40 percent and decreased the cancer death rate by 50 percent among subjects who took 200 micrograms of selenium daily over a four-year period. The incidence of lung cancer decreased by 38 percent, for colorectal cancer it dropped by 46 percent, and a 63 percent reduction occurred for prostate cancer.

8. CoQ10 (Ubiquinone)—100 Milligrams Twice Daily, 200 Milligrams Total. Everyone needs CoQ10 because it is essential to the production of cellular energy and is concentrated in the myocardium, or heart muscle. In dozens of clinical trails, supplementation with CoQ10 has dramatically reduced symptoms of heart failure, including congestive heart failure, and in some cases even restored

What About Vitamin C?

Sometimes held to be the nutrient that does it all, vitamin C boosts our immune system and is effective against bacterial infections, which is why it is useful in fighting colds. British researchers have found that people with high levels of vitamin C in their diets are less likely to develop rheumatoid arthritis. However, other research has found that taking too much vitamin C (more than 1,000 milligrams) can inflame joints and make arthritis worse. We recommend 400 to 500 milligrams a day, which should be in your multivitamin. If your multi has less than this, you might want to find a better one or add a separate vitamin C supplement.

the heart to its healthy state. Our ONA of 200 milligrams makes CoQ10 one of the more expensive items in your supplement arsenal, but having a strong heart makes it well worth the price.

9. Magnesium with Potassium—400 Milligrams Magnesium, 100 Milligrams Potassium After Meals. High levels of magnesium in the diet are associated with a reduced risk of metabolic syndrome, including all components: high blood pressure, high blood sugar levels, elevated blood fats, and low levels of HDL cholesterol. A significant study of 4,600 Americans found that the risk of developing metabolic syndrome over 15 years was 31 percent lower for those with the highest intake of magnesium. As a supplement, it is often paired with potassium, another champion of the cardiovascular system. Potassium helps maintain the correct fluid balance in the body; too much fluid increases blood pressure. Many medications, including diuretics for high blood pressure, deplete the body of both magnesium and potassium. Some doctors recommend more potassium, up to 600 milligrams. If this is the case with your doctor, you'll need to take additional potassium supplements or eat a lot of bananas. One banana has 80 milligrams of potassium.

10. SAMe, 200 Milligrams upon Waking and 200 Milligrams Before Going to Bed, 400 Milligrams Total. Boost your mood, lubricate your joints, and refresh your liver with SAMe (S-adenosylmethionine). Prescribed successfully for two decades in 14 countries where it has been approved as a drug, SAMe is a molecule that all living cells constantly produce. Because SAMe stimulates production of serotonin, it has been successfully used to treat depression. Because it acts as an NSAID (nonsteroidal anti-inflammatory drug), only without the gastric side effects of aspirin or ibuprofen, it is also prescribed to treat arthritis pain. German researchers gave patients either SAMe or a placebo for three months. MRI (magnetic resonance imaging) scans showed that SAMe recipients experienced measurable increases in cartilage in their hands. Other studies suggest it can help normalize liver function in patients with cirrhosis, hepatitis, and cholestasis (blockage of the bile ducts). SAMe has also been found to prevent or reverse liver damage. Even if you don't have liver problems, arthritis, or mild bouts of depression, we recommend this remarkable supplement because we think it can help prevent these problems from arising.

11. Phosphatidyl Serine (PS)—300 Milligrams. A naturally occurring lipid that is a component of cell membranes, phoshatidyl serine stimulates the cells in your brain to make new dendrites and axons and thereby enhance cognitive functions. People who take PS remember more names, faces, phone numbers, and written information. Thomas Crook, Ph.D., founder of the Memory Assessment Clinic, in Bethesda, Maryland, says PS "can turn back the clock 12 to 15 years."

12. Nattokinase—100 Milligrams (2,000 Fibrin Units). Derived from natto—a sticky, strong-tasting Japanese breakfast food made from fermented soybeans—nattokinase facilitates better blood flow throughout the body, including the brain, where it promotes memory and cognitive functions. Nattokinase breaks down fibrin protein deposits, preventing the formation of clots and improving blood viscosity. It is sometimes used to prevent deep-vein thrombosis—the type of large clots people get in their legs or ankles from flying in an airplane. We use it because nattokinase is a safe alternative to aspirin therapy for the prevention of heart attacks and strokes.

Using Supplements as Targeted Therapy

The preceding "big 12" are general-application supplements that we think every adult counting down his or her age should take. Depending upon your personal situation, you may need additional supplements as well to address specific concerns. If you are one of the millions of adults with sore knees, for instance, you should use the supplements glucosamine and chondroitin (discussed previously). Other targeted supplements we recommend are as follows:

■ **Prostate support—saw palmetto.** Superior to the drug Proscar for treating benign prostrate enlargement, saw palmetto relieves constricted urinary flow by blocking the enzyme that causes the prostate to enlarge. Oh, happy days—men who take this supplement often report a remarkable side effect: sexual rejuvenation.

■ **Liver concerns—milk thistle.** As a liver medication, milk thistle has been used to slash the death rate from cirrhosis by 50 percent and also improves the outcome of hepatitis treatments. If you worry about drinking too much alcohol, if you've had hepatitis, or if after a blood test your doctor expresses concern about your albumin levels (albumin is a protein made by the liver), then milk thistle is for you.

■ **Menopausal problems such as hot flashes or night sweats—black cohosh.** The influence that the active ingredients in black cohosh have on the body resembles that of estrogen. Just 16 milligrams daily for two weeks may diminish menopausal symptoms and alleviate menstrual cramps.

Fountain of Youth in a Pill?

A blend of two compounds extracted from blue-green algae harvested from Klamath Lake, in Oregon, StemEnhance has been shown in a "triple-blind study" to increase the number of adult stem cells circulating in the blood. By promoting stem cell migration, this supplement may enhance the body's ability to rebuild tissue, helping it to maintain optimal health. The people we talked to who take StemEnhance report remarkable increases in energy and fast recovery from various ailments. We'd like to believe this, but in the past some claims about blue-green algae have been proved to be false, and the "study" included only 15 volunteers. We're still watching this one.

■ **Eye health—lutein and zeaxanthin.** An unbeatable combination, these are the dominant carotenoids that protect the eyes. If you regularly eat kale, collard greens, spinach, and other leafy greens, you probably don't need to take the supplement. If not, we strongly recommend you take lutein and zeaxanthin: ward off cataracts, and cut the risk of macular degeneration by more than 50 percent.

■ **Chronic fatigue—NT factor.** Fatigue is one of the first outward signs of cellular deterioration. When a cell membrane deteriorates, it loses its fluidity, which is the ability to absorb critical nutrients into the cell for optimal health and energy production. NT factor delivers phospholipids that nourish and strengthen cellular and mitochondrial membranes and promote enhanced nutrient absorption for optimal energy production.

■ **Congestive heart failure—D-ribose.** A remarkable clinical study shows that D-ribose can effectively influence cardiac energy metabolism and provide patients a significant improvement in quality of life that is directly tied to observational improvements in physical functions. Another study, as yet to be published at the time of this writing, by Jacob Teitelbaum, M.D., showed that taking 10 grams (two scoops) of ribose a day increased energy by 45 percent. More information can be found at vitality101.com.

■ **Cancer protection—lycopene.** The pigment that colors tomatoes and watermelons, lycopene is the most powerful carotenoid for cancer protection. Of some 500 carotenoids tested in a study of prostate cancer risk among 47,894 men, it was the only one to demonstrate protective ability. If you eat lots of cooked tomatoes or regularly drink tomato juice, you don't need to take this supplement.

■ **Bone health—vitamin K.** Doesn't matter how much calcium you get from your diet or from taking calcium as a supplement, without vitamin K, your body can't form osteocalcin, the structural framework inside bones around which calcium crystallizes. Like lutein and zeaxanthin, vitamin K is concentrated in leafy green vegetables. If you eat enough, a supplement isn't necessary. Note: Vitamin K can counteract prescription blood thinners such as warfarin. Talk to your doctor before taking this.

■ **Blood sugar balance—chromium.** Called either chromium picolinate or chromium polynicotinate, this nutrient is pivotal for sugar metabolism. A chromium deficiency seems to correlate with insulin resistance and all the related medical conditions, including obesity, hypoglycemia, type 2 diabetes, stroke, high blood pressure, and multiple sclerosis. It is indispensable for controlling type 2 diabetes: once an optimal amount is circulating in the bloodstream, some people with diabetes find their blood sugar completely under control, while others find they need less diabetic medication or insulin.

■ **Anxiety and mild depression—theanine.** An amino acid derived from green teas, theanine is a wonderful treatment for anxiety that calms you while leaving your mind clear and your energy high. We recommend 200 milligrams.

■ **Hormonal boost—DHEA.** The mother of all hormones, DHEA (dehydroepiandrosterone) is made by the adrenal glands. It goes into the bloodstream and from there travels all over the body into cells, where it is converted into male hormones, known as androgens, and female hormones, known as estrogens. Our adrenal glands produce less and less DHEA as we age. Increasing DHEA will improve your sex drive, enhance your immune function, renew energy and stamina, brighten your mood, and give you a keener memory. Men need to be aware that DHEA can stimulate testosterone production. Any man with prostate cancer or who has a high risk of prostate cancer shouldn't take DHEA unless his doctor prescribes it.

Because research on supplements is on-going, we recommend that you regularly check our websites, longlife.com and vagnini. com, for the newest developments.

8 4 3
5 2
6
3 7
1
6 3
5
2
8

4

Better-than-Ever Fitness Plan

Soup Up Your Stamina, Double Your Strength, and Get Those Hormones Flowing!

Want to look and feel better than you ever have before? The Better-than-Ever Fitness Plan is a surefire means for achieving this goal. Stick with us and your risk of coronary artery disease will be reduced by 50 percent, your glucose tolerance and insulin sensitivity will improve, your odds of dying within the next 10 years will be reduced by more than 40 percent, your joints will be stronger and more flexible, you'll be less likely to suffer bone loss or fractures, your short-term memory will improve as your risk of getting Alzheimer's disease or dementia is reduced by 40 percent, you'll be sleeping better, and you'll be a happier person. The impact of the exercise program we recommend is immediate. You'll start seeing and feeling the results the very day you start on the plan.

Exercise is so powerful that a *lack* of exercise can be used to predict death.Researchers at Stanford University studied 6,213 men (average age 59) who were referred for exercise testing. Each man was hooked to an electrocardiogram machine to monitor his heart activity while he walked and ran on a treadmill. Based on their blood pressure, heart rate, exercise capacity, and medical records, the men were classified as having cardiovascular disease or not.

Six years later, the researchers used the Social Security death index to determine which of the men had died. They discovered that the men with the lowest exercise capacity were more than *four times likely to die* than the men with the highest. This was true even if the subjects had cardiovascular disease. Exercise capacity was the strongest predictor of death in men, outranking both smoking and history of chronic disease. But this study involved just men, as you may have noticed. What about women?

To find out if exercise testing could predict mortality in women, scientists tested 2,994 women between 30 and 80 years of age using the Bruce treadmill protocol, which measures the amount of oxy-

Smart Exercising Guidelines

The Better-than-Ever Fitness Plan is built around 15 "smart exercising guidelines."

1. Just get started.
2. Use your imagination.
3. You *can* do it daily.
4. Learn calorie awareness.
5. Build up your heart.
6. Pump iron.
7. Warm up, cool down.
8. Don't flout your limits.
9. Always be stretching.
10. Create your own routine.
11. Sweat out the toxins.
12. Make *no* excuses.
13. Dance your way to health.
14. Be an athlete, sort of.
15. Whip your brain into shape.

gen a person can consume and utilize. It's not too surprising that the results were similar to those for the men: mortality was higher among subjects with the least amount of endurance. Women who were below the median of all those tested had a 3.5-fold increased risk of cardiovascular death.

Exercise is also linked to a reduction in the risk of colon, prostate, and breast cancer. A 14-year study of 25,624 Norwegian women found that breast cancer was reduced by 37 percent among those exercising seven days a week.

Study after study has shown the beneficial effect of exercise in treating mild to moderate depression. Approximately 19 million Americans suffer from depressive orders; very few realize that a jog around the block will make them feel better. Even more eye-opening are the studies showing that seniors who engage in exercise at least three times a week can cut their risk of developing Alzheimer's and other forms of dementia by as much as 40 percent.

If you want to die early, just sit on your butt all day. However, you don't have to get old the way you might think, either; you can become a radically new person. More than 50 percent of all illnesses and injuries over the last third of your life can be eliminated! Instead of succumbing to the normal decay associated with aging—the sore joints, lack of energy, weakness, irritability—you can get stronger and feel younger. In fact, in a biological sense, you can *be younger.*

BIOMARKERS OF AGING YOU CAN CONTROL THROUGH EXERCISE

Research at the USDA Human Nutrition Research Center on Aging shows that people can reverse many of the physiological declines associated with aging through regular aerobic, flexibility, and strength-training exercise. By making positive changes in your own biomarkers, you can prolong vitality and prevent development of sarcopenia—a condition characterized by weakening of the body's muscles, loss of balance, reduced mobility, and frailty. This section lists the nine biomarkers you can change.

1. Muscle mass. No matter what your age, you can increase the strength and mass of your muscles through resistance training. Otherwise, muscle mass will decline, accelerating at an alarming rate after age 45.

2. Basal metabolic rate (BMR). BMR is the rate of your metabolism when you are sitting still or resting. Declines in BMR starting kicking in at age 20. Every decade, the number of calories needed daily to maintain a constant body weight declines as well, by roughly 100 calories. Since most people nevertheless continue to eat the same amount of food (if not more), this is one of the reasons they get fat. Aerobic exercise will speed up your BMR. Do enough of it and you can eat like a 20-year-old!

3. Body fat percentage. Just as people with a greater ratio of muscle-to-fat enjoy a higher metabolism, the opposite is also true: the fatter you get, the less efficiently you are able to burn off calories. According to the American Council on Exercise, a "fit" man should have no more than 14 percent to 17 percent body fat, and for a "fit" woman, it's 21 percent to 24 percent. Men are obese if their body fat is greater than 26 percent; for women it is 32 percent.

The most common tools for measuring body fat are the skin-fold method and bioelectrical impedance analysis. Your doctor or a trained specialist can measure you, or you can get a fat-percentage scale for home use. The best way to attack excess body fat is through a combination of exercise and moderate calorie restriction. In other words: *exercise more and eat less.*

4. Aerobic capacity. For healthy lungs, a strong heart, and an efficient vascular network, you need good aerobic capacity, which is the amount of oxygen your body can process within a given time. This capacity typically declines by 30 to 40 percent by age

65. Regular exercise can increase your aerobic capacity, but the positive change in older people comes almost entirely in the ability of muscles to utilize oxygen (oxidative capacity). Thus, you need strengthening exercises as well as aerobic exercises. When you build muscles, you create more muscle cells to consume oxygen. The more your body demands oxygen, the greater your utilization and the higher your aerobic capacity.

5. Blood-sugar tolerance. By age 70, some 30 percent of women and 20 percent of men have an abnormal glucose-tolerance curve, increasing their risk for type 2 diabetes (if they don't already have it). Factors related to glucose metabolism that you can control are the following:

■ Increase in body fat
■ Inactivity
■ Diet high in saturated fat

Resistance training is once again critical. Besides lowering body fat, resistance training has been shown to increase muscles' insulin sensitivity.

6. Total cholesterol/HDL ratio. To compute your ratio of total cholesterol to HDL cholesterol, you simply divide the total cholesterol number by the HDL number. (Of course, you first need to know these numbers.) For middle-aged and older men and women, the ratio goal should be 4.5 or lower.

LDL cholesterol can be lowered by the use of statins such as Atorvastatin or supplements such as niacin and red yeast rice. Or it can be lowered by reducing the amount of saturated fat in your diet. To increase HDL, however, you need to exercise. Aerobic exercise seems to be particularly effective for raising HDL.

7. Blood pressure. Controlling blood pressure is vital. Regular, vigorous exercise is one of the best tools for preventing and even treating high blood pressure.

8. Bone density. On average, a person loses 1 percent of bone mass per year. When this decline reaches the point where risk of bone fracture is substantial, we call it osteoporosis. The effectiveness of calcium supplements in fighting this decline is the subject of much debate; however, the effectiveness of weight-bearing exercise is not. Stress repeatedly placed on your bones through exercise makes them grow. Many studies have shown that a prolonged span of weight-bearing exercise—walking, running, or bicycling, for example—reduces the rate of bone loss. Research at Tufts University indicated that exercise also increases the body's ability to absorb dietary calcium.

9. Internal body temperature. Thermoregulatory ability is one more thing that diminishes with age. You have a harder time cooling off when you're hot or warming up when you're cold. The reasons are complex, but they include requirement of a warmer internal body temperature before sweating sets in, dehydration caused by impaired kidneys, and a lower overall amount of sweating. By exercising regularly, you sweat more and increase thirst and total body water content. Remind yourself to drink lots of water.

HEALTHY STRESS

It is a fact that *all* of the cells in your muscles are replaced three times a year. Your body is in a continuous process of growth and decay. When you exercise, you put "healthy stress" on your muscles, and in reaction to this stress, they send chemical messages that tell your body to grow new cells. These messages are delivered by your blood. When you are vigorously exercising, up to 80 percent of your blood flow goes through your muscles. When you are not exercising, it is only about 20 percent.

The chemical messages released into your bloodstream are regulatory proteins, called cytokines. There are many different cytokines, some involved with building up your cells, and others with tearing them down. An admittedly simplistic but accurate description is that *aging is a battle between decaying and growth.* As you grow older, you secrete more and more cytokines that turn on inflammation, which is a major factor in all age-related diseases.

Exercise is the best way to fight back. It tears you down to build you back up. Each time you work out, your muscles get a little stronger; enzymes and proteins flood into your bloodstream, creating a controlled inflammation that triggers the repair process: decay triggers growth. Your heart gets stronger, more blood flows to your brain, your blood vessels get more flexible, all your organs get more nourishment, and—most important—your immune system is invigorated, which may explain why exercise is linked with lower cancer rates.

Exercise makes up for most of your sins in other areas. If you do only one part of the Count Down Your Age program, do the exercise.

EXERCISE GUIDELINE #1: JUST GET STARTED

Don't procrastinate—walk! Walking is very simple: you don't need equipment or a gym; and if you walk far enough and briskly enough, you realize most of the benefits of aerobic exercise. Getting into the habit is the most important "step." Walk for 45 minutes to an hour every day for three weeks, and after that, you'll find it hard *not* to walk. Pick a regular time (mornings are best) so you won't put it off and skip days.

It doesn't take long to become *addicted* to exercise. Each time you go for that brisk walk, in addition to cytokines, your body is flooded with hundreds of other chemicals, including endorphins and serotonin. Endorphins are natural pain-medication hormones that improve your mood, make you feel better, increase pleasure, and minimize pain. When people have a low level of endorphins in their brains, they can feel anxious, and in response, they often will have a craving for fatty foods such as french fries or ice cream. Serotonin is also a beneficial hormone; it makes you feel calm, poised, confident, and relaxed. When your levels of serotonin are low, you can feel irritable and stressed out.

The same goes for swimming, bicycling, jogging, or whatever other form of exercise you use. The longer and more intensely you exercise, the more hormones are released. The runner's high that marathoners experience can be so euphoric, many say, that it's similar to an orgasm.

Tap In to Your Work Ethic

One fantastic way to get into the daily exercise habit is to tap in to your "go to work" habit. If you're like most people, you hardly ever miss (or missed) a day of work. Somehow, even when you were tired or sick, you still went. Right? Exercise is a job you have to do for your body (and your mind). If you've ever been fired or laid off from work, you know how miserable life can be when you're *not* doing your job. So, show up, exercise, and be glad you can.

If this doesn't get you started, take a week or two off and go on a "fitness vacation." Go somewhere where you can hike all day in the mountains, or try one of many fitness spas listed on the Internet. Typical of these health retreats is the New York Health Spa, which has a fully equipped gym, heated indoor and outdoor swimming pools, and a huge exercise studio for aerobics, Pilates, dance, muscle-conditioning, and stretch classes. It also offers nature walks in the nearby Shawangunk Mountains, tai chi, yoga, and meditation. The food is totally nutritious and awesome. Worldwide, there are thousands of health retreats—find one. For people who are into yoga, or would like to be, yogasite.com has links to the better yoga retreats around the world.

EXERCISE GUIDELINE #2: USE YOUR IMAGINATION

OK, your life is too complicated, you can't get away, your boss is a grump, the dog ate your cat, you haven't balanced your checkbook, and there is no way you can spend a whole hour in the morning hiking around your neighborhood. As a last resort, use your imagination. If you drive to the office, park as far away as you can and walk the rest of the way to work; time yourself and try to beat this pace on subsequent days. You can apply the same principle for running errands: the next time you drive to the post office or the coffee shop—park several blocks away.

Walk up stairs whenever possible instead of taking the elevator. Pick a restaurant about a mile away from your office, and walk to lunch. Take over the dog-walking chore at your house. Walk the neighbor's dog. Do a few sit-ups in bed before you get up—you'll be surprised to find it easier than doing them on the floor. After you get up, do a few stretches. Buy some dumbbells so you can do biceps curls here and there. Try jogging in place for a few moments before you get dressed. When you go to the grocery store, bag your own groceries and lift them into and out of the cart. Anything that will burn off a few extra calories and get your blood flowing is good. Exercise is cumulative—you don't have to do it all at once.

Buy yourself a fantastic little motivator: a pedometer. This electronic gadget, which you can put in your pocket or strap to your belt, will track the number of steps you take daily and will calculate the amount of calories burned. You'll find yourself trying to rack up more and more steps while burning off more and more calories.

Try Bouncing Up and Down

Take a longevity tip from Bob Hope: try rebounding. The comedian, who lived to 100, once said, "I keep a rebounder at the foot of my bed and use it daily." Rebounders are fun, and they help your lymphatic system pump and drain out the body's waste. Proponents claim rebounding boosts your immunity to viruses, circulates more oxygen to your tissues, increases red blood cell production, and provides relief from headaches and back pain. We're not so convinced, but you can jump, do aerobic exercises, custom jog, and run on a rebounder. People we know who use them love them. For more information: needakrebounders.com.

Many converts try to walk 1,000 steps a day. Pedometers are available most everywhere and at pedometer.com.

EXERCISE GUIDELINE #3: YOU *CAN* DO IT DAILY

It is much too easy to subscribe to the popular notion that "any exercise is better than none." We know many people who think a half-hour walk once or twice a week, or a weekend bike ride, or one weekly trip to the gym is all they need to stay healthy and keep the weight off. If you are in this category, you're not exercising nearly enough. You need to rethink your strategy and move exercise up the scale of things that are important in your life. Any exercise is better than none, but not that much better.

According to U.S. government dietary guidelines, which some fitness experts call conservative, you need at least 30 minutes a day of "moderate-intensity physical activity" to reduce the risk of chronic disease. And you need 60 minutes of "moderate-intensity" exercise most days of the week just to avoid gaining weight. If you really want to lose weight, you need 60 to 90 minutes *on a daily basis.*

We both made conscious decisions a few years ago to make exercise a priority in our lives and have stuck to it. Dave does a combination of aerobic exercise, stretching, and resistance training. Two or three days a week, he goes swimming (see "Dave's Swimming Routine"), and twice a week, he goes to the gym for weight lifting, followed by a 30-minute bout on the elliptical machine. At least once a week, he plays basketball and tennis with his grand-daughters, plus he goes on long bike rides (one to two hours) or rows in the Sausalito bay (sculling). Dr. V is what you might call a dedicated "gym rat." He loves the challenge of weight lifting and likes what it does for his physique—so he's been going five to seven days a week for weight lifting, aerobics, and some stretching for about 10 years.

One of the keys to staying on track with your exercise program is to constantly remind yourself of the benefits. One hour a day

Your Virtual Fitness Trainer

PumpOne (pumpone.com) is a portable, digital trainer that you can download and use on your iPod, Treo, or Blackberry. It houses 43 programs, including yoga, aerobic conditioning, and strength training. If you don't have a companion handheld device, you can choose from any number of virtual trainers available for use on your computer. We saw some good ones at virtualfitnesstrainer.com.

isn't really much when you consider that you are reducing the odds that you'll have a stroke or come down with heart disease, diabetes, Alzheimer's disease, cancer, or high blood pressure. It would really help, of course, if your employer and your family also recognized the importance of exercise. Workers who exercise miss fewer days of work because of illness, and they have more energy and can focus better than peers who don't. Grandparents, parents, spouses, and significant others who exercise are much nicer to be around than those who don't.

The Institute of Medicine recommends that adults spend at least 60 minutes a day doing "moderately intense" physical activity such as a brisk walk, because 30 minutes is not enough for most people to maintain an ideal weight or obtain maximum health benefits. It isn't realistic to exercise every single day; hardly anyone exercises on a regular basis without skipping sometimes. We both avoid missing more than two consecutive days, because by the third day off, lethargy sets in. It can be hard to get the momentum back.

Some days, after a previous day of intense exercise, Dave will go swimming and swim only about 12 laps (a third of a mile), which takes him less than 15 minutes. His thinking is, "Well, yesterday I had a really good workout, so I just need a quick tune-up—enough to keep my heart strong and to help me feel good." A tune-up is better than nothing. You might not burn as many calories, but you get your heart pumping, stretch your muscles, and oxygenate the

---

Will You Work Out More If You Have a Gym Membership?

A study in the *Journal of Sports Medicine* indicates that health club members are 34 percent more likely to work out than nonmembers. They work out longer and more vigorously. They are also three times as likely to have seen their doctor in the past year for a checkup and to have seen a dentist, optometrist, or nutritionist. The study's lead author, Elizabeth Ready, Ph.D., concludes, "People who are motivated to join a gym may be more motivated towards preventive health."

---

old system. Later in the day, if the opportunity comes up, you can go for a short but brisk walk or climb a few flights of stairs. No rule says you have to do all your daily exercise at one time.

Once you get started on a good exercise program, we want you to do more exercise, more often. In addition to aerobic exercise, it is vital for your routine to incorporate stretching and resistance exercise; in fact, the more variety, the better. We also urge you to exercise your eyes and your mind.

The goal is to exercise every single day.

EXERCISE GUIDELINE #4: LEARN CALORIE AWARENESS

Most people consume more excess calories than they can offset with just 30 minutes or even one hour of exercise. Dave knows he's a case in point. When he uses the exercise bike in the gym for 25 minutes, he burns off about 300 calories. Then, if he lifts weights for an additional 30 minutes, he'll use 500 or so calories. He feels great—and hungry—and by golly, his attitude is, "I worked so hard, I can eat a cheeseburger." Yikes, did you know that 500 calories is about the amount in a typical cheeseburger? As far as calories go, one Starbucks Caramel Frappuccino coffee with whipped cream will pretty much wipe out the benefits of an hour of intensive exercise. Likewise, have two scoops of Ben & Jerry's vanilla caramel fudge ice cream (580 calories), and it's time to go back to the gym.

The number of calories burned during exercise is partly a factor of your weight. Seems unfair, but the more you weigh, the more calories you will burn while exercising. A 125-pound person who swims laps for 30 minutes at a moderate pace will burn approximately 227 calories; someone who weighs 200 pounds will burn 363 calories. Odds are fairly good, however, that a 200-pound person will consume more calories during the day than a 125-pound person, so perhaps it balances out.

As a rule of thumb, if you are satisfied with your weight, you should exercise enough every week to burn a minimum of 1,200 calories. If you want to lose weight, raise this to 2,000.

We aren't suggesting you get fanatical about counting calories, but it makes great sense to have an approximate idea of how many calories you are eating daily and how many you are burning off during exercise. As we mentioned in the previous chapter, just to maintain your current weight, you need to use up as many calories as you consume. To lose weight, you simply have to use *more* than you consume. A great online resource where you can calculate how many calories you burn during exercise can be found at caloriesperhour.com.

EXERCISE GUIDELINE #5: BUILD UP YOUR HEART

Smoking is the worst thing you can do for your health. Aerobic exercise on a consistent basis is the absolute best. People who routinely walk, ride a bicycle, swim, or participate in any of a vast variety of aerobic exercises live longer than people who don't. Aerobic exercise, more so than any diet, helps you control your weight. It is primarily exercise for your lungs and your cardiovascular system, including your most important muscle—your heart. A strong heart and powerful lungs are the best insurance you can have against most of the health obstacles you'll be facing the rest of your life.

What is aerobic exercise? If you take a leisurely walk around the block, is this aerobic? The answer is no. If you get up from the couch and open another can of beer, is this aerobic? Hell no! What about sex? Well, it depends on how vigorous you are when having sex and, of course, how long you can do it. Five minutes isn't enough.

Some sports that you might think are aerobic really aren't because they involve too much stopping and going. This includes golf, softball, climbing, croquet, and bowling. Yoga and Pilates are really good for you, but they aren't aerobic.

The main purpose of aerobic exercise is to raise your heart *and* your breathing rates for a sustained period. True aerobic exercise occurs *only* when you *continuously* exert some, if not all, of the large muscles in your body (such as your leg or arm muscles) for at least 20 minutes during which your heart rate is elevated to between 60 percent and 80 percent of its maximum level. That specific range of elevation in your heart rate is referred to as your "training range."

This sounds more complicated than it is. Your maximum heart rate is simply your age subtracted from the number 220. If you're 60 years old, for example, then your maximum heart rate is 160 (220 minus 60 equals 160). If you're only 25, your maximum heart rate is much higher (220 minus 25 equals 195). Now calculate your training range by multiplying your maximum heart rate first by 60 percent and then by 80 percent. So, for a 60-year-old, the training range is 96 to 128 beats per minute (160 times 0.6 equals 96; 160 times 0.8 equals 128).

The easiest way to achieve the targeted 20 minutes of continuous aerobic exercise at your training range is to utilize the aerobic exercise equipment at a gym. Most gyms have equipment with built-in computer monitoring devices that measure your heart rate and provide other useful information, such as the number of calories you've burned. Our experience is that it takes 3 or 4 minutes on a stationary bike or jogging machine to raise the heart rate to the training range. And keeping it there can be a bit of a struggle until you are in good shape. Start by gradually building up to 20 minutes. No point in literally killing yourself in the gym. Ten minutes in the beginning is fantastic compared with nothing.

Once you've completed the aerobic portion of your workout, it is imperative to cool down gradually and not just stop. Pedal or jog slowly for 3 to 5 minutes so that your heart rate can scale down to a normal level. The minimum amount of time to spend on an aerobics machine in order to get 20 continuous minutes of aerobic exercise is 26 minutes.

People who use these machines soon learn to recognize when their hearts are beating within the training range. We don't need a monitoring device—however, many people find the feedback they get to be highly motivating. If you work out for 26 minutes and you pedal the equivalent of 5.6 miles, having a register of that accomplishment is good for your self-esteem, and it gives you a goal to beat next time.

Walking is the easiest and *cheapest* exercise, but unless you walk briskly or walk uphill, you may not really be getting the aerobic benefits you need to strengthen your cardiovascular system. You can't get your heart rate into its training range by strolling down the street and looking into the store windows or by leisurely hiking from your car to your office. The only way to know for sure if your walking exercise is aerobic is to measure your pulse. An excellent idea is to buy a good pulse meter, which will provide you a continuous readout of your pulse rate. Some of the best of these are imbedded into sport watches or pedometers.

Remember: to get 20 minutes of *continuous* aerobic benefit through walking, you need to either walk fast or climb hills, and it is good to walk for a longer period, as much as an hour. You can increase your heartbeat 10 percent by swinging your arms while you walk or, better yet, by carrying a weight in each hand (one to two pounds) and raising and lowering your arms. This technique, referred to as "heavy hands walking," is also a great way to strengthen your arms. Another technique is to speed up for a couple of minutes, slow down for a couple of minutes, and then repeat the process.

The faster you walk, the faster your heart beats and the more calories you burn. A 160-pound person will burn approximately 260 calories in one hour by walking three miles; at four miles per hour, calories burned rise to 322, and the number soars to 661 at five miles.

Jogging or running is extremely aerobic, but only if your body can withstand the stress. A high percentage of runners develop physical problems ranging from shin splints to tendonitis to stress fractures and bad knees. Don't be one of those fools who run on the hard surface of a street while inhaling the exhaust of traffic. Find a softer surface such as a track or grassy field (golf courses are perfect if you can run around the edges and not get whacked by a stray tee shot). Keep in mind that when you run, you inhale air into the deepest parts of your lungs, so you want to avoid polluted environments.

The Greatest Aerobic Exercise

Swimming is the greatest aerobic exercise; ask anyone who swims on a regular basis. Non-weight-bearing, it provides an excellent aerobic, whole-body workout that increases the flexibility and strength of your joints, and it's virtually injury free. Even if you don't know how to swim, you can participate. There is nifty aerobic swimming equipment that will let you take full advantage of the weightless effect of working out in the water. While the high end includes underwater treadmills and stationary bikes, there are also a number of inexpensive products to help you turn any pool into a gym without breaking the bank.

Most health clubs offer a variety of aquatic fitness classes, from water walking to high-intensity, deep-water aerobics. Students in these classes range in age from 20 to 90, but most are 50 and older. Anyone can benefit from water workouts, but they're especially good for people with injuries or physical conditions that make land-based exercise difficult. Many arthritis sufferers benefit from water-based fitness classes.

When you run, walk, or bike, the impact on your joints can be up to three times your body weight. If you're standing in shoulder-deep water, the water supports your body weight, so there's less pressure on your hips, knees, and ankles. With the aid of a flotation belt that holds you upright, you can essentially "jog" in deep water without hammering your joints. Heavier than air, water adds a resistance factor that is similar to that of weight lifting but not as intense. Many lap swimmers also work out with weights once or twice a week. Another advantage of swimming is you are less likely to become overheated, because the water is constantly cooling you down. However, you still *actually sweat*, so it is important to drink some water after swimming.

There are many other types of aerobic exercise, including cross-country skiing, kayaking, soccer, squash, dancing, and basketball. The cells in your body don't know the difference. As long as you get that heart rate up to the proper range for 20 minutes or longer, you are adding years to your life.

EXERCISE GUIDELINE #6: PUMP IRON

You're never too old to pump iron. Even if you are in your nineties, you can become stronger. A good resistance-training program will increase your strength by 25 to 100 percent or more within one year! In comparison, a good aerobic exercise program will increase your aerobic fitness by only 15 to 25 percent.

Resistance training increases muscle strength by pitting the muscles against a force, usually a dumbbell or barbell. Body weight itself can provide the resistance: pull-ups, sit-ups, and push-ups are a form of resistance training. Isometric exercises, in which you push your hands against a doorway or against the opposing limb of an exercise partner, also qualify. Of all forms, the use of free weights or resistance machines is by far the most effective method.

As anyone who belongs to a gym or who has walked by a gym window probably knows, the variety of resistance machines is vast. The most common machines use weight plates to vary the resistance, but others use hydraulic or air-cylinder engineering. The biggest advantage these machines have over free weights is that they are safer. You are much less likely to drop a weight on your foot or pull a muscle. Free weights, however, will increase your sense of balance and coordination.

The Bowflex machine you see advertised on late-night TV uses yet another system, one based on resistance rods. We're not opposed to home solutions like this, but most people are more likely to get into a habit of regular exercise if they go to a gym. There are too many distractions at home. And why should you have to bother with maintaining sports equipment when someone else can do it for you?

How does resistance training work? Basically, the cells in your muscles adapt to the extra workload by enlarging (thus the term *pumped up*) and by subsequently recruiting nerve cells to contract. After a muscle has been subjected to intense stress through maximal-force contractions over a moderate repetition range, hormones begin the growth process and muscle remodeling.

Levels of both testosterone and growth hormone can be increased through resistance training. When this happens, a cascade of highly beneficial events occurs, including an increase in glucose utilization, improved amino acid transport across cell membranes, improved protein synthesis and utilization of fatty acids, faster rate of fat breakdown, and enhanced immune function.

When using free weights or resistance machines, use a weight that allows 8 to 12 repetitions (reps) before maximum voluntary contraction sets in. This means your muscle has contracted to its peak. In fact, you should feel a burning sensation in your arm as you do the final rep—this is good. If you do three sets of 8 to 12 reps using the maximum amount of weight *and* you rest for only 60 seconds or less between sets, your muscles will release the maximum amount of hormones. They will grow in size and capacity (strength). This is so simple, which makes Dave wonder why so many people at the gym where he works out don't do it. They often sit around for five minutes or more between sets and fiddle with their iPods.

If you don't want to increase the production of hormones in your body because you are afraid you might start looking like Arnold Schwarzenegger, just do more reps with a lighter weight.

Parachutes for Runners Add Resistance Factor

Want to get in some resistance training while you run? Parachutes for runners, called power chutes, can strengthen your leg and arm muscles so you can spend more time on the track and less time in the gym. You wear the chute like a backpack, and while you're running, you can open it to provide resistance. After running this way for a while, you can release the parachute, which causes an "overspeed" effect. Runners say it feels as if you've been shot out of a cannon. We found a variety of these at Amazon.com and other websites, including competitiveedgeproducts.com.

High repetitions (15 to 30, or even more) won't give you bulging muscles and are best for building up endurance.

The most important message about resistance training is, You've got to get it right! This means a program of exercises that work your upper body, your lower body, and your core. And it is vital to do them correctly. If you're not already pumping iron, we strongly advise a bodybuilding class, or hire the trainer at your gym. If these options aren't available, find a friend to help you, or buy a book. Don't "just do it."

The two most common mistakes we observe in the gym are trying to lift too much weight and using your body's "momentum" to lift. These often go hand in hand. For example, if people try to perform a biceps curl with too much weight, they find they can't lift the weight without rocking their shoulders and elbows and jerking the weight up. You don't really exercise your biceps this way, and you leave yourself open to injury. Young men who think they are impressing people are most prone to this—we older folks stick to the basics.

EXERCISE GUIDELINE #7: WARM UP, COOL DOWN

Our observation is that many people fail utterly when it comes to warming up before exercise. At the pool where Dave swims, middle-aged people dive into the water and immediately start vigorous lap swimming. At the gym, someone walks in and sits at the lat pull-down machine and starts jerking a much too heavy weight, risking a serious shoulder injury. At the tennis court, an elderly couple will stroll out onto the court and, without so much as doing a single stretch, start banging the ball back and forth from the baseline. And so on.

Why? Are people in a hurry, or too lazy, or just plan ignorant? Warming up prevents injuries and makes for a better workout. It lubricates your joints, warms the connective tissues, activates your nervous system, and charges up your circulatory system. Always do some stretches before you do any exercise, and start out slowly, increasing your speed or intensity carefully.

Riding an exercise bike or running on a treadmill will get your heart pumping and cause you to sweat, but it won't warm you up for resistance training. This is because the related joints and connective tissues (your elbow or shoulder, for example) for most resistance exercises were not activated during the aerobic exercise. If you immediately try to do some biceps hammer curls with a heavy weight, you risk muscle strain that could keep you out of the gym for weeks.

Always start with a low weight or resistance that allows you to do 30 or more reps, so the specific muscles and joints that are being exercised can warm up. Then increase the weight or resistance to about 15 reps, and then increase it again to 10 or fewer. Gym instructors or personal trainers who tell you otherwise are idiots.

Before swimming, do a set of dynamic stretches (in or out of the water) that includes warming up your shoulders and stretching the muscles in your arms and legs as well as your lower back. Begin your swim with a few slow laps, and then increase the pace. If you play tennis, after stretching and jogging in place, warm up by hitting the ball inside the service box for a few minutes. Not only is this a safe way of getting your heart and lungs and your muscles and joints going, but also it's a good exercise in racket control.

Whatever your sport or exercise activity, stretch first, and start slowly. When you finish, don't just stop—cool your bod gradually.

Swim some slow laps; hit a few lobs; do some more stretches. Think of yourself as a machine that will function better when properly cared for.

EXERCISE GUIDELINE #8: DON'T FLOUT YOUR LIMITS

You can count down your age. At 60 you can have the physique, the stamina, and twice the strength you had when you were much younger. However, your joints will have lost some of their resilience, and your muscles won't be able to quickly recover from simple injuries. The hippy guru-philosopher Ram Dass is fond of saying, "Hang on tightly, let go lightly," and this is a good philosophy to apply to sports. There is a time to keep playing the game and a time to say to yourself, "I had a good run, and now I can move on to something else." If you have sore knees, stop running and take up swimming, biking, or rowing—there are plenty of low-impact choices. If you injure a rotator cuff from hitting that 90-mile-an-hour first serve, your body is telling you something. Let up on your hard serve, or take up a different sport, to avoid repetitive stress on your shoulder or elbow.

According to a survey by National Ambulatory Medical Care, sports injuries are the number two reason for visits to a doctor's office in the United States, right behind the common cold. It may be news to you that, among men, twisted or broken ankles from playing basketball are number one on the sports injury list. Take heed: if you are over 40, don't play this sport on a competitive basis—it is just too dangerous.

Dave likes to fool around on the basketball court as a way to warm up before lifting weights, but he always declines the invitations from college-age men to join in a pickup game. They see him hitting three-pointers and say, "Hey, that old man can shoot!" It's flattering, but when you're closing in on 60, it can take up to six months to fully recover from a serious ankle sprain.

EXERCISE GUIDELINE #9: ALWAYS BE STRETCHING

Stretching is vital to anyone's fitness routine. You can literally stretch all day long: a few stretches when you get up in the morning, before getting into your car, while you are sitting in a chair, while waiting for whatever, right after lunch and again before dinner, while you watch TV, before going to bed.

If you are a serious yoga practitioner, stretching can even be the main focus of exercising. However, yoga is a form of "static" stretching and is not the best way for warming up before you do aerobic exercise, resistance training, or any sport. Static stretching, in which you put your muscles into one position and hold it, forces the muscle to relax and temporarily makes it weak. This can create an imbalance between opposing muscle groups and make them prone to a strain or to a muscle tear or pull.

Dynamic stretching, on the other hand, involves constant motion; you stretch a muscle and release, and then stretch it again. A simple example is the neck rotation stretch, in which you slowly rotate your neck in a full circle as you keep your back straight. Everyone over 50 should do this stretch at least once a day. The best way is to rotate your neck completely around three times, stop and take a deep breath, and then rotate three times in the opposite direction. Repeat two or three times, or as often as you like. Think about backing out of a driveway or parking space: do you have difficulty turning your neck to see over your right or left shoulder? Many people do—and the simple neck rotation stretch will alleviate this problem.

We strongly recommend that you develop a set of basic, dynamic stretches that you routinely do before aerobic exercise or resistance training. After you exercise, you can do either dynamic or static stretches. With the dozens, if not hundreds, of possibilities, you can create something that works best for you, and all the information is readily available online or in books.

How Strong Is Your Backbone?

The main reason for stretching is to prevent muscle injuries, right? Preventing these injuries is certainly important, but reason number one for stretching has to do with your spine. At any one time, 65 million Americans suffer from back pain—usually centered in the lower back, which supports a lot of body weight. Americans with lower-back pain spend more than $50 billion a year in often futile efforts to lessen their suffering.

About 5 percent of back pain is so severe that it becomes debilitating. Either you've had or you know someone who's had a herniated disk, which occurs when too much torque is put on the spine and the disk bulges out. Sometimes the only solution is surgery. Keeping your spine flexible and healthy is mandatory if you want to live an active life. This includes your ability to move freely, to bend with flexibility, to do simple things like turn your neck to look over your shoulder, or even just to get up from a sitting position.

Hanging Upside Down

During the course of a normal day of sitting and standing, the weight of your body and the pull of gravity cause you to lose a quarter inch to a half inch in height. You regain this height when you are sleeping. One way to decrease pressure on intervertebral disks and increase the length of your spinal cord is through inversion—or hanging upside down. Dave has an inversion table, which he uses every day for about five minutes. Compared with when he began, he is one inch taller, his spine is more flexible, and he is free of any type of back pain. The use of these machines is controversial, but we think they are great. To learn more: teeterhangups.com.

Finally, stretching improves your balance and minimizes your odds of falling. About 12,000 mostly elderly Americans die annually as a result of falls, and more than 400,000 are hospitalized (250,000 with hip fractures). Falling is one of the chief hazards of growing older, and for the most part, it is preventable.

You don't have to start yoga classes to follow our fitness plan; however, yoga is fantastic and is highly recommended. Approximately 50 million people worldwide regularly practice one form of yoga or another, for both physical and spiritual reasons. Yet, despite this fact and yoga's long history, there's very little research to prove that it provides real benefit.

A small study sponsored by the American Council on Exercise at the University of Wisconsin found that after eight weeks, yoga improves flexibility, muscular strength, and balance. Yoga does little to improve aerobic fitness and doesn't burn many calories: a 50-minute session of hatha yoga burns approximately 140 calories, equivalent to a measly half cup of Whole Fruit brand lemon sorbet.

We want to emphasize this last point because the majority of people who practice yoga do not engage in other forms of exercise. For them, yoga is more than a stretching exercise: it is an all-

Are Yoga Classes Really Necessary?

Do you have to go to a yoga studio or take the yoga class at your local YMCA to do yoga? Hell no. Dave started practicing yoga in 1968 when he was a student at the University of Nebraska. Inspired by his grandmother, who did yoga, he picked up a copy of the classic book *The Autobiography of a Yogi*, by Paramahansa Yogananda, and learned how to do basic poses with his college roommates. Today the marketplace offers a wealth of yoga books and videos, as well as many online sources of step-by-step instructions (including http://santosha .com). If you can't teach yourself, another strategy is to take a few classes until you have the basics and then do it on your own. All it requires is a quiet room and a yoga mat.

consuming lifestyle choice. To improve aerobic fitness, which is the only way to strengthen your heart and your circulatory system, you need to be working in the aerobic training zone.

Researchers at the Fred Hutchinson Cancer Research Center examined the physical activity of 15,500 healthy, middle-aged men and women and found that people of normal weight who practiced yoga gained about 3 fewer pounds during a 10-year period than people who didn't practice yoga. A surprise was that overweight men and women who practiced yoga 30 minutes a week or more lost about 5 pounds over 10 years, while those who didn't gained about 14 pounds. Surprise because the calories burned by practicing yoga aren't enough to explain what is going on. The researchers think the reason has to do with state of mind. People who practice yoga, they suspect, feel better about themselves, and one consequence of this is that they don't overeat.

Another real benefit of yoga is that it strengthens the lower back muscles. Researchers at the University of Washington compared three remedies for people with chronic back pain: a yoga program, a self-care book, and an exercise regimen designed by a physical therapist. At 26 weeks, the yoga participants were less likely to take pain medication and reported less pain and more mobility. The yoga group also reported less pain than those who stuck to a more standard exercise routine.

If you have back pain, however, don't just sign up for the nearest yoga class. It could be too strenuous and end up causing you more pain. Look for a "therapeutic" yoga class that has been designed for dealing with this problem.

Please Buy Your Own Yoga Mat

If you take yoga classes, buy your own mat. Dermatologists and podiatrists are seeing more and more infections attributable to sharing dirty yoga mats, including jock itch, plantar warts, athlete's foot, and staph infections.

Best Kind of Yoga

For beginners, the best kind of yoga is hatha yoga, which involves basic stretching exercises that don't require much strength or balance. It is slow-paced and gentle, and you won't embarrass yourself by falling.

Vinyasa yoga, which is a bit more challenging than hatha yoga, has the advantage of focusing on "breath-synchronized" movements through a series of poses called sun salutations. Great for mental as well as physical balance, it is a calming form of yoga in which you work up to more intense stretching toward the end of a session.

Once you're comfortable with basic yoga poses and you want something more challenging, you should consider Bikram yoga (a.k.a. "hot yoga"), Ashtanga yoga (a.k.a. "power yoga"), or Kundalini yoga. These are all more demanding and will burn at least twice the calories of hatha yoga.

EXERCISE GUIDELINE #10: CREATE YOUR OWN ROUTINE

Dave has developed a unique stretching routine that he does before, *during*, and after swimming. It not only incorporates stretches with swimming but also adds some weight-bearing exercises, some eye exercises, and even a bit of meditation. You can follow Dave's routine or, even better, use these ideas as a "jumping-off" point for your own, special routine. This is a way to get aerobic, weight-bearing, and stretching work into one exercise period.

Dave's Swimming Routine

Before diving into the pool, Dave stands on the edge and does the following stretches:

■ **Neck rotation stretch.** Drop your chin straight down and slowly rotate your head 360 degrees in one direction (doesn't matter which), and then repeat in the opposite direction. Dave does this four or five times.

■ **Windmill stretch.** Spread your legs so that your feet are positioned just outside your shoulders. Hold your arms out straight. Bend down in a twisting motion so that your right hand touches your left foot. Straighten up and repeat in the opposite direction. Repeat up to 10 times.

■ **Simple shoulder stretch.** With your elbow bent, hold your left arm shoulder-high. Grip the elbow with your right hand and gently pull it across your chest toward your opposite shoulder. Release and pull three or four times. Reverse, with your left hand pulling on your right elbow.

■ **Lower torso twist.** Stand up straight and stare straight ahead. Slowly twist your upper body to the left as far as you can without moving your spine or turning your neck. Repeat in the opposite direction. Repeat four or five times.

■ **Swinging elephant trunk.** Keeping your legs straight, bend over and let your arms dangle straight down. Stay loose; swing your arms back and forth several times. Good for the shoulders, lower back, hips, groin, and hamstrings!

Dave then dives into the pool, turns around, and walks back to the edge. He does some more stretching:

■ **Deep knee bends.** With your back next to the wall of the pool, lower your body as far as possible by bending your knees. Raise your body and repeat. Dave does this exercise until the usual stiffness he feels in his knees goes away—about 20 repetitions. This is an excellent stretch for the quadriceps.

■ **Ankle rotation.** Squat with your back to the pool wall, and stick your right leg out. Using the slight resistance and buoyancy of the water, rotate your ankle clockwise and counterclockwise through a complete range of motion. Repeat several times with each ankle.

▪ **Toe stretch.** Stretch and flex your toes. It feels good.

▪ **Finger stretch.** Same as toe stretch.

▪ **Calf and Achilles tendon stretch.** Grab onto the edge of the pool, lean forward, and put all your weight on your left calf. Bounce up and down. Using your toes, raise and lower your foot. Repeat with the right calf. Also try doing this with your weight on both calves.

At this point, Dave takes a series of slow, deep breaths to oxygenate his body, and then he swims the entire length of the pool underwater. (If you can't stay under that long, it's OK to come up for a breath or two; the idea is to build up your lung capacity.) Once he reaches the far end, Dave does a few more stretches:

▪ **Lower back, hamstrings pull.** Gripping the edge of the pool with both hands, place your feet on the pool wall and push until your legs straighten out. Release, and repeat three or four times. You'll feel your lower back opening up, and you'll notice that this is also a good stretch for the back of your legs (hamstrings).

▪ **Splits.** With your hands still gripping the edge of the pool, gradually "walk" your feet out as far to your sides as possible. Walk them back in and then out again three or four times. This is a super stretch for the groin area.

▪ **Quadriceps stretch.** While floating on your back, bend your right knee. Reach up with your right hand and grasp your right ankle. Pull your leg back as far as possible without hurting yourself. Repeat with the other leg, and try to do this exercise, if you can, with both legs at the same time.

Time for Swimming

Dave is now ready for his aerobic workout. For the next 20 to 30 minutes, he swims laps using mostly the crawl stroke, though he varies this with a few backstroke and breaststroke laps. He swims briskly and gets his heart rate up to 80 percent of its maximum range. On a good day, he will swim one mile, which is 35 laps (back and forth) in the club pool. He swam 59 laps on his 59th birthday and is looking forward to swimming 60 laps, all the way up to 104!

Diving Board Exercises

Dave takes advantage of the one-meter high diving board at the Berkeley City Club, where he swims, using it as an exercise prop and platform for some yoga poses (static stretching). While treading water beneath the diving board, he pushes himself up so that he can grab the board with both hands. Then he does one or two sets of **chin-up exercises**. Again, the buoyancy of the water is an important factor, as it helps hold the body up. In the water, he can do 25 chin-ups.

Getting out of the pool, Dave uses the handrails on the ladder to do a set of **triceps dips**. Gripping the handrails, he bends his knees so that all his weight is supported by his hands, arms, and shoulders. He then lowers and raises his body four or five times, pumping up his triceps and also utilizing his pectoral muscles (chest) and deltoids (shoulder). Climbing up onto the diving board, Dave is ready for some static, yoga-type exercises:

■ **Forward bend pose.** Sit with your legs together and extended straight out. Slowly bend forward at the waist and grasp your feet (or your ankles, or shins, if you can't bend this far). Pull your head as close to your knees as possible and hold for 30 seconds or longer while breathing slowly and deeply. Repeat once or twice.

■ **Sideward bend pose.** Place your right foot against your left thigh so that your left leg is sticking straight out. Slowly bend to the side and grasp your left foot or ankle with both hands. Pull your head as close to your left knee as you can and hold for 30 seconds while breathing slowly and deeply. Repeat once or twice, and move on to your right leg.

■ **Restrained angle pose**. Sit on a diving board and bend your knees to draw your feet toward your torso. Place the soles of your feet together and, keeping your spine straight, bend forward and clasp your hands over your feet. Pull on your feet and push your knees to the surface of the diving board (or as close to the surface as you can get). Hold for 30 seconds while breathing slowly and deeply. Repeat once or twice.

■ **Cobra pose.** Lie on your stomach with your head turned to one side and your arms alongside your body. Turn your head and place your chin on the surface while swinging your arms around until you can place your hands just below your chin, with the palms down and the fingers nearly touching. Inhale slowly while pressing down on your hands and lifting your torso from the waist up off the floor, arching your spine backward and straightening out your arms. Keep your hips down, and tilt your head back. Hold this position for 30 seconds or more while breathing slowly. Repeat.

■ **Bow pose.** Start the same way as the cobra pose, but when your chin is on the surface, reach back with your arms and grasp your right ankle with your right hand and your left ankle with your left hand. Inhale slowly, and raise your legs by pulling your ankles up; simultaneously, lift your chest as much as possible. Tilt your head back and hold for as long as you can. Repeat.

Of course, there are many different yoga poses, and you can improvise an endless variation of Dave's routine. The most obvious benefit of his favorite poses is that they reinforce or restore flexibility of the spine, strengthen the lower back, and release tension and strain in the upper back and neck area. But there is more: the alternating stretching and releasing of the abdominal muscles that occurs with each pose increases blood flow and aids all sorts of digestive disorders and discomforts. Strain or fatigue in the legs is released, and the upper body is strengthened. Yahoo!

You'd think Dave would have had enough at this point, but he's not quite finished. Sitting up straight in a semi-lotus pose, he does a couple of eye exercises and then some breathing/meditation exercises.

▪ **Eye roll.** With your eyes open and without moving your head, look up as high as you can, and hold this position for three seconds. Rotate your eyes clockwise to a point midway between 12 o'clock and 3 o'clock, again looking up as far as possible. Hold. Rotate your eyes again to a 3 o'clock position. Continue until you have gone the full circle. Repeat, going counterclockwise. Perform this exercise two or three times in each direction.

▪ **Changing vision exercise.** Hold your index finger near the tip of your nose at the closest possible distance at which you can see it clearly without a blur. Raise your eyes slightly and find a point opposite the pool on which you can focus your eyes. Now focus on your fingertip, and then shift to the farther point in the distance. Repeat several times.

Eye exercises are an ideal way to relieve eyestrain while strengthening your eye muscles. People who do these exercises (and a few others) claim their vision improves as the ophthalmic nerves receive a richer blood supply. Some people have such success with eye exercises that they've been able to throw away their glasses (or so they say). Doctor V and Dave don't really believe this, but they definitely think eye exercises counterbalance the strain our eyes endure every day. This is particularly true if you spend much time before a computer screen.

After the eye routine, Dave stays in the semi-lotus position, closes his eyes, and breathes in slowly and deeply using his diaphragm muscles. Once he has stretched these muscles to the max, he lifts up and expands his chest muscles to let a bit more air into his lungs. He holds his breath for a moment or two, and then he exhales in a slow and controlled fashion.

During this breathing routine, Dave relaxes the muscles of his face and focuses his mind on his breathing until it is clear of all thoughts. On a good day, he is able to achieve a state of expanded consciousness in which, honest to God, he actually has the sensation that his body is floating weightlessly!

Dave's meditation lasts for about 5 minutes. This is probably not long enough to achieve all the benefits of meditation—20 minutes would be better—but it is still pretty darn fantastic.

Dave's swimming routine may seem like completely ridiculous overkill, but it isn't. From the time he checks in at the front desk of the swimming club until he leaves, about one hour and 20 minutes has transpired, so the actual swimming routine takes about an hour. He's succeeded in getting in a good aerobic workout, some resistance training, a lot of dynamic and static stretching, some eye and breathing exercises, and a bit of meditation.

He feels great. *Plus*, he's burned off 500 calories!

EXERCISE GUIDELINE #11: SWEAT OUT THE TOXINS

As a young man, Dave taught school on an Indian reservation in South Dakota, and one of his students, an Oglala Sioux named Vernell White Thunder, was and is today a follower of the "traditional ways," which includes frequent visits to the sweat lodge. ("Sweat bathing," as it is sometime referred to, is common among Native Americans.)

Dave's introduction to intensive sweating came from his participation in a purification ritual that always began with Vernell beating on a deer-hide drum while singing a prayer song in Lakota. The hissing steam, which can get extremely hot, is created by splashing water on red-hot rocks placed in a dirt hole in the middle of the lodge—a tentlike structure, the entrance of which always faces east (dawn of wisdom and source of life and power). The rocks are preheated in a bonfire.

The Sioux see the interior of the sweat lodge as representing the womb of Mother Earth, its darkness as human ignorance, the hot stones as the coming of life, and the steam as the creative force of the universe being activated. The health benefits were readily apparent to Dave, just as they were to the first European settlers. As early as 1643, Roger Williams, of Rhode Island, wrote, "Indians use sweating for two ends: first to cleanse their skin; secondly to purge their bodies, which doubtless is a great means of preserving them, especially from the French disease (probably influenza) which by sweating and some potions, they perfectly and speedily cure."

It seems ridiculous today to think sweating can cure influenza or even shorten the length of a cold, but it can help your body get rid of toxins, aid in weight loss, and, arguably, kill some viruses. And while you might think ridding the body of toxins is relevant only in our polluted, modern world, it was probably beneficial to Romans as well. Their elaborate baths may have counteracted the lead poisoning that affluent Romans contacted from leaded drinking vessels.

The Finns pioneered the use of dry heat more than 1,000 years ago, and today there are 700,000 saunas in Finland (one for every seven people). Both saunas and steam rooms are used to relax and unwind. Dry saunas will rid the body of more toxic metals, including any accumulation of lead, mercury, and nickel. The sauna is also more beneficial than steam for weight loss, because it uses up more calories by making the heart work harder to send blood to the capillaries under the skin. Studies show that a person can burn up to 300 calories during a sauna session, the equivalent of a two- to three-mile jog.

The German physical education professor Dr. Ernst Jokl wondered why none of the hundreds of marathon runners he had studied ever had any evidence of cancer. He found that their sweat contained a substantial amount of the toxins cadmium, lead, and nickel and thus concluded that athletes excrete potential cancer-causing elements by profusely perspiring.

We seriously doubt you can prevent cancer by regularly going to the sauna or practicing Bikram yoga, but it will improve blood circulation, reduce toxins, cleanse and rejuvenate skin, and help with weight reduction. However, you should approach this concept with caution. If you have high blood pressure or any cardiovascular problems, heat can make you dizzy and could even induce a heart attack or stroke. The very second you feel dizzy while sitting in a sauna, steam room, sweat lodge, or yoga class, you should get out quickly—and don't go back. Your body is telling you something: it's saying, "This is not for you, my friend."

One more caution: During just 20 minutes of intensive sweating, you can lose a quart or more of water. We advise anyone using this form of therapy or exercise to hydrate before and after—drink tons of water!

EXERCISE GUIDELINE #12: MAKE *NO* EXCUSES

If you think you're too busy to work out every day, think again. There are no more excuses: if Condoleezza Rice can find the time to work out, then you can too.

Dr. Rice is beyond doubt one of the busiest people on our planet, yet she manages to seriously work out on a daily basis, even when she's in the air or on the road (approximately 150,000 miles per month). How does she do this? The secrets to her successful exercise program were revealed recently by Barbara Harrison, one of the news anchors for WRC-NBC4, in Washington, D.C., who met the secretary of state at 5:30 A.M. at the State Department gym. There she filmed her workout, which you can still view at the WRC website (nbc4.com). We watched these reports in awe. To see this world-famous figure squat with some seriously heavy weights makes for riveting TV. The sit-ups she did while holding a large weight on her chest were mind-boggling.

We were doubly impressed to hear that the incredibly busy Dr. Rice does a daily cardio workout that usually consists of 40 minutes on an elliptical treadmill, pumps iron three days a week, and adds stretching and abdominal exercises. Her choice of an elliptical treadmill, by the way, is wise because the lower degree of impact is much easier on the knees, feet, and ankles. When an elliptical machine isn't available, the secretary favors walking over running. The trick, she says, is to "walk as fast as you can."

While on airplanes, she walks around as much as possible and does a lot of stretching. When she arrives at her destination, she resumes her workout routine. "I get up the next morning and work out before going off to meetings," she reports. It is probably a good thing for the country that our secretary of state is such a fitness buff, given that she acknowledged, "I think better when I exercise." No matter what your political persuasion, you must agree with Condoleezza Rice when she says, "Everyone should try to have the discipline to take care of themselves for a healthier life."

Fun, Fun, Fun on the Treadmill Today

The example of Condoleezza Rice provides us with some pretty powerful proof that everyone has time for exercise. If the busiest woman on the planet can work out most every day, so can you. The number two excuse we hear all the time is, "It's just too boring." We agree that exercise can be boring, especially if you do the same dull, unimaginative routine day in and day out, but there are at least 10 million ways to get around this and make exercise fun (OK, only 5 million). Let's start with the boredom of riding an indoor exercise bike or jogging on a treadmill. An alternative is to go to a gym with high-end equipment; the aerobic machines are likely to be outfitted with individualized TV screens so you can watch Oprah or CNN—or you can take your iPod or simply read a magazine. This is one reason we prefer gyms to working out at home. A good gym will have the latest, greatest, most fun equipment, and the employees are the ones responsible for maintaining this stuff, not you.

At one high-end gym, Dave tried out a virtual-reality-enhanced exercise bike called the Spark, which re-creates the experience of rid-

ing outdoors through various splendid settings, including a spectac-
ular ocean coastline. Not only does the scenic terrain unfold before
you on a computer screen, but also the sensation you get while riding is uncannily close to the real thing. The resistance of the pedals
smoothly corresponds to the terrain, navigating curves is similar to
what you would experience in the real world, and there is a shifter for
changing gears. For more information, visit expressofitness.com.

In the future, we envision "virtually reality" gyms where you
can race in Le Tour de France, run in the Boston Marathon, swim
the English Channel, play a round of golf at Saint Andrews, take a
turn at bat against Juan Marichal, hit a few balls with Venus Williams, and maybe even go a round or two with Muhammad Ali.

EXERCISE GUIDELINE #13: DANCE YOUR WAY TO HEALTH

Don't want to go to a gym, and you don't like walking, jogging,
or tennis, *and* you can't swim? Thousands of people who feel this
same way but want to maintain a healthy weight and stay in shape
have found a fun, social way of getting their main exercise: they
go dancing.

Traditionally, dance studios have catered to professional or serious amateur dancers who want to maintain their good form, but
in recent years, a new wave of customers has the dance business
booming across the United States and in many other countries.
These customers, mostly beginners, want to dance because they
have discovered that it is a great way to stay fit.

Through dancing, you exercise all the major muscle groups.
Provided you dance vigorously, it is also aerobic, burning off about
as many calories as riding a bicycle. Although not as low-impact
as swimming, dancing is still much easier on your knees and other
joints than jogging. We think the reason so many people lose weight
and improve their aerobic capacity by dancing is that, because it's
just so much fun, they tend to do it longer. A typical dance class is
one hour and is usually followed by a half hour of open dancing.

Of course, dance parties last much longer. Who knows, you might even find yourself dancing all night long.

If salsa, swing, or hip-hop doesn't provide you enough of a workout, you can go direct to aerobic dancing—Jazzercise. We particularly like Jazzercise because it is not just jazz dancing. Pioneered by Judy Sheppard in Chicago in 1969 as a blend of jazz, dancing, and exercise, it has evolved into a high-intensity mix of jazz, salsa, tango, hip-hop, and kickboxing—along with low-impact Pilates, ballet, and yoga. Hand weights and exercise bands, for strength work, are part of the mix.

According to *Consumer Reports*, a 200-pound person will burn 273 calories during 30 minutes of Jazzercise. The magazine picked it as the most beneficial among 15 forms of exercise—including walking, running, golf, and step aerobics—because it was the only one to provide benefits in all of the following categories: cardiovascular, resistant, weight-bearing, upper body, and lower body.

EXERCISE GUIDELINE #14: BE AN ATHLETE, SORT OF

Dave is not really an athlete, but he approaches exercise as if he were, and just like a little kid, he fantasizes about hitting the winning basket at the end of the big game. About once a week, he goes to the UC Berkeley Recreation Center to lift weights, but to warm up, he practices his three-point shot on one of the indoor courts.

One of Dave's all-time favorite NBA players is Latrelle Sprewell, who once hit nine for nine 3-point shots in a game against the L.A. Clippers. Dave's goal is to break this record! Granted, Latrelle did it during an actual NBA game with Corey Maggette waving his arms in Latrelle's face, and Dave is just puttering around in a gym shooting hoops by himself. Still, setting goals like this and trying to achieve them is one way to motivate yourself. By the way, Dave is up to five-for-five.

If you're like us, boredom can be a problem. Some people can do the same routine day after day, but we can't. In addition to swimming and basketball, Dave lifts weights, rides a bicycle, uses an elliptical training machine, plays tennis, and recently discovered ocean rowing. Dr. V frequently changes his weight-lifting routine and shifts from free weights to resistance machines to resistance cables.

You can create little exercise incentives as Dave does with his attempt to hit consecutive 3-pointers, or you can create great incentives around major events. Impress your friends and yourself by signing up for a long charity walk, bike ride, or run. Just make sure it is far enough in the future that you have achieved a level of fitness that will allow you to complete the event without hurting or embarrassing yourself. Dave swam from Alcatraz island in San Francisco Bay to the beach at the San Francisco Dolphin Club. This is an annual race, and while he didn't win, the fact that he did it floored everyone who knows him.

EXERCISE GUIDELINE #15: WHIP YOUR BRAIN INTO SHAPE

If you exercise your body on a regular basis, you will reduce your risk of getting dementia and Alzheimer's. A five-year examination of 4,600 men and women aged 65 and older found that regular exercise reduced the possibility of getting Alzheimer's by more than 30 percent. Another massive study found that, among more than 18,000 older women, those who were the most physically active had a 20 percent lower risk of cognitive impairment. In other research, magnetic resonance imaging scans showed that the brains of older people who exercise produce patterns of brain activity normally seen in 20-year-olds.

However, reducing your odds of getting dementia by a mere 30 percent isn't good enough for us. We want you to improve your odds even more—we want you to exercise your brain as well as your body. Unlike an old dog, your brain, no matter how old it is, can learn new tricks. A few decades ago, scientists believed that our brains were hardwired early in life and that, as we got older, cognitive decline was normal because the brain's architecture deteriorates. The conventional belief was that we could do nothing to resurrect the brain and our cognitive skills. We now know better. The brain is not hardwired; it has a quality called plasticity—like plastic, it can endlessly remodel itself.

Mental deterioration and restoration are the opposite ends of the same process: one is negative plasticity, and the other is positive plasticity. Negative plasticity occurs when the brain changes in a way that slows or impedes cognitive performance. It accounts for the "natural" decline characterized by memory lapses, slower thinking, and communication difficulties such as words getting "stuck on the tip of the tongue." Negative plasticity can become a self-reinforcing downward spiral of degraded brain function. The speed at which we process information declines, the accuracy decreases, and our ability to retain or "record" information becomes less reliable.

Research has demonstrated beyond doubt that with appropriate training, you can actually turn on positive plasticity, reverse the effects of cognitive decline, and improve the functioning of your brain. According to Michael Merzenich, Ph.D., a renowned professor at the University of California, San Francisco, and one of the pioneers of brain plasticity, to turn on positive plasticity, you need to engage in four types of brain exercises:

1. To combat the *disuse* associated with cognitive decline, you need activities that "engage the brain with new and demanding tasks."

2. To clear up the *fuzzy input* associated with cognitive decline, exercises "must require careful attention and focus." The right stimuli can sharpen neural pathways and speed up connections.

3. To restore the production of brain hormones called neuron modulators, engage in "rewarding or surprising" exercises, because they "trigger neuron-modulator production."

4. To counteract the tendency to avoid mental activities if they become difficult, do the opposite: engage in things that "confront challenges." For example, when Dave first tried to solve the Sudoku puzzles in the newspaper, he found them very difficult, but instead of giving up on them, he purchased a Sudoku book that gave him some hints on how to solve the puzzles and also provided some easy examples to get started. After completing the puzzles in the book, he found he could master the ones in the newspaper.

Stimulating the brain isn't just about mental activities. Physical challenges that require the progressive mastery of *new* motor skills can increase brain vitality and actually cause your brain to grow new dendrites (the branches on nerve cells). Dendrites receive information from other nerve cells across connections called synapses. If you use these connections irregularly, they atrophy and reduce your ability to remember new information and retrieve old information. Research at Duke University has shown that unexpected and novel experiences involving vision, smell, emotions, coordination, and balance create new dendrites and also cause an increase in the production of neuron modulators.

What matters is that you do things you've never done before. For example, you take up archery. Intensive, repetitive, and progressively challenging, archery requires specific motor skills involving eye-hand coordination, strength, breath control, and steady nerves. Your brain will actually "rewire" itself as you become more proficient, and because archery is such a novel and rewarding activity for you, you'll get a flood of brain chemicals, to boot!

Dave joined the Open Water Rowing Club, in Sausalito, where he learned the sport (and art) of sculling. He was using muscles he didn't know he had and found he needed to develop his sense of balance to keep the scull from turning over. The hardest part, he discovered, was simply getting in and out of the damn thing. There were many surprising rewards, including the day a seal followed him across the Sausalito bay and the day he rowed into a

Cross-Train Your Brain

A wonderful way to cross-train your brain is to take up the task of helping your grandkids do their homework, or volunteer to tutor children at the local elementary or junior high school. You'll be struck by how difficult a subject such as math can be and how much class work has evolved since you were in school. To stay ahead of your student or students, you'll have to focus, think fast, and employ some mental agility. And the big plus is the emotional reward you'll get, which will stimulate your neuron modulators.

buoy, tipped over in the water, and discovered he had the strength to crawl back into his scull.

The are many types of exercising in addition to archery and sculling that you might try. If you aren't much of a dancer, taking dance lessons will help you not only control your weight and keep your cardiovascular system in top shape but also ward off dementia. The important point is this: if you have been playing golf most of your life, playing more golf isn't going to do nearly as much for your brain health as it would if you had never played before.

Aerobics for Your Brain

Lawrence Katz, a leading neurobiologist at Duke University, has created a series of activities designed to rewire your mind without requiring that you learn a whole new sport. He calls these activities "neurobics."

■ **Use your nondominant hand for routine tasks.** If you are right-handed, use your left hand to brush your teeth, comb your hair, shave, and so forth. Next time you do a crossword puzzle, use your nonwriting hand.

◼ **Close your eyes while you shower to stimulate your tactile senses.** Try this with other daily routines. You can't do it while you're driving, of course, but you can enter and get ready to start the car with your eyes closed. Using your sense of touch and your "spatial" memory, try to find the right key, unlock the door, sit down, buckle your seat belt, insert the key into the ignition, and even locate the radio dial or turn the windshield wipers on and off. These exercises employ rarely used but important brain pathways that are suppressed when you rely solely on sight.

◼ **Whether you are driving, walking, or commuting, break out of your daily routine and take a different route to your destination.** When you proceed the usual old boring way, your brain goes, "duh" and pretty much stays on autopilot. The unfamiliar route, though, is challenging, so your brain wakes up as it attempts to integrate new sights, smells, and sounds into a new brain map.

◼ **Read aloud to your significant other or to your grandchild.** Alternate the role of reader and listener. When you read aloud or listen to someone reading, as opposed to reading silently, your brain uses very different circuitry.

These are a few examples of the many neurobic exercises you can do. Katz has published a book of 83 exercises, titled *Keep Your Brain Alive*, and you can find others on the Internet. Or you can make up your own. A true neurobic exercise should involve one or more of your senses in a novel context, engage your attention, and break a routine activity in an unexpected, nontrivial way.

Build Your Memory Skills

Another way to exercise your mind and build up memory skills is to make an effort to memorize details that are important or interesting. Dave memorized his Visa credit card number, including the expiration date and the security code. Now when he wants to order something from the Internet, he doesn't have to search around for his wallet. He also memorized the words to the Bobby Dylan song "Blowin' in the Wind" and taught them to his granddaughters.

Dave also made a conscious decision to remember the names and faces of people he meets. When he meets someone, he listens carefully to the name and takes a mental snapshot of the person's face. Sometimes he finds associations that will help him recall who the person is the next time they meet. For example, a waiter at one of his favorite restaurants is named Amanda. Upon meeting her, Dave briefly focused his eyes on the details of her face and took a "virtual photo" of her. He remembered he has a young male friend who has a girlfriend named Amanda. This girlfriend is about the same age as the waitress, and they both have light brown hair. Next time Dave was in the restaurant, it was easy to recall the waiter's name, and when he said, "Hi, Amanda," she was surprised. She in turn made an effort to remember Dave's name. Because Dave now knows the names of most of the waiters, bartenders, and hosts at his favorite place, he believes he gets better service (knowing the *owner* doesn't hurt, either).

Here's a great memory exercise. Before you go to the grocery store, make a list of the items you need, but leave the list in your

---

Computer Games for Your Brain

Posit Science, of San Francisco, has a computer fitness program designed by video game programmers that focuses on the speed, accuracy, and strength with which our brains record what we hear. The theory is that, as users improve their performance, short-term memory will also improve. The software includes instances of surprise, rewards, and focuses that stimulate the brain to increase its production of key biochemicals. Dave has tested this software and thinks it really works. For more information: positscience.com.

car. You'll be amazed at your ability to recall most if not all of the items. Writing things down stimulates your ability to recall information. When you go to a movie, make an effort to remember the names of the actors, the director, the screenwriter, and as many others as you can; when you get home, jot down these names. Then see how many of them you remember the following day.

Mental decline and short-term memory loss are *not* a necessary evil. You can fight back and become sharper and even smarter than you have ever been. Send your mind back to college, virtual or otherwise!

Take Charge of Your Medical Care

Conspire with Your Doctors, Take Notes, and Accelerate the Countdown

You eat all the right foods, exercise like crazy, get adequate sleep, and take all the right supplements; everyone says you look fabulous—then you die from skin cancer. Whoops, you didn't think to get an annual exam from a dermatologist, and your melanoma had metastasized by the time it was discovered.

We want you to be realistic about today's health care system. Frankly, it will not provide all the crucial services you need to count down your age if you simply go to the doctor for an annual checkup. You need to be extremely *proactive* about your medical care so you can collaborate with your primary doctor and with the specialists and other health care professionals, including the dentist, the chiropractor if you have one, and even the massage therapist.

We want you be a "coconspirator" in the plot to extend your "health span" beyond all reasonable expectations. You shouldn't be comfortable being a patient in today's health care system with only a doctor and no collaborator. Outside of an occasional consultation with a specialist, there really isn't anyone for your doctor to collaborate with but *you*. You need to jump on board, roll up your sleeves, get your hands dirty, take your turn at the wheel, belly up to the bar, and all the rest! Our job is to show you how.

YOUR VERY OWN HEALTH JOURNAL

Information is power. To take command of your medical care, you first have to get your hands on the data. If you are like most people, your medical data aren't even in one place; the information is scattered among different health care providers. In some offices, it's nicely organized in a computer file, and in others, it's a stack of handwritten notes in a file folder. You might think that with today's advanced information technology, medical records could be linked. To see which prescriptions you are taking, your dentist should be able to access the file at your doctor's office. Instead, the receptionist will ask you to list them on a form. If you forget one or two—oh well, that's just par for the course. The health care world has the greatest technology when it comes to diagnosis and treatment of various conditions and diseases, but when it comes to medical records, prescriptions, scheduling, and communications, the industry is barely out of the horse-and-buggy days.

Until this dire situation is resolved, the only real option you have is to actively put together your own health record, which we refer to as your "personal health journal." It will be extremely useful to you when you go to a new doctor's office. When they ask you about your medical history, you can simply hand them a copy of your journal. The information will be accurate and up-to-date. And there's one more major benefit: the act of creating the journal will encourage you to be more proactive about your health. You'll learn a great deal about yourself, and you'll be better prepared to discuss the state of your health with your doctor or any other health care provider.

An important point: Provided you have your personal health journal with you or you've made it remotely accessible on an Internet database, it could save your life in an emergency situation. Dave stores his on a miniature UBC flash memory drive, a.k.a. thumb drive, that hooks right on to his key chain. The device is labeled "In Case of Emergency" and includes his journal plus scanned-in images of his most recent lab results and some of the more relevant handwritten notes from his medical files.

Many online services are set up to store individual medical records. Some provide a printable access card for your purse or wallet; in case of emergency, the medics or doctors can use the coding on the card to access your record. These sites have explicitly stated privacy and security policies, which they display at the point of registration. One of the better ones, WebMD Health Manager (https://healthmanager.webmd.com), is free for the first six months and then charges $29.95 a year. Also, there are online storage services, such as xdrive.com, where you can store any documents you want.

After testing a few personal medical record sites, we decided it is just as easy and, in many ways, more flexible and useful to create our own journal. Prepackaged systems require you to keep track of items you might not need and leave out other things that might be important. The overall amount of work and time is about the same.

To get started, create a contact list of the various doctors, clinics, dentists, therapists, and so forth, who have treated you over the past few years or so. Store this list in a notebook or on your computer. The computer is preferable because it makes it easier to update the list. Keep in mind that any type of health record is a living, breathing document that will need to be updated from time to time.

You can call your health provider's office and request your medical records; however, this approach is rarely successful. Medical personnel may not know that you have a legal right to these records and that they are obligated to provide them to you at no fee except for the actual costs of photocopying and mailing. A more productive approach, we found, is to send letters (not e-mails) directly to your doctors. Tell them you're compiling a personal health record, and ask them to send your records to you by e-mail, fax, or snail mail. If any ask you to fill out an "authorization for release of information" form, they are misguided. These forms need to be filled out only when a third party (such as another doctor) is requesting your records. However, fill it out anyway, as doing so is less stressful than trying to convince someone it isn't necessary. Then, each time you have an appointment, be sure to ask for copies of any notes or new records your health provider makes. Once the staff gets used to your asking, it will get easier.

You can put anything you want in your personal health journal, but try to keep it concise. No doctor is going to look through a huge stack of papers. If your journal is online, you can scan in any number of documents, including lab reports, doctors' notes, and even x-rays, which can reside in a file folder separate from the main document. No scanner? Skip this step, or go to Kinko's, where you cheaply rent one.

As you create your personal health journal, imagine that you pass out on the sidewalk in some strange city (*not* outside a bar, let's hope), or that you have an automobile accident and you're unconscious. Someone finds you and calls an ambulance. What would you want the medical team who attends you to know about your health history? Put this information in your health journal.

Your health journal should include the following:

- Your complete contact information.
- Birth date and Social Security number.
- Health insurance information.
- Weight, height, and blood type.
- Emergency contacts.
- A statement about any medical documents you have signed and where they are located. A copy could be on your computer or in a file folder, or simply at your lawyer's office.
- Names and contact information for all the health care specialists you deal with, as well as your lawyer if you have signed a living will, a DNR (do not resuscitate) order, a power of attorney, an organ donor form, or other relevant documents.

■ A statement about any medical allergies.

■ Existing conditions that are being treated.

■ Medications you are currently taking, including frequency and dosage.

■ Immunizations. Include name of doctor and date if you can remember; otherwise, just list them.

■ Supplements you are taking, including frequency and dosage.

■ Summary of lab testing results, DNA testing results, and vital statistics.

■ Summary of your medical history, including major illnesses and surgeries or extended hospitalizations.

■ Family history, including known hereditary conditions.

■ Current concerns, including untreated medical conditions you are worried about.

■ Notes from your last doctor visit. Jot down anything you think that might be useful to review before your next visit or that might be useful in an emergency. Also, the act of taking these notes will help you remember details about any medical problems you have.

To make it easier, we've provided an example of what a journal might look like.

Once you've completed your health journal, we recommend you send a copy of it to each of your health care providers with a note asking them to put it in your file. If nothing else, this tells them you are an involved patient who requires some extra attention. About once every six months or so, send them an update.

THE POWER OF NOTE TAKING

Your doctor and your therapists (if applicable) take notes, and you should too. Whenever you go to any health-related appointments, pack a notebook. And don't take notes just during your visit: while you're waiting in the reception area, jot down any concerns or questions you want to address. Include as much detail as possible

My Sample Personal Health Journal

[Include date of most recent update.]

Jonathan Barber
1130 Shearing Road
Berkeley, CA 94707
510-555-1646 home
510-555-7287 cell
jonathan@barber.com

SS#507-85-1782

Born 6/25/45
5 feet 8 inches
175 pounds
Blood type B

Mid-West Cheapo Health Insurance Co.
Health ID: 2403853451
Association ID: 2493857890
Rx ID: 2403853444

Emergency Contact
Jenny Barber
Wife
510-421-4641 home
510-222-6345 cell

I am an organ donor
I have a living will
Scanned copies include the folder that contains this file
Copies also with my wife and my lawyer

Dr. Denise Stanford
Primary doctor
3031 Telegraph Avenue, Suite 235

Berkeley, CA 94705
510-318-1046

Dr. Arnold S. Vandever
Cardiologist and antiaging doctor
1600 Drumm Avenue
San Francisco, CA 94301
415-517-2650 office
514-369-2040 cell

Dr. Camella S. McCain
Dermatologist
6955 Fairmont Avenue, Suite 10
El Cerrito, CA 94530
510-782-8865

My Personal Attorney
Patrick Alvarez
Attorney at law
3362 Sampson Street
San Francisco, CA 94603
415-987-4321

Medication Allergies
I have no known medication allergies

Existing Conditions
High blood pressure treated with hydroclorothiazide—25 mg daily
Metabolic syndrome treated with metformin—100 mg daily
Low testosterone levels treated with Androgel, 1%—4 pumps daily
I am not being treated for any other medical problems, and I have
    no other known medical problems

Medications
Hydroclorothiazide—25 mg daily
Metformin HCL—100 mg daily
Androgel, 1%—4 pumps daily

Immunizations

11/05—Flu shot; Dr. Stanford

7/8/96—Tetanus/diphtheria, hepatitis A, polio, typhoid, meningitis;
   Dr. Eric Weiss, San Francisco Airport

Childhood: Polio, measles, mumps

Supplements

DHEA—25 mg   EPA & DHA—600 mg, 2 caps

Ginkgo phytosome—80 mg   Multivitamin

Vitamin B complex—1,000 mg   Vitamin E

Vitamin C—1,000 mg   Selenium

Folic acid—1,600 mcg

Vital Statistics/Most Recent Lab Numbers

Last physical: 10/27/05

Blood pressure—130/87, cholesterol—220, LDL—160, HDL—60,
   ratio HDL/total 3.7:1, triglycerides—180 mg/dL, C-reactive
   protein—4 mg/dL, homocysteine—14 μmol/L

Note: My most recent lab report has been scanned into the same
   folder as this file

Personal Medical History

11/04 Basal cell carcinoma on upper right cheek removed by Dr.
   McCain

9/04 Periodontal surgery—Dr. Swan

1996 Diagnosed with sleep apnea, Stanford Sleep Laboratory; used
   CPAP machine for 2 years and then was fitted for a dental device
   by Dr. Farley in 11/99

Sleep apnea has completely abated

1986 Surgery on left wrist to repair tendon severed in accident
   during vacation in St. Lucia; doctor unknown

Current Concerns

Mild arthritis in hands and knees

I am eating much less meat and much less saturated fats in a quest
   to lower my LDL cholesterol and my homocysteine levels.

I want to reduce my drinking to 1 or 2 glasses of wine a day and days of not drinking.

I am exercising vigorously most days—swimming, weight lifting, cycling, rowing, basketball, tennis, and aerobic machines.

I would like to lower my blood pressure and get off the medications.

I continue to work on losing weight and eating less; I have lost about 40 pounds over the past 2 years.

Family Medical History

Mother died at age 82. She was alcoholic and had dementia. She died a year after hip fracture.

Father died at age 90 from old age.

Sister is diabetic and has high blood pressure.

Grandfather died of a heart attack in his 70s.

Aunt lived to 99.

Notes

4/14/06 went to see Dr. Stanford about lingering illness . . . seem to have caught a virus from my granddaughter 10 days prior and haven't been able to shake it . . . no fever, just chest congestion and lots of fatigue . . . haven't been able to work much and have been sleeping during the day . . . feeling irritable and crabby . . . Dr. Davis checked the glands in my neck and said they were fine; she checked my blood pressure—it was a bit borderline 130/75 but not bad; checked my lungs and they were clear . . . she said it was probably a virus that many people have and the symptoms can linger for as much as 6 months! Gave me a prescription for an antibiotic called "azithromycin." A few days later I was better—no signs of the illness.

without sidetracking into irrelevancies, such as your Aunt Glenda had the same little itch on her bottom, except it was psychosomatic—*your itch is real*! When seeing your doctor, be ready to discuss the following topics:

- **Cause**—If you've noticed, what triggers your symptoms?
- **Severity**—How bad is it, really? Is it absolutely horrible, moderate, or slight?
- **Previous or current treatments**—Have you tried any over-the-counter drugs, dietary changes, or other treatments? Have they made any difference in your symptoms?

Jot Down That Prescription!

Your doctor may send you off for a heart scan using a multislice computed tomography scanner, which in 20 seconds will produce about 600 clear images of your heart and its arteries and valves. After some really cool software analyzes these images, you receive a prescription for Lipitor in horribly unreadable handwriting to take to your pharmacist. This is like flying to St. Louis and then hitching a ride to town in the back of a horse-drawn wagon. Text messaging, anyone?

In the United States alone, more than a billion little slips of paper with hand-scrawled prescriptions are annually carried out of doctors' offices by patients. Another billion-plus are phoned in. The Institute for Safe Medical Practices estimates that 3 million "adverse drug events" occur each year as a result of illegible handwriting, unclear abbreviations and doses, and unclear telephone or other spoken orders. Many efforts are under way to create electronic health records and provide doctors with tools to allow them to electronically order prescriptions, but the vast majority of doctors still use the old-fashioned methods.

If your doctor is one of these old-fashioned hand scrawlers, ask for the spelling of the prescription; write it down, along with the dosage amount and frequency. Ask about side effects and any problems you might have because of the other medications or supplements you are taking; write this down too. When you pick up the prescription from your pharmacy, compare your note with the label on the bottle: if it's not an exact match, call the doctor to make sure there hasn't been a mistake. This could literally save your life.

Always remember: collaboration is the key. You are working together with your health care providers to solve specific problems and improve the overall state of your health. As you conspire with these wonderful people, you will become more knowledgeable and intelligent about your body, and more insightful about what to ask and what to be concerned about. If your doctor recommends a test, you will want to know how frequently this test returns false positives, what the alternatives are, and whether it is covered by insurance. How is the test performed? How should you prepare? How long after the test before you can return to your normal life? When will you get the results?

DO YOU HAVE THE RIGHT DOCTOR?

Can you communicate with your doctor without making an appointment? If, for example, you are considering aspirin therapy but you are taking a medication for blood pressure, can you call your doctor and talk to him or her directly? Can you e-mail your doctor and get a response? Does your doctor even have e-mail? If you can't talk to your doctor, will someone in the office relay your message and get back to you? The best doctors are those who *want to have* frequent two-way communications with their patents. They don't mind talking to you on the phone or answering some e-mail. If your concerns merit a face-to-face visit, they'll tell you to come in.

If you see your doctor for something minor like a tick bite, does your doctor ask you a few unrelated questions about your state of mind, what you're eating, whether you're exercising, your family life, and even your sex life? Is your doctor enthusiastic about some new health information you might benefit from knowing? Or does your doctor simply look at your tick bite and tell you that you needn't worry about West Nile disease; it's been nice to see you; good-bye, and don't forget to stop at the desk and pay your bill on the way out? The best doctors are holistic; they realize that treating specific ailments is not enough. They look for signs of depression, sleep deprivation, nutritional deficiencies, stress, lack of exercise, and many other factors.

What's your doctor's attitude toward supplements? If you tell your doctor you're taking CoQ10 to boost your cardiovascular health, does your doctor ask how much you are taking, or shrug and say something like, "Gee, that's nice."? Any doctor who doesn't know about CoQ10 hasn't been keeping up with the literature or

Some Really Cool Doctors

The Family Medical Specialists of Texas is a small clinic run by three outstanding board-certified family physicians in Plano, Texas, who have embraced the power of the Internet. Even if you don't happen to live in Plano, we think you might benefit by taking a peak at their website, fmstexas.com.

The two founders of the clinic, Dr. Christopher Crow and Dr. Sander Gothard, were named the "Best Doctors in Texas" by *Texas Monthly* magazine. If you decide to become a new patient, you can set up an appointment online and submit the necessary forms. If you take your laptop to the office, you can use their free Wi-fi service while you wait—you don't have to look at a bunch of old magazines that might be infected by who-knows-what.

Patients are encouraged to e-mail their doctor anytime with non-urgent medical questions and are guaranteed a reply within 24 hours; *plus*, they have online access to their electronically maintained medical records, including past and present medical conditions, medications, drug allergies, and pharmacy information. Other online services include automatic appointments, prescription renewals, referrals to specialists, and even billing questions.

These doctors believe the most important service they provide is listening to their patents. The idea, according to their website, is to create a "strong doctor-patient relationship based on mutual trust, confidence and communication."

We think all doctors should be like this.

has a not uncommon attitude that all supplements, with the possible exception of a multivitamin, are a waste of time. A knowledgeable doctor will know that your body produces less CoQ10 as you age and that the only nutritional source of any substantial quantity is organ meat. Unless you eat a lot of calves liver and lamb kidneys, you're probably deficient in CoQ10. A good doctor will want to know how much you are taking and may suggest you change your dosage. Or a good doctor might express concern that little of the CoQ10 is actually getting absorbed into your bloodstream, perhaps recommending that you switch to a liquid CoQ10 or an emulsified formulation to increase absorption.

We're not advocates of swallowing hundred of pills every day, but a careful selection of supplements can help you stay disease resistant, young, and energetic. Having a doctor who helps you select the right supplements is a big plus. Therefore, if you have one of those "fuddy-duddy" doctors who think supplements are just a way of having "expensive urine," you may need a new doctor.

What Makes for a Great Doctor?

Can you distinguish a great doctor from a mediocre or average doctor? To find out, take our test.

▪ **1. Which best describes the demeanor of a great doctor?**

Ⓐ Arrogant
Ⓑ Unapproachable
Ⓒ Congenial
Ⓓ Nosy

▪ **2. When it comes to discussing your medical concerns, what will a great doctor do?**

Ⓐ Hurry you along to the important parts
Ⓑ Try not to yawn
Ⓒ Listen attentively
Ⓓ Ask penetrating questions

■ **3. How does a great doctor respond when you ask about alternative or nontraditional therapies?**

Ⓐ Is polite but dismissive
Ⓑ Laughs
Ⓒ Seriously considers your suggestions and will either agree to try the therapy or explain why it isn't a good idea
Ⓓ Readily agrees, "Yea, baby!"

■ **4. Does a great doctor know everything?**

Ⓐ No doubt about it
Ⓑ Might not be that astute on a putting green, but untouchable when it comes to medicine
Ⓒ Knows his or her limits and is always learning
Ⓓ No, but is really good about looking things up on the Internet

■ **5. How would you characterize a great doctor when it comes to spending time with patients?**

Ⓐ Efficiently handles large patient load by not wasting time with any one person
Ⓑ Lets assistants do most of the work so he or she can zero in on the important matters
Ⓒ Wants to know you and will ask questions about your general health as well as your specific problem
Ⓓ Loves to chat

■ **6. Will a great doctor care whether you are knowledgeable about health-related issues?**

Ⓐ Patients who think they know too much can be a danger to themselves
Ⓑ When you put your health in the hands of a great doctor, you don't need to worry about what you know

Ⓒ The best doctors want smart patients and always take the time to educate them

Ⓓ The best doctors want patients who take care of themselves except for emergencies

■ **7. What happens when a great doctor prescribes medicine?**

Ⓐ It is always spot-on

Ⓑ The doctor's assistant will tell you how many pills to take

Ⓒ The doctor will fully explain the purpose of the medication, how it works, and what the potential side effects are

Ⓓ A truly great doctor will ask you if there is anything else you want so you won't have to make extra trips to the drugstore

■ **8. What kind of staff people work for a great doctor?**

Ⓐ Protective of the doctor's time

Ⓑ Cold but professional

Ⓒ Friendly, helpful

Ⓓ Will always offer you a drink or ask if you want to step outside for a smoke with them

YOUR SCORE _____

Score: If your answer is Ⓒ for at least seven questions, you know what a great doctor is. If you answered Ⓒ for only five or six questions, you know what an average doctor is. Fewer than five would describe a mediocre doctor.

HOW TO FIND THE RIGHT DOCTOR

You need a doctor who will partner with you in your quest to live a longer, healthier life—someone who cares about preventive medicine and who is open to alternative solutions, the use of the right supplements, and the value of a healthy lifestyle. Conventional wisdom says finding the right doctor is like searching for a needle in a haystack, but we disagree. Using a combination of referrals from healthy friends or knowledgeable people you trust (your pharmacist, a nurse who works in the ER, or perhaps someone who runs a health food store), a bit of online researching, and some old-fashioned "gumshoe" detective work, you can find the right doctor.

First, you need to establish criteria for the type of doctor you are seeking. Assuming you are looking for a primary doctor, you need someone who is either a general practitioner, family practitioner, internist, or doctor of osteopathic medicine (D.O.).

Whichever type of doctor you seek, we recommend that you find one who is board-certified by the AACOM or in one of the 24 areas of specialty recognized by the American Board of Medical Specialties (ABMS). You can quickly check this out for any of the doctors you are considering by calling the ABMS at (866) 275-2267 or by clicking on abms.org. If you already know that your candi-

---

What the Heck Is a D.O.?

Osteopathic medicine is holistic medicine based on the idea that the role of the physician is to facilitate the body's inherent ability to heal *itself*. D.O.s, as opposed to M.D.s, use manipulation to align the musculoskeletal system, not unlike chiropractors. D.O.s are complete physicians, licensed to prescribe medication and perform surgery throughout most of the world. To learn more about D.O.s, look up the American Association of Colleges of Osteopathic Medicine's website, aacom.org.

date is an internist, you can go directly to the American Board of Internal Medicine, abim.org.

Why board-certified? A board-certified doctor has passed some tough exams in his or her area of specialty, an indication of a high level of skill and education. Doctors don't have to be board-certified to practice, and some fine doctors simply choose not to bother. In our book, however, this is a criterion that matters and helps weed out some really bad doctors (those who *failed* the exams).

Questions to Consider When Looking for a Doctor

Does the prospective doctor:

- accept new patients?
- spend a lot of time seeing patients, or mostly either manage a large office, build up celebrity status by appearing on the "Larry King" show, or work on lowering a golf handicap?
- come from a prestigious, accredited medical school and residency program, or hold a degree from the Mail Order Academy of Medicine in Tobago?
- mostly see patients similar to you, or mostly see gangsters recovering from gunshot wounds?
- accept your insurance plan?
- have hospital privileges at the major, accredited hospitals in your area?
- have an equally qualified doctor to cover the office when vacationing in the French Riviera, or have Uncle Billy fill in?
- focus on preventive medicine, or tell people not to come in unless it's terminal?

Of course, you also want someone who is friendly and accessible, as well as at least semi-aware that there has been a personal-computer revolution and even old ladies have e-mail. Once you have the criteria in mind, start looking for candidates by asking friends and associates—and by searching online. Some of the better online resources that we know about are the following:

▪ **Integrativemedicine.arizona.edu.** On this website you'll find a referral service for medical doctors who have graduated from the University of Arizona's Program in Integrative Medicine, which is the famous holistic school of medicine founded by Dr. Andrew Weil.

▪ **Worldhealth.net (click on "Directory").** A worldwide directory of more than 6,000 doctors who are members of the American Academy of Anti-Aging Medicine. These doctors specialize in preventive medicine and in life-extending technologies, including the use of "bio-identical" hormone therapy.

▪ **Http://doctor.webmed.com.** An extensive doctor database maintained by WebMD. The information is a bit sparse, but many of the doctors listed have links to their own websites, and you can use WebMD's online appointment service if you want to see one of them.

▪ **Http://webapps.ama-assn.org/doctorfinder.** The American Medical Association's doctor finder service, which includes 690,000 doctors.

You can also check the yellow pages, or better yet, check out community online chat services to see if any of them have a doctor-ranking discussion board (you might be pleasantly surprised). Once you have some names and related contact information, the final phase of your search begins—the gumshoe detective phase.

Gumshoe Step #1

Call the doctor's office and see if you can strike up any kind of conversation with the person who answers the phone. If you're successful (a huge assumption), you can say that you are looking for a new doctor and ask questions. A good sign would be a straight-forward, friendly person who answers your questions. Bad signs would be that the person is just too busy to talk to you, or the doctor has only an answering service. Ask if you can come to the office to meet the doctor for a two-minute interview—and if the phone goes blank, the person to whom you are talking has just fallen off the chair. If the person laughs out loud but actually agrees to ask the doctor, at least he or she is listening and finds you mildly interesting. Finally, if the response is, "Yes, you can come in next Tuesday at 9:30 A.M.," you've got yourself a lively prospect.

Before making an initial appointment to see a new doctor, check the doctor out at healthgrades.com. HealthGrades is a company based in Golden, Colorado, whose sole business is to compile and provide health care ratings and profiles of doctors, hospitals, and nursing homes. A "Physician Quality Report" on the doctor you've selected will cost you $12.95, but it's well worth the price. To see for yourself, check out one of the free sample reports. The report will tell you which schools the doctor attended; where the residency and internship were completed; in what specialties the doctor is board-certified; any sanctions or governmental disciplinary actions received, including the nature of the complaint and any actions that have been taken; ranking compared with national data on several criteria; fluency in foreign languages; how hospitals in the area rank in terms of various kinds of treatment; and more. HealthGrade reports on 650,000 doctors and provides quality reports on 5,000 hospitals and 16,000 nursing homes.

If you feel up to being a real sleuthhound, call a hospital or medical center where the doctor has privileges and ask to speak to someone who knows Dr. So-and-So. See what the colleague has to say. Ask if you can talk to one or two of the doctor's patients. The more people you can interview who actually know the doctor and have directly or indirectly experienced his or her work, the more you will know. Don't get carried away, however; talking to the doctor's mother isn't going to help much ("Oh, my boy Tommy—he is such a fine doctor. He gives me these fantastic little pink pills.")

The next step is for you *and your health journal* to go on an actual site visit. Your primary purpose is to find out if this doctor is someone you can *really* trust for long-term collaboration—not quite the same thing as getting married after the first date, but almost. First notice the reception area: Does it look as if someone wants patients to be comfortable and well cared for? Is there plenty of fresh air and natural light, or is it dark, stuffy, and slightly toxic. Are the magazines new and interesting, or old and grimy? Are there some useful fliers and newsletters with health tips written by the doctor or the doctor's partners? Do you find yourself not wanting to touch anything for fear of infection? Does the receptionist act friendly and professional, or just hand you a clipboard, ask for your insurance card, and not even look you in the eyes? Doctors who care about the quality of their reception areas and the professionalism of their support personnel are more likely to care about the quality of their medical service to patients, and vice versa.

Assuming the reception experience doesn't cause you to storm away, next is the initial consultation with the doctor. How's the chemistry: Do you and the physician have compatible communication styles? Do you feel comfortable with the doctor's general demeanor? Does the doctor seem genuinely interested in hearing what you say, or do you sense that the doctor's mind is somewhere else? Is he or she up to speed on medical trends and hip to the benefits of good nutrition, exercise, the use of supplements, and alternative approaches? Is the doctor willing to listen to you if you want to know about an alternative medical solution? And, yes, ask about the fees: Can you afford this person? The final decision is really subjective, involving your intuition and good sense—but the more homework you do and the more you know about the doctor, the more likely you are to make the right decision and select the right doctor.

COUNT DOWN YOUR AGE PHYSICAL

Once this is settled, you need to start the collaboration process by going in to see your doctor for a complete "Count Down Your Age

Physical Exam." It's a sad fact that most medical checkups involve only routine diagnostic and blood tests, if any at all. Dr. V believes this situation has to do with fear of economic reprisal from health maintenance organizations, but he doesn't let any such reservation stop him from providing his patients with the absolutely best testing available. The one caveat is to not waste time and money on tests that return a high number of false positives.

Our exam, designed by Dr. V, includes the tests you need to best guarantee you won't fall prey to some unforeseen medical disaster. We urge you to discuss these tests with your doctor, who may want to make adjustments to meet your individual needs. The point you want to get across is that you are serious about getting an in-depth analysis of the current state of your health. As much as possible, you want to be in control of your medical future.

Annual blood and diagnostic testing can help aging adults prevent life-threatening disease. With results in hand, you can catch critical changes before they manifest as heart disease, diabetes, and cancer. The proper tests can empower you and your doctor to design treatments and scientifically based programs that could add decades of healthy living.

Count Down with These Blood Tests

The annual blood tests Dr. V recommends for all adults can be done with one visit to the lab. Here's a rundown:

1. **Comprehensive metabolic profile.** Tests electrolytes, liver function, kidney function, and lipids (total cholesterol, HDL cholesterol, LDL cholesterol, and trigylcerides).

2. **Comprehensive thyroid panel.** Thyroid function affects your energy level, heart rate, weight control, and more. Thyroid-stimulating hormone (TSH) helps identify an overactive or underactive thyroid state. A comprehensive evaluation should include T3 uptake, T4, T7, TSH, free T3, free T4, and reverse T3.

3. High-sensitivity C-reactive protein. C-reactive protein (CRP) is a substance made by the liver and secreted into the bloodstream, increasing when inflammation is present.

4. Homocysteine. Increased concentrations of homocysteine have been associated with an increased tendency to form inappropriate blood clots.

5. Lipoprotein subfraction test. Separates HDL and LDL into "subfractions," based on their size and density. Studies have shown that small, dense LDL particles are more likely to cause atherosclerosis, or "clogging of the arteries," than light, fluffy HDL particles. The presence of small, dense LDL could be one of the reasons that some people have heart attacks even though their total and LDL cholesterol are not high.

6. Heavy metals. Dr. V has found that an overwhelming number of his patients have toxic levels of arsenic, lead, mercury, and aluminum.

7. Coagulation profile. This includes fibrinogen, prothrombin time, and platelet count. Results of these tests are markers for inflammation and clotting. Reduced concentrations of fibrinogen may impair the body's ability to form a stable blood clot.

8. Uric acid test. Too high of a level of uric acid is an indication of gout—characterized by painful inflammation of the joints, especially the feet and hands.

9. Chromium and CoQ10 levels. Chromium supports the normal function of insulin and plays a role in decreasing blood lipids. A natural product of the human body, CoQ10 is essential for good heart health. A deficiency in either of these can easily be corrected with supplements.

10. Fasting blood glucose. This is a series of blood glucose tests. After you've fasted for 8 to 10 hours, blood for this test is collected. Then you drink a standard amount of a sweet, gooey glucose solution, wait an hour, and get another blood test. This is followed by one or more additional glucose tests performed at specific intervals to track glucose levels over time. This will reveal if you are diabetic or prediabetic.

11. Hormone status *for women*. Tests for levels of FSH, prolactin, LH, estradiol, progesterone, testosterone, DHEA sulfate, and IgF1. Estradiol is particularly important, as increased levels may indicate an increased risk for breast or endometrial cancer, whereas diminished levels correlate with low levels of bone mineral density, which is a strong risk factor for osteoporosis.

12. PSA test *for men*. While not a diagnosis of prostate cancer, elevated levels of PSA are a concern. They may also be seen with prostatitis (inflammation of the prostate) and benign prostatic hyperplasia (BPH).

13. Testosterone test *for men*. In addition to experiencing a decrease in sexual desire and erectile function, men with a lowered testosterone level may notice changes in mood and emotions, a decrease in body mass and strength due to loss of muscle tissue, and an increase in body fat. The "grumpy old man" phenomenon (andropause) is the result of decreased testosterone.

14. DHEA sulfate test. DHEA is frequently referred to as an "antiaging" hormone, as low levels have been associated with erectile dysfunction in men and loss of libido in women. Healthy levels of DHEA have antidepressant effects and help boost immune function, bone density, libido, and healthy body composition.

For problems with fatigue, Dr. V recommends a "fatigue profile," which checks for Epstein-Barr, herpes, mycoplasma (an antibiotic-resistant microorganism similar to bacteria), chlamydia, Lyme, and candida. For gastrointestinal problems, he always performs a candida immune panel and checks for food allergies. If you have sore joints, he recommends an arthritis profile.

There are many other sophisticated blood studies that are usually not done on a regular basis unless indicated by your specific medical condition. Want to know more?—the website labtestson line.org is a nonprofit service with detailed, easy-to-comprehend information about every blood test known to civilization (almost).

Blood Numbers *You* Should Know

It is not necessary for you to fully understand the results of your blood tests; however, there are a few vital numbers we think you need to be aware of, which we suggest you keep track of in your personal health journal. These include the following:

■ **Cholesterol.** The unit of measure for cholesterol is milligrams per deciliter (mg/dL). A milligram is $\frac{1}{1,000}$ of a gram, and a deciliter is $\frac{1}{10}$ of a liter. A total cholesterol count under 200 mg/dL is desirable and supposedly reflects low risk of heart disease; 200 to 240 mg/dL is considered a moderate risk; and anything over 240 mg/dL is considered high risk. Getting your total cholesterol below 200 mg/dL should be one of your highest priorities.

■ **LDL (low-density lipoprotein).** This is the bad cholesterol. If you have heart disease or diabetes, a reading of less than 100 mg/dL is highly desirable. Otherwise, an LDL of 130 mg/dL or less is optimal for most people. "Normal" would be 130 mg/dL to 160 mg/dL, while anything over 160 mg/dL is alarming.

■ **HDL (high-density lipoprotein).** The good stuff. An optimal level of HDL is 60 mg/dL or greater, while 40 mg/dL to 60 mg/dL is associated with an average risk of heart disease. Less than 40 mg/dL and you are dead meat.

■ **Total cholesterol/HDL ratio.** Some laboratories report this number, but it is easy to calculate: just divide your total cholesterol number by your HDL number. A ratio of 4 or less (4:1) is nirvana. Over 5 (5:1) is not good.

■ **Triglycerides—a.k.a. "fat."** A normal level for fasting triglycerides is less than 150 micrograms per deciliter (mcg/dL). You consume no food for 12 to 14 hours before the test. When triglycerides are higher than 1,000 mcg/dL, there is a risk of developing pancreatitis. Treatment to lower triglycerides should be started immediately.

■ **C-reactive protein.** CRP is a sensitive marker of systemic inflammation (meaning it affects your entire body) that has emerged as a powerful predictor of coronary heart disease and other diseases of the cardiovascular system. It is linked with the onset of type 2 diabetes, age-related macular degeneration, loss of cognitive skills, and rheumatoid arthritis. A CRP reading of less than 3 mg/dL is considered optimal, and over 5 mg/dL is "elevated."

■ **Homocysteine.** The optimal level of homocysteine for both men and women is less than 7.2 μmol/L. A number over 16 μmol/L for men and 14 μmol/L for women is considered elevated.

What the Flying Burrito Is a "μmol/L"?

If you haven't already guessed, μmol/L stands for "micromoles per liter." A micromole is one-millionth of a mole. A mole is the amount of substance that contains 600 sextillion molecules (600,000,000,000, 000,000,000,000.) Six hundred sextillion molecules sounds like a lot, but it really isn't. A micromole is therefore one of the smallest units of measurements there is. It is tiny, tiny, tiny.

Diagnostic Testing Too

Sorry, blood tests are not enough. The Count Down Physical Exam also includes diagnostic testing. Fortunately, you don't need to take all these tests annually. Unless your personal medical situation dictates otherwise, the first test is a once-in-every-10-years royal pain, beginning at age 50. Everyone hates it, and yet it is absolutely crucial.

1. Colonoscopy. Worldwide, colon cancer kills more than one-half million people annually—56,000 in the United States. When detected early, it is highly treatable. Even if it has metastasized, it can be effectively treated with an innovative, targeted drug from the biotechnology company Genentech called Avastin. Used in combination with chemotherapy, Avastin shrinks tumors by preventing the growth of new blood vessels and helps people live longer. (For more info: avastin.com.)

Everyone 50 or older should get a colonoscopy. Assuming the gastroenterologist or "endoscopist" gives you a clean bill of health, you won't need another one for 10 years. By then, "virtual colonoscopies," which are currently not as accurate as the real deal, will be significantly improved. With any luck, next time, you can go virtual. Meanwhile, three new developments have made colonoscopies more endurable. We suggest you *tell* your doctor you want to be referred to a gastroenterologist who uses these:

▪ **Visicol tablets.** Anyone who has had a colonoscopy will tell you the absolute worst part is the horrible-tasting bowel-cleansing agents you must drink the day before. The Mayo Clinic says that an unwillingness to take a bowel preparation is "the single largest barrier to colorectal cancer screening." But now you can simply take a pill. OK, you have to take 32 of them (over time), but it still beats drinking the standard "gallon jug" preparation. Manufactured by Salix Pharmaceuticals, Visicol is still not universally used, so make sure you get it.

■ **Entonox.** An inhaled sedation, Entonox is a 50/50 percent mixture of nitrous oxide and oxygen administered through a mask. It's much better than the conventional intravenous sedation. Patients who use it report less pain and are discharged more quickly when the colonoscopy is finished. Another advantage: you can drive yourself home.

■ **NeoGuide.** First introduced in Germany in 2006, NeoGuide is a computer-guided colonoscopy system that requires half the force of a conventional system. More flexible because the tubing has articulated hinges, it won't "bunch up" as it is inserted into your colon and is therefore less uncomfortable.

If you still can't make yourself go for a colonoscopy, at least do the next-best thing: get a virtual colonoscopy. Newer and less invasive, it does not require the scope used in traditional colonoscopy. Instead, it uses computed tomography (CT) scans to create computer-generated images of the colon. However, a tube does have to be inserted into the rectum to fill the colon with air, and studies have shown virtual colonoscopy to not be as thorough as traditional colonoscopy in finding polyps, which are usually nonmalignant tissue growths, though they can also be cancerous. Polyps are not removed during this procedure.

2. Fecal Immunochemical Test (FIT). Not to be confused with the fecal occult blood test (FOBT), the FIT is a newer kind of test that detects occult (hidden) blood in the stool and produces fewer false positives. Vitamins or foods do not affect it, and some forms require only two stool specimens (as opposed to three for FOBT), so people may find it easier to use. You can do this test at home with the CARE Home Colon Cancer Test, available from Home Health Testing (homehealthtesting.com) for $24.95—and actually get the results within 10 minutes. This test should be taken once a year. Be sure to share the results with your "coconspiring" doctor.

3. Cardiac Imaging (Heart Scan). The number one cause of death in most industrialized countries, heart disease can be reversed if it's detected in time. One reason it isn't detected enough is that the technologies for detecting it are inaccurate. Stress tests, MRI (magnetic resonance imaging) tests, and traditional CAT (computerized axial tomography) scans miss most early symptoms and often return false positives. A cardiac CT scan can provide an image of the heart and its arteries so detailed that the presence of plaque, narrowing (or stenosis) of the arteries, calcium scoring, and abnormal heart vessels can be determined with the detail and accuracy previously available only through invasive procedures such as angiography. The cost is about $500 and may not be covered by insurance—but it is an incredible technology that could very well save your life. Hey, Oprah had a heart scan, and you should too. To see a video clip of Oprah's heart scan: heartscanofchicago.com.

4. Carotid Artery Screening. The carotid arteries are the main blood supply to the brain, and plaque buildup in these arteries is the leading cause of stroke. A simple test using ultrasound technology will provide images of the carotid arteries on both sides of your neck and measure the velocity of the blood flow through these vessels.

5. Stress Echocardiogram (Stress ECHO). This is a noninvasive test that combines two tests: a treadmill stress test (TST) and an echo-

---

How to Save 90,000 Lives per Year

Proposed carotid artery exams of most American men over 45 and most women over 55 could prevent 90,000 deaths from heart attack a year, according to a report in the *American Journal of Cardiology*. The expert task force recommending this universal screening estimates that they would also save $21.5 billion a year in medical costs by identifying people at risk much earlier.

cardiogram (ECHO). An echocardiogram, which uses sound waves (ultrasound) to provide an image of the heart's internal structures, size, and movement, is done while you are at rest and then again at peak heart rate. This test will help your doctor evaluate your cardiac condition related to irregular heart rhythms, decrease of blood and oxygen supply, overall cardiovascular conditioning, how hard your heart has to work before any symptoms develop, and how quickly your heart recovers after exercise.

6. Annual Digital Tomosynthesis (for Women). Digital tomosynthesis creates a three-dimensional picture of the breast using x-rays and is radically better than standard mammograms, which are two-dimensional. When a mammogram is taken, the breast is pulled away from the body, compressed, and held between two glass plates, which creates a problem because cancer can be hidden in the over-lapping tissue. Mammograms miss up to 17 percent of tumors in women who have breast cancer.

Digital tomosynthesis takes multiple x-ray pictures of each breast from many angles. The information is sent to a computer, where it is assembled to produce clear, highly focused three-dimensional images throughout the breast. Cancer lesions are easier to see among dense fibro-glandular breast tissue, and this test can catch minute tumors that could never be seen on a mammogram. We recommend this for women 45 and older once a year—discuss with your doctor.

7. Bone Density—a.k.a. Bone Mass Measurement Test. Safe, totally painless, and noninvasive, a bone mass measurement (BMM) is the only way to know if you have serious bone loss or osteoporosis. There are several types of BMM tests, some measure your hips and spine, and others measure your wrist and/or your heel. Your doctor will know which one is right for you. The National Osteoporosis Foundation (nof.org) recommends all women aged 65 or older get this test regardless of risk factors. We agree. Moreover, anyone, regardless of age, who has two or more of the risk factors itemized here should consider this test:

■ **Age.** The older you are, the greater your risk of osteoporosis.

■ **Gender.** Your chances of developing osteoporosis are greater if you are a woman.

■ **Family history.** Susceptibility to fracture may be, in part, hereditary.

■ **Race.** Caucasian and Asian women are more likely to develop osteoporosis.

■ **Bone structure and body weight.** Small-boned and thin women (under 127 pounds) are at greater risk.

■ **Menopause/menstrual history.** Normal or early menopause increases the risk of osteoporosis. In addition, women who stop menstruating before menopause because of conditions such as anorexia or bulimia, or because of excessive physical exercise, may also lose bone tissue and develop osteoporosis.

■ **Lifestyle.** Cigarette smoking; drinking too much alcohol; consuming an inadequate amount of *dietary* calcium, magnesium, and potassium; or getting little or no weight-bearing exercise increases your chances of developing osteoporosis.

■ **Medications.** A significant and often overlooked risk factor in the development of osteoporosis is the use of certain medications to treat chronic medical conditions such as rheumatoid arthritis, endocrine disorders (i.e., an underactive thyroid), seizure disorders, and gastrointestinal diseases.

8. Annual Gynecological Exam (for Women). It is vital for women to have a great gynecologist. If you don't already have one, ask your primary doctor for a referral, and check with friends you trust. Gynecological (or "GYN") exams are exactly the same for each patient; typically, they include a medical history, brief physical exam, breast exam, pelvic exam, STI (sexually transmitted disease) tests, and other lab tests and counseling. For most women, the pelvic exam is at worst mildly uncomfortable and a bit awkward. You can tell your doctor what you're feeling during the exam so he or she can slow down or make adjustments to keep you as comfortable as possible. A good gynecologist will take the time to describe exactly what is going on, and you have an absolute right to stop the procedure if you want. A GYN exam can detect many medical problems, including breast abnormalities, pelvic infections, and cervical cancer.

For some women, their gynecologist is their primary doctor, and this is fine with us. Just don't forget to take notes to add to your personal health journal each time you go in for a visit.

9. Annual Skin Exam. Everyone over 40 should have an annual skin exam by a qualified dermatologist, who will examine the skin over your whole body, looking for suspicious growths, moles, or lesions. The exam is performed using a bright light and occasionally a magnifying lens. The scalp is examined by parting the hair, and the dermatologist will even look between your toes. By taking notes and sometimes photographs, the doctor will create a "map" of your skin so that when you return the following year, any changes in a wart or mole can be detected.

In the United States, about 800,000 new cases of basal cell carcinoma and 200,000 new cases of squamous cell carcinoma are

---

New Sunscreen Provides More Protection

The U.S. Food and Drug Administration (FDA) has finally approved sunscreen containing mexoryl, an agent that shields skin from shortwave UVA rays—something sunscreens available in the United States have been unable to do. Besides skin cancer, UVA causes skin aging. Sunscreens containing mexoryl have been available in Europe, Asia, and Canada since 1993. Anthelios SX, made by L'Oreal, is the first sunscreen with mexoryl marketed in the United States.

diagnosed annually. *Basal cell* is the most common type of skin cancer. It grows slowly and rarely spreads, but it can damage nearby tissue. Basal cell cancer usually appears as a pink or white pearly bump or as an irritated patch. *Squamous cell* is less common, but it can be more dangerous because it grows more quickly and may spread. Squamous cell cancer may appear as a raised pink bump or scaly patch with an open sore in the center.

An estimated 62,000 Americans are diagnosed with melanoma, the most serious type of skin cancer, each year, according to the American Cancer Society, and nearly 8,000 people die from the disease annually. A changing mole is the most important warning sign that a melanoma could be developing. A little dose of melanoma could really mess up your longevity plans, but all skin cancers are completely treatable if detected before they metastasize.

10. Eye Exam by an Ophthalmologist. After age 40, you need to have your eyes examined once every two years (over 60, every year). The reason for seeing an ophthalmologist and not just an optometrist or optician is that you want to rule out any signs of presbyopia (a condition in which the eye is unable to focus in all directions), cataracts (cloudy areas in the lens), glaucoma (elevation of pressure inside the eyes that can progress to a dangerous level before symptoms appear), diabetic retinopathy (a condition that occurs when blood vessels stop feeding the retina properly), or macular degeneration (gradual distortion and sometimes complete loss of central vision).

The numbers are frightening. Some 1.1 million Americans are legally blind. According to the World Health Organization, 100 million people in the United States are visually impaired, of which 80 million suffer from potentially blinding eye disease. Cataracts affect 5.5 million Americans, 2 million Americans are visually impaired by glaucoma, 230,000 Americans are blind from age-related macular degeneration, and 700,000 out of 7 million people with diabetes suffering from diabetic retinopathy are presently at risk for blindness. The American Federation for the Blind has an excellent website where you can learn everything you will ever need to know about eye disease—afb.org.

11. Dental Exam. We don't know if gum disease initiates other illnesses, including heart disease and diabetes, or if it exacerbates them. Dr. Michael Rethman, president of American Association of Periodontology and a periodontist, says it has been known for more than 10 years that people with periodontal diseases are more likely to experience heart disease. Gum and related periodontal diseases have also been associated with strokes, type 2 diabetes, and even early delivery of babies. You need to aggressively take care of your teeth by getting regular dental exams, having your teeth cleaned on a regular basis (we recommend every six months), brushing regularly, flossing, and using toothpicks, Water-Piks, gum stimulators, floss picks, mouthwash, chewing sticks, and whatever other devices strike your fancy.

CHECKUPS YOU CAN DO AT HOME

If you have been diagnosed with diabetes, you probably know all about home medical testing because you need to monitor your blood glucose levels. There are hundreds of glucose testing systems, which have made this chore easier, more convenient, and more accurate. If you need information on some of the most advanced systems and also a resource for reasonably priced testing strips, check out the Home Diagnostics website at homediagnostics.com.

There are literally hundreds of home medical tests. People sometimes opt for these tests because they are concerned about protecting their privacy, but the tests are also often less expensive than the tests a doctor might order, and they help in becoming more proactive about health. Why run to the doctor every time you are worried about something if you can order a simple test on the Internet?

Home Blood Pressure Testing

If you have high blood pressure, or if your doctor tells you that you have "prehypertension," we urge you to routinely measure your blood pressure at home. You can find home testing systems at drugstores or on the Internet. Because blood pressure can rise and

What Do Blood Pressure Numbers Mean?

Blood pressure measures the pressure of blood against the walls of your arteries. There are two readings: systolic and diastolic pressure. Systolic pressure is the higher figure and is the pressure while the heart contracts to pump blood to the body. Diastolic is the lower number and represents the pressure when the heart relaxes between beats. A reading *below* 120 over 80 mmHG (millimeters of mercury) is considered healthy. A reading *higher* than 140 over 90 mmHG is considered high blood pressure. Anything in between, and you have—guess what—prehypertension.

fall during a day, it's helpful to know your pattern so you and your doctor can adjust the timing of any medications you're taking, if necessary. In addition, taking your own blood pressure will engage you in the process of controlling and even resolving this situation. Next time you see your doctor, take your blood monitor with you so you can see if you get the same reading as the doctor.

Testing for Breast Cancer

If you're female, you surely know about self-examination for lumps in your breasts, and we hope you are doing the exam once a month. What you may not know about is i-Find, a handheld imaging device, about the size of a deck of cards, that detects cancerous tissue by using infrared light to measure how much blood is flowing in different locations in the breast. Because tumors need blood to grow, cancerous areas have more blood. Tests found the device to have a 96 percent sensitivity rate in detecting cancer—which is much higher than the rate you get with standard self-examination. Projected to cost $100 retail, these devices were on the fast track for FDA approval at the time we were writing the book.

Testicular Cancer

Testicular cancer, which is very treatable, is the most common cancer in American males between the ages of 15 and 34, which doesn't mean it doesn't appear in older men. It is easily detected by self-examination, but unfortunately, men seem reluctant to talk about testicular cancer or to examine themselves. Men under age 50 should be checking for testicular cancer about once every three months, and for older men, it's once or twice a year. The best time to do this is after taking a shower or bath. The simple instructions are as follows:

1. Support the testicles in one hand, and feel each with the other hand.
2. Feel for swelling or lumps.
3. If you detect swelling or lumps, see a physician immediately.

The Other Tests

Here's a sample of some of the other tests you can take at home:

- For women, a simple home menopause urine test that is quick and easy to use. It tells you if your FSH (follicle-stimulating hormone) levels are elevated in the menopausal range, which would mean you have menopause. See menocheck.com.
- Stool sample colon test, with results available in just five minutes. See healthtestingathome.com and click on "Colon Testing."
- Home cholesterol tests that determine your overall cholesterol level in a few minutes using one or two drops of blood from your fingertip. If you want to know LDL, HDL, and triglyceride levels as well, you can do this: just send the "collection kit" to a lab. BioSafe is widely available in drugstores and online at Amazon.

- A kidney test that allows you to collect a urine sample in the privacy of your home and mail it to a licensed clinical laboratory for microalbumin (a type of protein) testing. The results are quickly mailed to you, and your physician will determine if you have a kidney disorder that needs to be treated. A good source is homehealthtesting.com.
- Prostate (PSA) test. Using the provided finger lancet, you collect three drops of blood and mail the sample to a certified lab. Test results are available in approximately five days. High levels of PSA don't necessarily mean you have prostate cancer, but they are cause for concern. BioSafe has one of these that you can order at homehealthtesting.com, and some drugstores carry them.
- Simple saliva test for women to assess estradiol, progesterone, and testosterone levels. BodyBalance (bodybalance .com) sells a product called FemaleCheck that can be ordered online for about $65.
- MineralCheck from BodyBalance measures your body's level of 11 minerals and nine toxic elements, including aluminum and mercury. You send in a hair sample to the company's testing lab.

To see what else is available, check out websites that exclusively sell home testing kits:

- Healthtestingathome.com
- Homehealthtesting.com
- Testsymptomsathome.com

GETTING TO KNOW YOUR DNA

A home DNA test is easier than most people think—and it can be very useful. What exactly is involved? The answer is fairly simple: You swab the inside of one of your cheeks with the provided buccal swab, which looks like an oversized Q-tip. Drop it into the provided envelope to mail back to the lab. The lab looks at a cell sample to see if it contains a specific biochemical, chromosomal, or DNA marker. These markers can indicate if you are at risk for a genetic disease and can often tell if you would benefit from a specific drug therapy. The results are totally valid, despite any bacteria in your mouth when you swab your cheeks. You can do this right after eating a piece of chocolate cake, and it won't matter.

Many online companies provide home genetic testing, several of which focus on establishing the paternity of a newborn child. The would-be father (or not) has to send in a swab from his cheek as well as that from the child. Other companies, including DNAdirect (dnadirect.com), focus on providing tests that can tell if your DNA makeup predisposes you to various medical problems. For example, approximately 160 million people worldwide are carriers of an inherited disorder called Alpha-1 antitrypsin deficiency, which can cause asthma and even lung or liver disease. DNAdirect sells a home testing kit for $330 that reveals if you are an Alpha-1 carrier or not. Consultation with a board-certified expert is included by e-mail or toll-free phone, along with lab analysis at a premium laboratory, and a personalized report explaining the results, which "interprets your genes in context" of your lifestyle, family concerns, preventive steps, and more.

There are three genetic tests for breast and ovarian cancer that will tell you if you carry an increased risk. The first is for women who have a family member who has tested positive for an altered BRCA1 or BRCA2 gene. The second is for women of Ashkenazi Jewish (Eastern European) ancestry, and the third is for women with a family history of breast or ovarian cancer who do not have Ashkenazi Jewish ancestry. Approximately 1 in every 40 people with Ashkenazi ancestry carry a genetic change that bears a high risk for breast and ovarian cancer.

People with Ashkenazi Jewish ancestry are more likely to have cystic fibrosis (CF), an inherited disease that can cause male infertility and wreak havoc with your lungs, digestive system, and sweat glands. More important than your ancestry is whether you have a relative with this condition. If one of your parents or one of your children has CF, your odds of being a carrier are 100 percent. If you have an aunt or uncle with CF, your carrier odds are 33 percent.

The most common genetic disorder that runs in families is hereditary hemochromatosis (HH), which is more commonly known as "iron-overload disease." Symptoms start with tiredness and muscle and joint pain, but they escalate to much more serious problems. HH actually mimics liver disease, heart disease, and diabetes. In fact, hemochromatosis accounts for approximately 15 percent of cases of adult-onset diabetes. One out of 10 people in the United States carries the gene related to HH, and among people with Celtic ancestry, the rate is 1 out of 4.

The home tests for these conditions and others vary in price from $199 for the HH test to $3,325 for one of the breast or ovarian cancer tests. People may avoid genetic testing because they would rather not know if they are predisposed to getting some disease. This attitude is very shortsighted. Testing can provide you with useful information for treating or preventing a disease—and it can help your children. Since genes are inherited, children need to know what they might be up against. Knowing about your genes and your kids' genes can empower you to take action that could prevent life-threatening diseases down the road.

DON'T GO TO THE HOSPITAL

One of the reasons for going to all the trouble, time, and expense to perform the testing just discussed is that it is hoped you won't have to spend time in a hospital. People not only die in hospitals but also are often killed there. As a rule of thumb, it is a good idea to avoid them except as a last resort. Every year an estimated 200,000 people in the United States die needlessly in hospitals due to preventable medical errors. To put this appalling problem in perspective, 200,000 is more than four times the number of Americans who die annually in automobile accidents—and it is more than three times the number of Americans who died in the Vietnam War.

To be completely fair, the Institute for Healthcare Improvement, a Massachusetts-based nonprofit organization, challenged health care leaders to improve care quality and prevent mistakes in hospitals, and its work is helping. About 3,100 hospitals participated, sharing mortality data and carrying out study-tested procedures to help prevent infections and mistakes. Experts say the cooperative effort was unusual for a competitive industry that traditionally doesn't like to publicly focus on patient-killing problems.

What can we do about this? For one thing, if you go to a hospital, you can ask your doctors and the other medical staff if they've washed their hands before entering your room, and if they haven't, request that they do so. And make sure they are using an alcohol-based hand sanitizer, such as Purell, which is much more effective than regular soap. Don't be shy about insisting that the doctors and medical staff wash their hands; chances are you have to mention this only once and they will comply.

While we recommend that you don't go to the hospital, there are obviously times when you may have no real choice. If and when you do go to the hospital, you can make a number of decisions that will minimize your risk. Unless you live in a rural area, the first decision is, Which hospital? If you are having surgery, look for a hospital that has a lot of experience in the procedure you are going to have. For example, if you are having a total hip replacement and Hospital A does 350 of these a year, while Hospital B does only 25, go to Hospital A. (If you have to change surgeons to do this, fine.)

For a comprehensive quality report on the hospital you are considering, you can download an online report from healthgrades. com. As with the doctor reports we discussed earlier, the hospital reports give you a lot of useful information. Included is patient safety issues such as "avoidance of severe infection following surgery," mortality rates for various procedures, average length of hospital stay, and average costs. The hospitals with the lowest infection rates are the ones with the best overall rates when it comes to preventing all kinds of medical errors. These hospitals, which receive the highest ratings from Health Grades, have a "culture of safety" that puts them a notch above all the rest.

Once you've chosen your hospital, the single most important way to prevent errors is for you to be your own advocate. Take part in the decisions about your health care. Ask questions, and don't accept things you don't understand. If you are too sick to be your own advocate, the next best thing is have a friend or relative act in this capacity—ideally, someone who can be with you throughout your stay. You want someone who is smart enough to ask good questions and strong enough to insist that you get the best care.

You or your advocate should check your medications to verify what they are and what they do. Get to know their colors and shapes, and find out if the hospital has a computer-based pharmacy-dispensing system. Request the shortest possible postoperative stay. The less time you spend in the hospital, the less chance you have of getting an antibiotic-resistant infection. Question any procedure or test you are being given. Is it really in your best interest, or is the hospital merely trying to "cover its tracks"? Tests are often used only to rule out unlikely conditions; you don't have to take them if they don't make sense to you.

Also, always make sure your name wristband is visible, and if it breaks, ask for another one. Don't make a pest of yourself, but remember three things:

- Staying in a hospital costs a lot more than a luxury hotel: you have a right to be fussy.
- Your life might depend upon your ability to fend for yourself.
- Finally, get the hell out of there as soon as possible.

IS THERE AN EASY WAY *OUT*?

Is there a way to look and feel younger without modifying your eating habits, exercising like crazy, and bothering with all the medical issues we bring up? In a way, there is. Treatment with injectable human growth hormone (hGH) has been approved by the FDA to treat adult growth hormone deficiency, and thousands of people are using it as an antiaging therapy. Studies published in the *New England Journal of Medicine* show that hGH may reverse aging in at least a dozen, measurable ways. Here are chief examples:

- Restoring muscle mass, lost hair, and size of the liver, heart, and other organs that shrink with age
- Decreasing body fat
- Increasing energy, sexual function, and cardiac output
- Improving cholesterol profile, vision, and memory
- Thickening skin and reducing wrinkles
- Normalizing blood pressure

Wow, what's the downside? you may wonder. Costing up to $10,000 a year, human growth hormone therapy is expensive and probably not covered by your health insurance. And there are risks of side effects, including increased insulin resistance (particularly if you don't exercise), carpal tunnel syndrome, joint aches, and edema among women. Some doctors think there is also an increased cancer risk.

We're not opposed to using hGH to correct deficiency. Life without adequate hormone levels can be of poor quality and can lead to increased inflammation and early death. If you do want to use it for antiaging, we say: proceed with caution, and don't think of it as a substitute for healthy living. Make sure you have the right doctor, one who will monitor you for any side effects. Some people we know inject hGH every other week or month, and some use it for three months and then stop for three months. The results can be dramatic.

Estrogen replacement therapy using "bio-identical" rather than synthetic hormones can provide several antiaging benefits for women approaching menopause and after. Besides reduction of menopausal symptoms, these include prevention of osteoporosis and Alzheimer's disease; improved cholesterol profile, concentration, and sleep; and increased libido. As a result of an increase in heart attacks, strokes, and breast cancer among women using synthetic hormones such as Prempro, bio-identical hormones have gained favor, and millions of women have turned to them. To learn more about this and related issues, including the use of progesterone and compounded bio-identical hormones, see womento women.com.

Finally, there is testosterone therapy. Women are sometimes prescribed small amounts in skin creams to stimulate declining libido and restore their ability to achieve orgasms. For men with low testosterone levels, this therapy can do wonders to fight depression, fatigue, and erectile dysfunction while lowering cholesterol and decreasing insulin resistance. Men on this therapy must undergo regular prostate cancer screenings with blood tests for PSA, as testosterone can stimulate prostate growth.

Besides hormone replacement therapies, the other "easy way" out is to turn to cosmetic surgery. If you follow our plan, you will look dramatically better, but if you want more, we say, go for it! Anything that boosts your self-esteem and makes you feel younger is fine with us. Just be smart and realize it is an artificial solution. A forehead lift may take years off your face, but it won't count down your age. A good place to start learning is plasticsurgery.org.

8 4 3
5 2
6
3 6 7
1
6 3
5
2
8

6

The Antiaging Plan

Your scores from the antiaging test in Chapter 1 should give you a fairly good idea about the current state of your health and some clues about what you need to do. Combining these results with all the information you've now gleaned about nutrition, fitness, lifestyle, and medical care, you are ready to come up with your very own plan—your personal "Count Down Your Age Plan." To help you do this, we have compiled a set of recommendations that may apply to you.

In each of these five lists, circle *all* of the recommendations you want to follow, filling in the blanks as appropriate, and *add* a few items of your own. For the online version, go to countdown yourage.com.

Nutritional Recommendations
- Eat breakfast every morning.
- Find a good whole grain cereal with little or no sugar.
- Start eating oatmeal ____ days a week.
- Eat raw fruit every morning.
- Add blueberries to my diet.
- Stop drinking juice.
- Stop putting sugar in my coffee and/or tea.

- Switch to whole grain toast.
- Give up on the jam.
- Make grapefruit part of my life.
- Make sure I'm getting enough fiber—at least ＿＿ grams a day.
- Eat eggs once and no more than three times a week.
- Cut way back on the bacon and/or sausage.
- Reduce my coffee consumption to one or two cups a day.
- Start drinking green tea.
- Drink more green tea.
- Add yogurt to my universe.
- Increase my consumption of raw and cooked vegetables so that on average, I'm eating ＿＿ servings a day.
- Stop eating french fries.
- Give up the ketchup.
- Eat salad for lunch at least ＿＿ times a week.
- Eat more chicken.
- Drink more water—at least ＿＿ glasses a day.
- Give up on sodas.
- Learn to read nutrition labels on packaged food.
- Avoid high-fructose corn syrup.
- Eat organic.
- Reduce my consumption of beef to no more than ＿＿ times a week.
- Switch to red wine.
- Limit my drinking of alcoholic beverages (including wine) to no more than two glasses a day.
- Stop drinking alcoholic beverages.
- Learn to replace simple carbohydrates with complex carbohydrates.
- Eat low-mercury-contaminated fish at least ＿＿ times a week.
- Eat dessert only occasionally.
- Cut back on starchy food.
- Sharply reduce my consumption of saturated fats.

- Cook with olive oil.
- Try to eat at least one serving of the following foods at least once every two weeks (Circle *all* that apply):

  Ⓐ Blueberries
  Ⓑ Grapefruit
  Ⓒ Almonds
  Ⓓ Apples
  Ⓔ Avocados
  Ⓕ Beets
  Ⓖ Broccoli
  Ⓗ Cranberries or cranberry juice
  Ⓘ Flaxseeds
  Ⓙ Garlic
  Ⓚ Olive oil
  Ⓛ Onions

  Ⓜ Oranges
  Ⓝ Salmon
  Ⓞ Soy
  Ⓟ Tea
  Ⓠ Tomatoes
  Ⓡ Whole grains
  Ⓢ Red wine
  Ⓣ Beans
  Ⓤ Sea vegetables (a.k.a. "seaweed")
  Ⓥ Cabbage
  Ⓦ Kale

- Eat more slowly so that I will eat less.
- Put less food on my plate.
- Develop a strategy for eating less when I go to a restaurant—such as ordering two appetizers, skipping the dessert, and putting a portion of my meal in a doggie bag.
- Gradually reduce my daily consumption of calories to _____ per day. (Note: This is a decision you must make based on your body size, how much exercise you do, and how aggressive you want to be about losing weight. We recommend that everyone eat fewer than 3,000 calories per day and more than 1,500.)
- Other recommendations? On a separate piece of paper or on your computer, write out any other nutrition-related guidelines you'd like to follow. For example, if you've decided to become a vegetarian, you might write, "Stop eating meat."

Supplement Recommendations

- Find a good multivitamin and start taking it every single day.
- Add the following supplements to my daily routine:

Ⓐ Omega-3 (fish oil)
Ⓑ Vitamin B complex
Ⓒ Alpha lipoic acid
Ⓓ Acetyl-L-carnitine
Ⓔ Curcumin
Ⓕ Vitamin D
Ⓖ Vitamin E
Ⓗ CoQ10
Ⓘ Magnesuim
Ⓙ Selenium
Ⓚ SAMe
Ⓛ Phosphatidyl serine (PS)
Ⓜ Nattokinase
Ⓝ Glucosamine and chondroitin

Ⓞ Saw palmetto
Ⓟ Milk thistle
Ⓠ Black cohosh
Ⓡ Lutein and zeaxanthin
Ⓢ Lycopene
Ⓣ Vitamin K
Ⓤ Chromium
Ⓥ GABA
Ⓦ DHEA
Ⓧ _____
Ⓨ _____
Ⓩ _____

▪ Other recommendations? On a separate piece of paper or on your computer, list any other supplements you think you should take.

Fitness Recommendations

▪ Start exercising on a regular basis—at least _____ days a week.
▪ Start walking—at least _____ minutes a day.
▪ Buy a pedometer.
▪ Increase the intensity of my exercise.
▪ Set a goal of burning off _____ calories per day on average through exercise.
▪ Increase the duration of my average exercise session to at least _____ minutes.
▪ Engage in *true* aerobic exercise (20 minutes or more during which my heart rate is elevated to between 60 and 80 percent of its maximum capacity) at least _____ times a week.
▪ Go swimming on a regular basis.
▪ Warm up properly before strenuous exercise, and cool down once I'm finished.
▪ Join a gym or similar organization offering exercise-related facilities.

- Engage in resistance training at least ____ times a week.
- Start stretching on a regular basis.
- Join a yoga studio or other form of exercise such as _____
  _____.
- Take a sauna (or go to the steam room) once every _____
  _____.
- Go dancing on a regular basis.
- Create an exercise routine that I can follow.
- Reduce my body fat percentage to ____ percent.
- Take up a new and demanding sport or exercise activity.
- Exercise my eyes.
- Consciously exercise my brain.
- Take up a new and demanding activity that requires me to use my mind in a new and demanding way.
- Other recommendations? On a separate piece of paper or on your computer, write out any other fitness-related guidelines you'd like to follow.

Lifestyle Recommendations
- Determine how much sleep I need by keeping a sleep diary.
- Establish a goal to get ____ hours of sleep on average every night.
- Create a sleep-friendly bedroom.
- Follow a sleep-conducive routine before going to bed.
- Try melatonin.
- Seek professional help for my sleep problems.
- Forget nightcaps. No alcohol two hours before going to bed.
- Avoid bedtime arguments or stressful conversations.
- Make sure I don't have sleep apnea.
- Get some help to stop smoking.
- Get some help to stop drinking.
- Deal with my depression.
- Start being honest with myself.
- Enjoy life more.
- Have more sex.
- Talk to my doctor about sex.

- Practice deep breathing.
- Meditate _____ days a week.
- Learn to leave the moment.
- Join a community group.
- Find some real meaning in my life.
- Look for humor in ordinary daily events.
- Seek out comedy (movies, books, comedy club, TV).
- Err on the side of caution (don't be reckless).
- Protect my hearing from loud noise.
- Stop kicking the dog (control my anger).
- Don't ever be bored.
- Other recommendations? On a separate piece of paper or on your computer, write out any other lifestyle-related guidelines you'd like to follow.

Medical Care Recommendations
- Create my personal health journal.
- Carry a medical response card in my wallet or purse or somewhere on my body.
- Learn to collaborate with my doctor.
- Find a new doctor.
- Go in for the Count Down Your Age Physical.
- Learn what my cholesterol count is.
- Find out what my LDL and HDL numbers are.
- Take action to lower my cholesterol count.
- Make sure my fasting triglyceride level is normal.
- Get treatment to lower my triglyceride levels.
- Ditto C-reactive protein.
- Ditto homocysteine.
- Take notes whenever I see a health care professional.
- Jot down the name of any prescriptions I get, and double-check the label to make sure I've received the right one.
- Set a goal to reduce the size of my waist by _____ inches.
- Do everything possible to reduce the risk of heart disease.
- Follow my doctor's advice to manage my prediabetic or diabetic condition.

- Know my blood pressure reading.
- Regularly check my blood pressure.
- If I have hypertension or prehypertension, do everything possible to reduce and control my blood pressure.
- Schedule a colonoscopy.
- Self-examine my skin on a regular basis.
- Self-examine my breasts on a regular basis.
- Ask my doctor about a heart scan.
- Ask my doctor about getting a digital mammogram or a digital tomosynthesis.
- Get a bone-mass measurement.
- Schedule a gynecological examination.
- See a dermatologist.
- Have my eyes examined by an ophthalmologist.
- Talk to my doctor about a PSA test.
- Don't go to the hospital.
- If I do go to the hospital, follow the advice in this book about how to choose a hospital and how to manage the situation once there.
- Find out about my family medical history.
- Look into DNA testing.
- Other recommendations? On a separate piece of paper or on your computer, write out any other medical-related actions you'd like to take.

YOUR VERY OWN PLAN: THE NEXT STEP

It's your plan. From this point, you have to do the work—we've done our part. Using your computer or a notebook (it could be a section in your personal health journal), write a short description of your personal goals for the next few months or years. It could be that you want to stabilize your weight; increase your energy; get fit; run a marathon; start dating hot, younger people; restore your mental sharpness; or any number of other things—it's entirely up to you.

Next, write down the following: "In order to achieve my plan, I will follow these nutritional recommendations."

Under this sentence, list the recommendations you think you should follow, *in order of their importance*. Why? The process of determining the priority of the recommendations and then actually writing them down will reinforce their significance and help keep them fresh in your mind. The odds that you will follow through are much improved by virtue of this simple step.

Do the same for the supplement recommendations, fitness, lifestyle, and medical. Once you've completed this, read the entire plan aloud to yourself, and then put it someplace where you can easily retrieve it.

YOUR VERY OWN PLAN: HOW TO FOLLOW THROUGH

Turning to the appointment calendar that you normally use (could be in your computer, your date book, or on the wall), pick a day and time once every two weeks or once a month when you can check the progress you are making. Mark your calendar ahead for at least six months (for example, every other Saturday morning at 10 A.M.) with the following: "Important—Check My Plan."

When the designated time comes, check off each of the recommendations you have been following and write a brief progress report, including the recommendations to do better. Perhaps you have started an aerobic exercise program but you haven't yet found a program for resistance training; if so, then you would note, "I need to find a resistance program."

After following your plan for six months, and every six months thereafter, retake the test (countdownyourage.com). If your total score is going up faster than your actual age, you are making real progress. You are, in essence, reversing your age—and, in a real biological sense, you are getting younger! You are counting down your age.

Appendix A

Fiber Content of Basic Foods

Almonds (handful—¼ cup) = 4.5 grams of fiber
Apple (one medium) = 3 grams
Asparagus (1 cup) = 3 grams
Avocado (one medium) = 2 grams
Banana (one medium) = 3 grams
Barley (1 cup) = 13 grams
Beets (1 cup) = 3.5 grams
Bell pepper (1 cup) = 2 grams
Black beans (1 cup) = 15 grams
Blueberries (1 cup) = 4 grams
Broccoli (1 cup) = 4.5 grams
Brussels sprouts (1 cup) = 4 grams
Cabbage (1 cup) = 3.5 grams
Cantaloupe (1 cup) = 1 gram
Carrots (1 cup) = 3.5 grams
Cashews (handful—¼ cup) = 1 gram
Cauliflower (1 cup) = 3 grams
Celery (1 cup) = 2 grams
Collard greens (boiled—1 cup) = 5 grams
Corn (1 cup) = 4.5 grams
Cucumber (1 cup) = 3 grams
Eggplant (1 cup) = 2.5 grams
Garbanzo beans (1 cup) = 12.5 grams

Grapefruit (one-half) = 1.5 grams
Grapes (1 cup) = 1 gram
Green beans (1 cup) = 4 grams
Green peas (1 cup) = 9 grams
Kale (1 cup) = 2.5 grams
Kidney beans (1 cup) = 11 grams
Leeks (½ cup) = 0.5 gram
Lentils (1 cup) = 15.5 grams
Lima beans (1 cup) = 13 grams
Mushrooms (handful—5 ounces) = 1 gram
Mustard greens (1 cup) = 3 grams
Oats (1 cup) = 4 grams
Onion (1 cup) = 3 grams
Orange (one medium) = 3 grams
Papaya (one-half medium) = 3 grams
Peanuts (handful—¼ cup) = 4 grams
Pear (one medium Bartlett) = 4 grams
Pinto beans (1 cup) = 15 grams
Potato (medium—baked with skin) = 3 grams
Pumpkin seeds (handful—¼ cup) = 1.5 grams
Raisins (handful—¼ cup) = 1.5 grams
Raspberries (1 cup) = 8 grams
Rice (1 cup brown) = 3.5 grams
Romaine lettuce (2 cups) = 7.5 grams
Rye (⅓ cup) = 8 grams
Soybeans (1 cup) = 10 grams
Spinach (1 cup) = 4 grams
Strawberries (1 cup) = 3 grams
Sunflower seeds (handful—¼ cup) = 4 grams
Sweet potato with skin (one medium) = 12.5 grams
Swiss chard (1 cup) = 3.5 grams
Tomato (fresh—1 cup) = 2 grams
Walnuts (handful—¼ cup) = 1.5 grams
Wheat (1 cup) = 8 grams

Appendix B

Selected Online Resources

General Health

Medstory (medstory.com): Search engine like Google, only engineered specifically for looking up articles and research on health and medicine.

Family Doctor (familydoctor.org): A library of accessible health information on all topics.

WebMD (webmd.com): Big, sprawling website with a wealth of information and tools related to all aspects of health.

Physicians Committee for Responsible Medicine (pcrm.org): Website by physicians who *really* believe in preventive medicine.

Health Central (healthcentral.com): Insights from Dr. Dean Edell, including audio and video clips from his radio and TV appearances. Plus the latest medical news.

Medical Breakthroughs (ivanhoe.com): The latest medical research.

Blood Tests Direct (health-tests-direct.com): Full line of diagnostic blood tests you can take at home.

Specific Health Issues

Alzheimer's Association (alz.org): Voluntary health organization dedicated to finding prevention methods, treatments, and an eventual cure for Alzheimer's.

Spine Health (spine-health.com): What to do about common causes of back pain and neck pain, such as a herniated disk, degenerative disk disease, osteoarthritis, and other conditions.

Dr. Blood Pressure (blood-pressure-hypertension.com): Everything you could ever want to know about hypertension and how to treat it.

HealthyPlace (healthyplace.com): Consumer mental health site with information on all types of psychological disorders and psychiatric medications. Includes active chat rooms, hosted support groups, and subsites focused on depression and anxiety.

Prostate Health (prostatecare.com): Comprehensive guide to prostate health.

Imaginis: The Breast Cancer Resource (imaginis.com): Covers areas relating to breast cancer such as prevention, screening, diagnosis, and treatment. Also contains extensive information about medical procedures such as angiography, biopsy, CT, MRI, nuclear medicine, ultrasound, x-ray imaging, and radiation therapy.

Knee1 (knee1.com): Guide to knee care including topics such as knee fitness, knee surgery and recovery, and advances in arthritis care.

Alternative Health Care

Annie Appleseed Project (annieappleseedproject.org): Alternative and complementary therapies for treating cancer.

WholeHealthMD (wholehealthmd.com): A great library of articles on complementary and alternative medicine developed by a team of leading board-certified doctors and specialists. Good searching tools.

HealthWorld Online (healthy.net): The original network for "wellness, healthy living, alternative therapies, and mind-body-spirit" health.

Holistic Health Yellow Pages (findhealer.com): Find someone in your neighborhood.

Supplements

Vitasearch (vitasearch.com): The latest research on vitamins, minerals, and other supplements.

Linus Pauling Institute Micronutrient Center (lpi.oregon state.edu/infocenter): If you want to know the "truth" about supplements, this is a highly regarded source.

Nutrition

Tufts Health and Nutrition Letter (healthletter.tufts.edu): Excellent nutrition information based on the latest research from the Friedman School of Nutrition Science and Policy at Tufts University.

The World's Healthiest Foods (whfoods.com): Developed by the founder of Whole Foods, George Mateljan, through his private foundation. Extremely accessible information on the nutritional value of healthy foods based on scientific research.

NutritionData (nutritiondata.com): Nutrition breakdown of most foods, including processed and fast foods. Includes a "fullness" factor as well as number of calories and glycemic index.

Harvard School of Public Health—Nutrition (hsph.harvard .edu/nutritionsource): Resource for the latest information on nutrition according to some very smart people at Harvard University.

The Glycemic Index (glycemicindex.com): The "official website" of the glycemic index includes the world's most thorough glycemic index database.

Traineo: Weight Loss Community (traineo.com): Pick four friends to receive e-mail messages about the progress you are making to achieve your weight-loss goal. Free online diet and exercise tracker.

Epicurious.com (epicurious.com): The world's greatest recipe collection. Online home of *Gourmet* and *Bon Appétit* magazines. Featuring recipes, menus, chefs, wine, drinks, cooking demos, food forums, gourmet shopping, and much more.

CalorieKing (calorieking.com): The best calorie counter and a whopping-big database.

The Calorie Restriction Society (calorierestriction.org): If you are considering a calorie-restriction diet, start here. Tells you how and gives you tons of motivation.

Grass-Fed Beef: These three grass-fed beef producers sell steaks that, for the *New York Times* reviewer Marian Burros, "brought back memories of the beefy flavor meat had before cattle were stuffed with grain in feedlots."
- Tallgrass Beef (tallgrassbeef.com)
- U.S. Wellness Meats (uswellness.com)
- Whippoorwill Farm (allenandrobin.com)

Fitness

CaloriesperHour.com (caloriesperhour.com): Terrific calculator for tabulating calories burned by almost any activity, based on your body weight. Also includes a "weight loss calculator" and other tools and tips.

American Council on Exercise (acefitness.org): For professionals but has plenty of useful information for everyone else. Includes "find a health club or personal trainer" service and an impressive library of exercises with illustrated, step-by-step instructions.

Fitness Jumpsite! (primusweb.com/fitnesspartner): Great calculator for determining calories burned, based on your weight and amount of time you exercise, for more than 200 activities—plus fitness information.

Netfit Health and Fitness Team (netfit.co.uk/netfit.htm): Started by an ex–British Royal Marine commando, the Netfit team includes some impressive athletes. If you want personalized training but can't afford your own trainer, this could be for you. Cost is $95 for one year.

Exercise and Muscle Directory (exrx.net): Great drawings of muscles and skeletal components. High-production video how-tos featuring "professional exercise models" for dozens of exercises—weight-lifting and aerobic.

FitDay (fitday.com): Diet and exercise tracker that provides calorie and nutrition information. You can set a weight goal and keep track of your progress. Very good free service.

How to Exercise Your Eyes (wikihow.com/exercise-your-eyes): Step-by-step instructions for simple eye exercises.

Personalized Gym Workout Program (hyperstrike.com): Creates a personalized workout program for you to do at the gym, and 3-D animations show you how to do each exercise.

Fifty-Plus Lifelong Fitness (50plus.org): Senior fitness and health site that promotes exercise for people over 50 years old. Started at Stanford University, it has evolved into a nonprofit organization that sponsors "50+ Fitness" events and provides some great information.

Longevity

The Longevity Info Center (longevityexperts.com): Tells you "how to live to 110 or longer" with an exclamation point. Sells products but has links to antiaging experts such as Ray Kurzweil.

Gerontology Research (grg.org): Physicians, scientists, and engineers dedicated to the quest to slow and ultimately reverse human aging within the next 20 years.

Anti-Aging Guide (anti-aging-guide.com): Here you'll find a vast array of antiaging strategies. Claims you can add 40 to 50 years to your life by fasting.

Immortality Institute (imminst.org): The lofty goal of this organization is to defeat death so we can live forever. Very scientific, based on the ideas of Dr. Aubrey de Grey.

Alliance for Aging Research (agingresearch.org): Nonprofit organization for promoting the development of antiaging technologies and medicine.

Government

Healthfinder (healthfinder.gov): Broad-based health information from the U.S. Department of Health and Human Services.

National Institutes of Health (nih.gov): Great library of consumer health information on all topics.

World Health Organization (who.int/en): Track the progress of bird flu. Rich with general health information as well as pandemic topics.

U.S. Food and Drug Administration (fda.gov): *FDA Consumer* magazine tells you how to "get healthy and stay healthy." Good source for the latest FDA approvals of new drugs and warnings about existing drugs or supplements.

Authors' Websites

Vagnini.com (vagnini.com): Cutting-edge information on heart care, diabetes, and weight loss as well as antiaging medicine from Dr. V.

LongLifeClub (longlifeclub.com): Founded by Dave Bunnell and dedicated to helping people live longer, happier lives. Includes blogs, interactive tools, interviews with centenarians, and the latest longevity-related health news. You can go to this site to take the Count Down Your Age test.

Count Down Your Age (countdownyourage.com): Takes you to the Count Down Your Age test on the LongLifeClub site.

Selected References

Preface

Perls, Thomas T., and Margery Hutter Silver. *Living to 100*. New York: Basic Books, 1999.

Chapter 1

Crowley, Chris, and Henry S. Lodge. *Younger Next Year*. New York: Workman, 2004.

Oge, Eray. *Counterclockwise*. Internet: New York: Third Millennium Publishing, 2004.

Chapter 2

Bunnell, David. "Are You Really Sure You Don't Have Sleep Apnea?" LongLifeClub, February 25, 2006: online.

Dement, William C., and Christopher Vaughan. *The Promise of Sleep*. New York: Dell, 1999.

Heller, Richard F., et al. *The Carbohydrate Addict's Healthy Heart Program*. New York: Ballantine, 1999.

Khalsa, Dharma Singh, and Cameron Stauth. *Meditation as Medicine*. New York: Fireside, 2001.

Levy, Daniel, and Susan Brink. *A Change of Heart.* New York: Alfred A. Knopf, 2005.

Maas, James B. *Power Sleep.* New York: HarperCollins, 1999.

Mayo Clinic. "Skin Cancer Reaching Epidemic Status." *Mayo Clinic Health Letter,* April 2005: 20–24.

Messinis, Lambros, et al. "Neuropsychological Deficits in Long-Term Frequent Cannabis Users." *Neurology,* November 2005: 737–39.

Rush University Medical Center. "Melatonin Most Effective for Sleep When Taken for Off-Hour Sleeping." News Release, May 1, 2006.

Thornton, Mark. *Meditation in a New York Minute.* Boulder, CO: Sounds True, 2004.

Chapter 3

Atkins, Robert C. *Dr. Atkins' Vita-Nutrient Solution.* New York: Simon & Schuster, 1998.

Balch, Phyllis A. *Prescription for Dietary Wellness.* New York: Avery, 2003.

Bounds, Gwendolyn. "After Bottled Water? Purified Ice Cubes." *Wall Street Journal,* July 25, 2006: B1.

Brand-Miller, Jennie, et al. *The New Glucose Revolution.* New York: Marlow & Company, 2003.

Bunnell, David. "Are You Drinking Enough Water?" LongLifeClub, September 24, 2005: online.

Campbell, T. Colin, and Thomas M. Campbell II. *The China Study.* Dallas: Benbella Books, 2004.

de Vrese, M., P. Winkler, et al. "Effect of *Lactobacillus gasseri* PA 16/8, *Bifidobacterium longum* SP 07/3, *B. bifidum* MF 20/5 on Common Cold Episodes: A Double-Blind, Randomized, Controlled Study." *Clinical Nutrition* 24, no.4 (2005): 481–91.

Faloon, William. "Blueberries—the World's Healthiest Food." *LifeExtension Magazine,* Winter 2005/2006: 2–6.

———. "Dietary Supplements Attacked by the Media." *LifeExtension Magazine*, June 2006: 7–18.

Harvard University. "Dietary Fiber and Colon Cancer: The Pendulum Swings (Again)." *Harvard Medical International*, August 2005.

Iso H., M. Kobayashi, et al. "Intake of Fish and Omega-3 Fatty Acids and Risk of Coronary Heart Disease Among Japanese." *Circulation* 113, no. 2 (2006): 195–202.

Johnson, Nathan. "Swine of the Times: The Making of the Modern Pig." *Harper's*, May 2006: 47–56.

Joyal, Steven V., and Dale Kiefer. "Calorie Restriction Without Hunger!" *LifeExtension Magazine*, July 2006: 21–25.

Khalsa, Dharma Singh. *Food as Medicine*. New York: Atria Books, 2003.

Nestle, Marion. *What to Eat*. New York: North Point Press, 2006.

Netzer, Corrine T. *The Complete Book of Food Counts*. New York: Bantam Dell, 2006.

Oliff, Heather S. "Why Lutein and Zeaxanthin Are Becoming So Popular." *LifeExtension Magazine*, September 2005: 38–45.

Perricone, Nicholas. *The Perricone Promise*. New York: Warner Books, 2004.

Pratt, Steven G., and Kathy Matthews. *SuperFoods HealthStyle*. New York: William Morrow, 2006.

Rosick, Edward R. "Antioxidants, Mitochondrial Damage, and Human Aging." *LifeExtension Magazine*, February 2006: 63–67.

Shahani, Khem. *Cultivate Health from Within*. Danbury, CT: Vital Health Publishing, 2005.

Staelin, Earl. "Strong Bones or Osteoporosis." *Well Being Journal*, March/April 2006: 1, 34–41.

Tufts University. "Shaking the Salt Habit." *Health & Nutrition Letter*, February 2006, Supplement.

———. "Vitamin D May Protect Against Breast Cancer." *Health & Nutrition Letter*, July 2006: 1–2.

Tuttle, Dave. "Protecting Your DNA from Lethal Mutations." *LifeExtension Magazine*, September 2005: 31–32.

Weil, Andrew. *Eating Well for Optimal Health.* New York: Alfred A. Knopf, 2000.

Willett, Walter C. *Eat, Drink, and Be Healthy.* New York: Free Press, 2001.

Chapter 4

Anderson, Bob. *Stretching.* Bolinas, CA: Shelter Publications, 2000.

Braverman, Eric R. *The Edge Effect.* New York: Sterling, 2004.

Bunnell, David. "Having Fun, Fun, Fun on an Exercise Bike." LongLifeClub, August 20, 2005: online.

———. "Pumping Iron with Condi." LongLifeClub, March 6, 2006: online.

Hu, Gang, et al. "Leisure Time, Occupational, and Commuting Physical Activity and the Risk of Stroke." Department of Epidemiology and Health Promotion, National Public Health Institute (Helsinki, Finland), August 4, 2005.

Katz, Lawrence C., and Manning Rubin. *Keep Your Brain Alive.* New York: Workman, 1999.

Larson, Eric, et al. "Exercise Is Associated with Reduced Risk for Incident Dementia Among Persons 65 Years of Age and Older." *Annals of Internal Medicine*, January 17, 2006: 73–81.

Mason, Douglas J., and Michael L. Kohn. *The Memory Workbook.* Oakland, CA: New Harbinger, 2001.

MensHealth Magazine. Total Body Guide. Emmaus, PA: Rodale, 2001.

Mora, S., et al. "Ability of Exercise Testing to Predict Cardiovascular and All-Cause Death in Asymptomatic Women." *Journal of the American Medical Association*, September 24, 2003: 1,600–07.

Richardson, Caroline R., et al. "Physical Activity and Mortality Across Cardiovascular Disease Risk Groups." *Medicine and Science in Sports and Exercise*, November 2004: 1,923–29.

Robinet, Jane-Ellen. "Regular Exercise Can Help Young and Old Fight Depression." LongLifeClub, February 4, 2005: online.

Roizen, Michael F., and Mehmet C. Oz. *You: The Owner's Manual.* New York: HarperCollins, 2005.

Sherman, Karen J., et al. "Comparing Yoga, Exercise, and a Self-Care Book for Chronic Low Back Pain." *Annals of Internal Medicine* 143, no. 12 (December 20, 2005): 849–56.

Small, Gary. *The Memory Bible.* New York: Hyperion, 2002.

Chapter 5

American Academy of Dermatology. "You Really Need to Learn How to Spot the Warning Signs of Hidden Melanomas." News Release, May 1, 2006.

Baron, Penny. "The 10 Most Important Blood Tests." *LifeExtension Magazine*, May 2006: 43–51.

Doheny, Katherine. "Technology May Bring Kinder, Gentler Colonoscopy." HealthDay, May 24, 2006: online.

Edelson, Ed. "Self-Monitoring of Blood Drug Helps Patients." HealthDay (February 2, 2006): online.

Isaacs, Scott, and Frederic Vagnini. *Overcoming Metabolic Syndrome.* Omaha, NE: Addicus, 2006.

Kurzweil, Ray, and Terry Grossman. *Fantastic Voyage: Live Long Enough to Live Forever.* New York: Penguin, 2005.

Landro, Laura. "Hospitals Combat Errors at the 'Hand-Off.'" *Wall Street Journal*, June 26, 2006: D1.

Raucher, Megan. "Be Assertive to Stay Safe in the Hospital." Reuter's Health, April 20, 2006: online.

Reinburg, Steven. "New Sunscreen Promises More Protection." HealthDay, July 25, 2006: online.

Robinet, Jane-Ellen. "Cancer Screenings, Prevention Efforts Pay Off in Declining Death Rates." LongLifeClub, June 10, 2004: online.

———. "Here Are Ways to Lower Your Risk of Getting Colon Cancer." LongLifeClub, February 13, 2005: online.

Roizen, Michael F., and Mehmet C. Oz. *You: The Smart Patient.* New York: Free Press, 2006.

Vagnini, Frederic, and Barry Fox. *The Side Effects Bible.* New York: Broadway Books, 2005.

Weil, Andrew. *Healthy Aging.* New York: Alfred A. Knopf, 2005.

Wurman, Richard Saul. *Diagnostic Tests for Men.* Newport, RI: TOP, 2001.

Index

Home Health Testing
(homehealthtesting.com), 217,
226
Homocysteine, 45, 114, 115, 125, 137,
212, 215
Honey, 102
Hope, Bob, 155
Hospitals, 228–30
Hot flashes, 68, 143
HTTP-5, 72
Http://doctor.webmed.com, 208
Http://santosha.com, 170
Http://webapps.ama-assn.org/doctor
finder, 208
Https://healthmanager.webmd.com,
193
Huevos de la Casa, 90–95
Human growth hormone (hGH),
230–31. *See also* Growth
hormones
Human Nutrition Research Center,
USDA, 149
Hunger, avoiding extreme, 131
Huntington's disease, 106
Hydrogenated fats. *See* Trans fats
Hypertension. *See also* Blood
pressure
chromium and, 145
exercise and, 157
heat and, 180
home monitoring of, 223–24
meat and, 114
pre-, 223, 224
sleep disturbances and, 53
soy and, 125
sugar and, 101

I-Find, 224
Ice, 101
Immune system
exercise and, 153, 164
garlic and, 124
probiotics and, 96
vitamin B_6 and, 137
vitamin C and, 141
Incomplete proteins, 111
Indole-3-carbinol, 124
Infertility, 68
Inflammation, 125, 138, 153, 215
Insoluble fiber, 126
Insomnia, 68

Institute for Healthcare
Improvement, 229
Institute of Medicine, 81, 157
Institute for Safe Medical Practices,
200
Insulin, 41, 101
carbohydrates and, 84, 86
chromium and, 145, 212
exercise and, 151
fiber and, 80
fructose and, 102
vegetarianism and, 110
Insulin resistance, 77, 84, 94, 145,
231
conjugated linoleic acid and, 116
sugar and, 101
testosterone therapy and, 232
Insulin sensitivity, 80, 86, 110, 151
Integrativemedicine.arizona.edu, 208
Internal body temperature, 152
*International Classification of Sleep
Disorders, Diagnostic and Coding
Manual, The*, 56
Inuit people, 104
Inversion tables, 169
Iodine, 127
Ionizers.org, 100
Irritable bowel syndrome, 138
Isometric exercises, 163

Japan, cancer rates in, 127
Jazzercise, 183
Jogging, 162
Johns Hopkins University, 124
Johnson, Lori, 129
Johnson, Ron, 129
Joint pain, 98
Jokl, Ernst, 179
*Journal of the American Dietetic
Association*, 87
Journal of Sports Medicine, 158
Juvenon (juvenon.com), 139

Kale, 127–28
Katz, Lawrence, 187, 188
Keep Your Brain Alive (Katz), 188
Kellogg's Smart Start cereals, 102
Kelp, 127
Kidney tests, 226
Kidneys, 97, 115
Kifir, 97

Teitelbaum, Jacob, 145
Television, 51, 57
Testicular cancer, 225
Testosterone, 62, 146, 164, 213, 226, 232
Tests/quizzes
  Antiaging Test, 1–37
  Borg Scale Test, 14
  Count Down Your Age Laugh Test, 64–66
  Food-Buying IQ, 77–79
  What Makes for a Great Doctor?, 203–5
Testsymptomsathome.com, 226
TetraPak International, 96
Texas Monthly, 202
Theanine, 145
Thiamine, 136
Thrifty gene, 130
Thyroid gland, 127
Thyroid panel, 211
Toe stretch, 174
Tomatoes, 91, 126, 145
Tortillas, 94, 107
Total cholesterol/HDL ratio, 151, 214–15
Training range, 160–61
Trans fats, 92, 108–9
Transcendental Meditation, 68
Treadmill stress test (TST), 218
Treadmills, 180, 181
Triceps dips, 175
Triglycerides, 103
  fiber and, 80
  grapefruit and, 123
  niacin and, 133, 136
  omega-3 fatty acids and, 104, 135
  onions and, 91
  saturated fats and, 106
  tests for, 215
Triticale, 90
Tufts University, 152
Turmeric, 138
Type 2 diabetes, 84, 101, 145, 151, 215, 223

Ubiquinone. *See* CoQ10
Ulcers, 124, 127, 138
Uncle Sam's whole wheat cereal, 89
Union of Concerned Scientists, 116

University of Arizona, 208
University of California, Berkeley Recreation Center, 183
University of California, San Francisco, 115, 185
University of East London, 124–25
University of Maryland Medical Center, 64
University of Maryland School of Medicine, 66
University of Toronto, 132
University of Wisconsin, 170, 171
Uric acid test, 212

Vagnini, Frederic J. ("Dr. V" author)
  breakfast of, 95
  dinner with, 117–18
  exercise routine of, 156, 184
  laughter therapy and, 67
  lifestyle changes made by, 40–43
  on physical exams, 211, 212, 213
Vagnini.com, 146
Vegans, 110, 111
Vegetables
  cooked *vs.* raw, 113
  fiber in, 82
  importance of, 109–12
  pigmentation of, 112–13
  sea, 126–27
  serving size, 110
  skin of, 113
Vegetarians, 110–12, 124, 137
Vinyasa yoga, 172
Virtual colonoscopy, 216, 217
Virtual fitness trainers (virtualfitnesstrainer.com), 157
Visicol tablets, 216
Vital Vittles 12 Grain bread, 81–82
Vitality101.com, 145
Vitamin B_1, 136
Vitamin B_2, 136
Vitamin B_3. *See* Niacin
Vitamin B_5. *See* Pantothenic acid
Vitamin B_6, 136, 137
Vitamin B_7. *See* Biotin
Vitamin B_{12}, 112, 136, 137
Vitamin B complex, 136–38
Vitamin C, 141
Vitamin D, 135, 139–40
Vitamin E, 140